D0515847

ODD AND ECCENTRIC PEOPLE

Cover: His distinctive mustache cunningly adorned, surrealist artist Salvador Dali is captured in a peak moment of ornamental eccentricity in 1969.

ODD AND ECCENTRIC PEOPLE

By the Editors of Time-Life Books

TIME-LIFE BOOKS, ALEXANDRIA, VIRGINIA

CONTENTS

ODDNESS IN HIGH PLACES

Eccentric means, literally, off-center, and that is what eccentric people are—off-center, on the fringes, out of step in the way they believe or behave. By choice or happenstance, they march to drumbeats that they alone can hear. In difficult or turbulent times, eccentrics are persecuted or cast out; in good, stable times, they are celebrated for their differences, for the charm and piquancy that they frequently lend to a world of drab conformity. Like all independent thinkers, eccentrics grow best in a democracy; totalitarian regimes lock their nonconformists away or even kill them.

Most eccentrics are ordinary people whose lives are merely out of phase with the majority of others, and they come and go almost invisibly, leaving no great impression on their era. But wealth, power, and position tend to amplify and encourage oddness: In a ruler, a religious leader, a politician, or a press lord, oddities and obsessions can alter the very topography of an age.

Thus, the chronicles of human affairs are filled with eccentrics in high places—odd archbishops, idiosyncratic socialites, self-styled statesmen, barmy billionaires. Their foibles have ranged from chats with dead pets to dreams of ruling the entire world. Some, by their singularity, have achieved great things; others have destroyed or been destroyed. Whatever their individual fates, however, they all share a curious distinction: In the recipe of human history, they are the spice.

A sixteenth-century mural in a Cyprus church shows an overdressed Saint Simeon atop the pillar he occupied for thirty-seven years: The real Simeon wore a simple leather tunic or skins.

Upward Bound

To many early Christians, asceticism was the surest route to the kingdom of God. But few worshipers carried self-denial and mortification of the flesh to the extremes of a Syrian named Simeon. His life, purged of even the smallest worldly comfort, was lived on another plane—literally.

Born into a Christian family in AD 390, Simeon was a shepherd as a child. He entered a monastery at the age of thirteen to work as a servant while training to be a monk. Two years later, he entered another monastery, where he followed a strict regime of prayer, meditation, and fasting. But even as a boy, Simeon was drawn by the hardest paths to virtue. Once he twisted a rope so tightly about his body that it dug deep into his flesh, causing skin ulcers that nearly killed him. For this perilous penance his abbot dismissed him, apparently deciding that the lad was a little prone to extremes.

Simeon eventually repaired to a hermitage near the city of Antioch, where he very nearly killed himself again by virtually total abstinence from food and water during the forty days of Lent. After three years in Antioch, Simeon moved to a nearby mountaintop, where he lived by himself, without shelter, clothed only in animal skins. To further demonstrate his sincere dedication to bliss through mortification, Simeon had his right leg shackled to a rock by a chain.

Gradually, word of this extraordinary holy man spread, and people came to the mountain to hear him speak, receive his blessing, and be healed by his touch. Fame prompted yet another removal—upward, this time. He built a pillar six cubits—about ten feet—high, beyond the reach of tugging hands. The top, accessible by a rope ladder, was an open platform less than six feet across. Spurning furniture, he fitted out his perch with a post that gave him some support when—often remaining upright—he rested or briefly slept. Twice a day he delivered sermons. All through the night, he prayed.

He now became known as Simeon Stylites, from *stylos*, the Greek word for "pillar." From time to time over the years, his aerie was raised, lifting him ever nearer to God. The final version, built by Simeon's followers in three drumlike sections that represented the Holy Trinity, was almost seventy feet high.

Altogether, he spent thirty-seven years standing in worship on pillars, utterly steadfast in his pious suffering. People from every walk of life sought him out; three Roman emperors traveled to the spot to obtain his advice and prayers. When he died at the age of sixty-nine, much of the Syrian populace attended his funeral, and a church was erected around the ruined base of the original pillar. But Simeon the determined sufferer left something more: a tradition of stylite martyrs that continued to produce an occasional pillar-bound penitent into the nineteenth century. □

Mad Monk

According to Zen Buddhism, true enlightenment is gained by fighting free of the reasoning mind, moving beyond words and logic to find the unity in all things. One of Japan's most renowned Zen masters, a fifteenth-century monk named Ik- kyū Sōjun *(below)*, pursued this or- thodox goal in highly unorthodox ways—by frequenting taverns and bordellos, for instance. Adopting the sometimes comical, always heretical attitudes of what is known as mad Zen, the monk flouted con- vention at every turn. A moralist and ascetic who was also a libertine and voluptuary, Ikkyū demonstrated that the road to enlightenment could be a very quirky path.

Ikkyū's origins are obscure; it is believed that he was the product of a shadowy union between the em- peror Gokomatsu and a low-ranking woman of the court. In any event, he was placed in a Zen temple at an early age. There, he absorbed the re- ligion's precepts, received an excel- lent education, and, by the time he was twelve years old, had demonstrated singular gifts as a poet.

But these were tur- bulent times for Japan. The fifteenth century was marked by war, famine, plague, and peasant uprisings that shook the very foundations of the country. Amid these upheavals, Zen monasteries be- came worldly and even corrupt: They owned large es- tates and business-

es; they functioned as bankers, pawnbrokers, and even sake brew- ers; and they were closely allied with the rulers of the land.

Ikkyū rejected every effort to draw him into this wealth-seeking fraternity. Instead, by both word and deed, he steered toward deeper values. To illustrate the transience of life, he burst in on a New Year's festival in a temple waving a human skull on the end of a bamboo stick. "Be careful, be careful," he shouted to the shocked assemblage, remind- ing them that one day they too would be reduced to skeletons. He also habitually wore a long, red- lacquered scabbard when walking in town. Asked, "What kind of priest is it that carries a sword?" Ikkyū would then draw a wooden sword from the scabbard and say, "Don't be afraid; it is counterfeit, like the other priests." The implication was that Ikkyū's colleagues followed "wooden Zen," not his own "keen- as-steel" variety.

Eventually, Ikkyū left his temple for a time and lived the life of a bo- hemian. As a parting shot, he wrote to his superi- or: "If you come an- other day and ask for me,/ Try a fish shop, tavern, or else a brothel." He meant it: Pleasure and enlightenment were one, he believed. He frequented bars and brothels for many years, wandering from city to city, sleeping in humble

huts and hermitages, simply clad in his black habit, straw hat, and rain- coat. All the while, he continued to write poetry, much of it highly erot- ic. A favorite subject was a blind woman—a young singer—named Mori, with whom Ikkyū fell diffident- ly in love in his late seventies.

Although such behavior was un- heard of in a Zen monk, he won many disciples. His craziness—as he himself described it—was a route to discovering that the true nature of the world possessed a unity that eluded reason. One seem- ingly nonsensical poem put the matter this way: "That old Zen mas- ter's words are worth a thousand pieces of gold,/ Do no evil, do much good./ It must have been something the Elder sang while drunk."

At the age of eighty-two, the iconoclast was restored to the mainstream: He was asked to be- come the abbot of Daitokuji, the Zen temple where he had learned the rigors of his faith and which he had spent a lifetime criticizing. □

Skirting Danger

In the year 1702, the colonies of New York and New Jersey welcomed their latest governor, Edward Hyde, Lord Cornbury. A cousin of the royal proprietress, Queen Anne of England, Cornbury had served for a time in Parliament and at first seemed to bring the colonies the benefits of his high connections. Unfortunately, as one historian put it, Cornbury had been "hunted out of England by a host of hungry ▷

Academic debate persists over the subject of this unsigned eighteenth-century painting, but some scholars believe it was the cross-dressing governor of New York and New Jersey, Lord Cornbury.

attire. He was said to have worn queenly raiment to his wife's funeral and to official balls, and he sometimes conducted business dressed as a woman. Reports also circulated that he roamed the streets at night in woman's finery. Apologists suggested he was simply taking his position as the representative of a lady—the queen—too literally. But the outraged colonists demanded the recall of what one of them called a "peculiar but detestable maggot."

When she learned the particulars, Queen Anne readily agreed to remove her cousin, and in December 1708, Cornbury was recalled. Unhappily for the cross-dressing governor, the move stripped him of royal protection, and his creditors immediately threw him into jail. There he stayed until the following year, when the death of his father, the earl of Clarendon, restored his aristocrat's immunity to the law. Unrepentant, he gathered up his skirts and, leaving his American debts permanently unpaid, stormed off to England—and, evidently, to forgiveness: The new earl of Clarendon was seated on the queen's Privy Council. □

creditors" and sent to the New World by his royal cousin as an alternative to a term in a debtor's prison. The appointment not only failed to repair Cornbury's fortunes, it proved to be an outright disaster.

Anticipating, quite correctly, that this aristocrat had expensive tastes, the colonists greeted him with an award of £2,000 to pay for his voyage, plus a seven-year advance on projected living costs. Although quite large, the sum was not nearly enough to support Cornbury's lordly habits in entertainment and domestic comfort. To make ends meet, the governor began taking bribes; he also embezzled funds

that had been appropriated to build fortifications; and he imposed a variety of special fees, even charging clergymen for the right to preach. But the money continued to run out much faster than it came in. Within a few years, Cornbury's debts had mounted to as much as £10,000. The colonists had encountered corruption and despotic ways in other governors. Somewhat benumbed by graft, they might have tolerated even Cornbury's rotten administration—but they could not forgive the man his taste in clothes.

The governor was regularly seen patrolling the ramparts of Fort Anne, his residence, in full female

Cold and austere, nineteenth-century American President John Quincy Adams relaxed with an arduous hour or two in the swift currents of the Potomac River. On most summer mornings in Washington, Adams would rise before the sun, strip off his clothes, and swim naked in the river—a custom he continued until well into his seventies.

Putting on the Dogs

On history's long list of well-heeled eccentrics, Francis Henry Egerton, eighth earl of Bridgewater, ranks high for both foibles and funds. Born in London in 1756, the aristocratic Egerton attended Eton and Oxford, then took up what promised to be an important career in the Anglican Church. But early in the nineteenth century, Egerton left England and never returned—a lifelong exile many attributed to some unspeakable transgression at home. With an estimated income of £20,000 a year, he was able to set himself up in grand style in Paris, where he attracted a circle of students, literary figures, artists, and publishers—although, his French neighbors noted, no Englishman ever visited Egerton's home. In 1823, upon his elder brother's death, he acceded to the earlship of Bridgewater, and his income more than tripled. But even as his fortunes rose, his behavior turned more and more toward extravagant caprice.

An ardent lover of books, he would send back a borrowed volume in his finest carriage, attended by liveried footmen. He wore a new pair of boots everyday, having his servants line the daily castoffs along a wall, creating a kind of footwear calendar. As he became too feeble to hunt properly, he stocked his urban garden with hundreds of rabbits, partridges, and pigeons for a spot of shooting when the impulse seized him.

Although his life was largely solitary, the table at his splendid establishment was typically set for twelve. When it no longer attracted his artistic friends, Egerton turned to alternative company: His dining companions finally consisted only of dogs, each fashionably dressed, with linen napkins around their necks and a footman behind every chair. The earl tolerated no misbehavior at his well-laid table. Should a dog show ill manners—noisily wolfing down food, for instance—it was banished to the servants' hall and required to wear livery until its dining habits improved enough to warrant inclu-

sion in polite society once again. According to a French journal article, Egerton kept his dogs shod in expensive boots (four per dog) and frequently took the animals out riding in his landau.

Despite such treatment, the dogs seemed to enjoy no particular affection from the earl. When he died at seventy-two in February 1829, he left none of his vast fortune to sustain his canine friends. □

At the head of the table, the earl of Bridgewater presides over dinner with his stylish canine guests.

Lord Tim

Timothy Dexter lived in the era when the American nation was trying to find and form itself. In a kind of personal parallel, Dexter too sought to shake off old bonds and win position and respectability in the eyes of the world. But in his case, the transforming impulse went curiously awry.

Dexter was born into an impoverished Massachusetts family in 1747, went to work on a farm at the age of nine, and was apprenticed to a leatherworker in South Carolina at sixteen. He received almost no education and did not emerge from servitude until he was twenty-two.

Though illiterate and unmannered, he was resourceful. Settling in Newburyport, Massachusetts, in 1769, he married a widow with four children and set up a shop as a leather dresser. By the time the colonies had won their independence from Britain, he had saved several thousand gold dollars, which he used to buy up quantities of the almost-worthless Continental dollars that had been issued during the Revolution. The in- ◊

vestment seemed like financial lunacy—until Alexander Hamilton, America's first treasury secretary, persuaded Congress to back the Continental currency by establishing a national bank. Suddenly, the leatherworker was a rich man.

In the years that followed, Dexter added to his fortune by all sorts of unlikely transactions: He shipped surplus cats to the tropics, where they were badly needed to control mice; and he sold thousands of warming pans, used to take the chill out of New England beds in winter, to molasses makers in the ever-warm West Indies. Defying the message of a cliché, he even sent Virginia coal to Newcastle, England's coal-mining center—and made an enormous profit because the miners were on strike. No one knows whether Dexter possessed an acute, but eccentric, entrepreneurial sense or survived through dumb luck. But prosper he certainly did.

With his ever-growing wealth,

Dexter bought one of the biggest houses in Newburyport, acquired fine clothes and a carriage, and invested in a large wine cellar. But Newburyport society merely sneered at his presumption. When he offered to pave the main street through town (if its name were changed to Dexter Street) or erect a large municipal market building (if it were called Dexter Hall), his proposals were brusquely dismissed.

Dexter began to drink heavily and vent his frustrations in odd ways. He made a policy, for example, of referring to Elizabeth, his long-suffering wife, as a ghost, insisting that she was an illusion and pointedly ignoring her existence. Years later, he shot at a passerby who was looking at his house and spent two months in prison for the deed.

In 1796, he sold the house and left Newburyport for Chester, New Hampshire, a poorer community that was only too glad to have a wealthy resident. Dexter returned to

Newburyport a year later, however, and installed himself in another mansion. This time his social aims were on an entirely new level. He declared that New Hampshire ("hamsher state," as he referred to it in his distinctive free-form spelling) had made him a lord—"the first Lord in Americake." He had been willing to accept this title, he said, because it had been thrust upon him by the "voise of the peopel and I cant Help it."

As befitted his nobility, he hired a poet laureate in New Hampshire, a local fish peddler who composed such verses as: Lord Dexter is a man of fame;/ Most celebrated is his name;/ More precious far than gold that's pure./ Lord Dexter shines forevermore.

He then decided to make his house "an outdoor museum" and commissioned a local craftsman to carve forty large wooden figures—history's greatest personages, in his estimation—that would be placed

Self-styled Lord Timothy Dexter embellished his Newburyport mansion with lifelike wooden figures of the famous, including two of himself (circled).

around the grounds. The effigies, completed in just over a year, included Louis XVI of France, Adam and Eve, Aaron Burr, Benjamin Franklin, the emperor of China, a figure representing Motherly Love, and—in the two choicest spots—statues of Lord Timothy Dexter, one marked with the modest inscription, "I am the first in the East, the first in the West," the other with "I am the Greatest Philosopher in the Western World."

As a token of his philosophical genius, he published a nearly incoherent book about his life, his grievances, and his global political plan. Not a single punctuation mark marred the text of *A Pickle for the Knowing Ones, or Plain Truths in a Homespun Dress.* However, Lord Dexter obligingly added a pageful of commas, periods, question marks, and semicolons at the end of subsequent editions of the book, instructing the readers

to "peper and solt it as they plese."

As his health declined, Dexter staged an elaborate funeral, complete with eulogy and the lowering of an empty coffin into the ground. The purpose, apparently, was to see whether people would mourn him properly at his passing. His poor ghost of a wife did not, and he beat her afterward.

He died in 1806 at the age of fifty-nine and was buried not in his elegantly appointed mausoleum, but in an ordinary grave, marked by a simple stone. When his will was read, his wealth proved somewhat diminished by his various quirky indulgences, and he surprised his snobbish neighbors with his generosity toward his adopted town. (He left, for example, a fund to aid the local poor.) The two-score statues stood until 1815, when a gale knocked most of them down. Some were sold for a small sum. The rest—including those of Lord Dexter—fueled a large bonfire. □

Flat City

Even in the beginning, Zion City, Illinois, was not exactly the kind of place most people would go to have a good time. The fundamentalist community was built in the late 1890s by about 5,000 followers of a faith-healing Scot by the name of John Alexander Dowie—Elijah the Restorer, as he styled himself. Within the ten square miles of Dowie's domain, only fifty-four miles from sinful Chicago, there were no theaters, dance halls, drugstores, or physicians' offices. Life insurance was forbidden as an unseemly hedge against the will of God. Oysters were banned in accordance with Old Testament injunctions against shellfish.

Despite such restrictions, Zion City was relatively wide open compared to what it became after an Indiana-born preacher named Wilbur Glenn Voliva wrested it from the ailing Dowie's control in 1906. Under the new regime, cigarettes, alcohol, lipstick, and high heels were outlawed. Bacon and ham were added to the list of taboo foods. (Voliva himself lived mostly on Brazil nuts and buttermilk, a diet he claimed would enable him to live to 120.) A strict 10:00 p.m. curfew was imposed. Police with *Patience* written on their helmets and doves outlined on their sleeves patrolled the streets carrying Bibles, which they used as clubs. Humming was strictly prohibited.

Voliva was determined to tighten things up. In his view, the world beyond the confines of Zion City was bound for hell in a handbasket, and his flock must remain separate and uncontaminated at all costs. Thus those who lived in Zion City would think and believe as he did, shar- ◊

Flat-earther Wilbur Glenn Voliva, shown here about a year before his 1935 ouster, ruled Zion City, Illinois, by making everyone say no to whiskey, ham, shellfish—and almost everything else.

ing, among other things, his peculiar view of scientific truth.

Especially critical to Voliva's cosmic schematic was the shape of the earth. He had determined that it was flat, like a phonograph record, with the North Pole at the center and the South Pole consisting of a barrier of ice around the rim. As for the rest of the universe, the sun, stars, and moon were fastened to the sky and were much closer than claimed by astronomers ("poor, ignorant, conceited fools," he called them). "The idea of a sun millions of miles in diameter and ninety-one million miles away is silly," he declared, shaving an initial couple of million miles from the actual distance. "The sun is only thirty-two miles across and is not more than three thousand miles from earth. It stands to reason that it must be so. God made the sun to light the earth and therefore

must have placed it close to the task it was designed to do." Its rising and setting, he added, is an optical illusion.

Self-doubt was utterly alien to Voliva. He offered a $5,000 reward to anyone who could prove to him that the earth was round. Those who bothered trying invariably came up short, of course. He discouraged others by his truculence; during a court challenge, for example, he screamed, "Every man who fights me goes under. Mark what I say. The graveyard is full of fellows who tried to down Voliva."

What finally downed Voliva was competition for his flock. He had predicted that the world would end in 1923. When noth-

ing happened, he picked various other years, including 1935—the year his unique universe collapsed around him. Taking advantage of unrest brought on by financial hardship during the Depression, rival preachers moved into Zion City and ousted him. Still, it could have been worse. Voliva had been absolute ruler of his curious little kingdom for almost thirty years. He died in 1942 at the age of seventy-two, his Brazil nuts and buttermilk having evidently fallen somewhat short of his expectations. By the time he presumably made the short hop to the nearby heaven that he had envisioned, medieval Zion City had joined the twentieth century. □

Loose Canon

Richard Whately *(below)*, a London-born Oxford don and Anglican archbishop of Dublin from 1831 to 1863, was a serious and energetic man, the author of more than two dozen books on subjects ranging from religious matters to the British constitution. He was also famously nonconformist—a Christian leader with a pervasive contempt for humankind, and a social disaster whose odd physical blundering made him the terror of hostesses.

At Oxford, this large man in a large white hat and rough white coat, accompanied by a large white dog, earned the nickname the White Bear. Despite his unconventional appearance, however, Whately had an altogether superior mind, and he spent his life making that quite clear to everyone he met. To underscore the point, he also took care to denigrate any intellect belonging to someone else. He publicly ranked the intelligence of his dogs higher than that of many university students, and he tended to dismiss the intellectual opinions of others with the remark, "I went through that when I was twelve."

An unappreciative attitude toward fellow mortals had surfaced early: Whately was said to have been "a weird and sickly child, with no appetite, except for arithmetic, and no care for the society of other children." The great man's own society, in return, was not easily borne. Brilliant though he was, Whately could be uncommonly graceless in company. At gatherings, he would stand in front of the fire and spread his coattails, capturing the lion's share of the heat. While in conversation he might take out scissors and begin to trim his fingernails. If the gathering grew lively, he vented his nervous energy by pivoting his chair on a single leg, which took its toll on fragile furnishings. One of his hostesses, Lady Charlotte Anglesey,

arranged to have a chair especially built for the archbishop, with legs, according to one account, "like the balustrades of Dublin Castle."

Whately's feet obeyed no rules of decorum. He would lean back in his chair and rest them among delicate objects adorning the mantelpiece. He was seen to raise his right foot and grasp its instep "as though he were strangling some ugly animal," an observer noted. Alternatively, he would place a foot in the lap of a neighbor. At one social gathering, Ireland's chief justice reached for a handkerchief and discovered that the archbishop's foot had strayed into his pocket. People flocked to hear his sermons, less for his wisdom than to see what he might do with his wandering legs, which sometimes strayed up and over the pulpit's edge.

Behind the veil of eccentricity, however, Whately was shy and self-conscious to a painful degree and simply unable to feign interest in his fellows. He lacked, as one writer said, "the instinct which is the oil of society," adding, "Many men could not see his great honest heart for the roughness of the rind under which it lay." Beneath that rough rind lived a happy family man who—sometimes wearing worn-out vestments as work clothes—gloried in horticultural experiments, hard outdoor labor, and dogs as unusual as he was. He was fond of climbing trees to hide a personal object—a handkerchief, perhaps—so that his tree-scaling canines could go after it. And crowds invariably gathered to watch his favorite spaniel, Sailor, climb a tree and dive into a river.

Whately died in 1863 at the age of seventy-six, and one writer's subsequent assessment could be a motto for many highly placed eccentrics: "The sparks which flew from his wheel attracted more attention than the effect he produced upon the material in his hand." □

Heart in San Francisco

When a thirty-year-old merchant named Joshua Abraham Norton arrived in San Francisco on November 23, 1849, opportunities beckoned on all sides. As the gateway to California's newly discovered gold fields, the city spawned fortunes by the score, and the newcomer had never lacked ambition. Born in London in 1819, he had migrated with his family to South Africa two years later, where he lived until his father's death. Selling the family business, Norton moved on to Brazil, hoping to invest his modest inheritance advantageously. Once there, however, he learned of the gold strikes in California and immediately headed for San Francisco.

Using a $40,000 stake, he traded in commodities such as coffee, tea, coal, and flour; he dealt in real estate; he built a huge warehouse and, when it burned down, built another. By 1853, Norton had become a rich man, with a fortune of $250,000 in his grasp. Then he made a bold bid for greater riches. Having witnessed the price of rice increase eightfold in times of shortage, Norton took advantage of a Chinese embargo on rice shipments to California. Sensing that a shortage was in the offing and that prices would rise, he began buying all the rice he could lay his hands on. His goal was to corner the market. But the shortage never came. Suddenly, rice seemed to pour in from every quarter. With the market glutted, Norton was forced to sell his rice at a huge loss. Then, unable to meet his debts, he spiraled into bankruptcy. In 1857, stunned and disoriented, he became a recluse, his entrepreneurial spirit irreparably shattered.

But three years later, the former prince of commerce emerged with a new, imperial idea for himself, spelled out in an announcement he had published in a local newspaper. "At the peremptory request and desire of a large majority of citizens of these United States," he wrote, "I, Joshua Norton, declare and proclaim myself Emperor of these United States."

Soon the new ruler was striding about the city in his royal attire, a light blue, secondhand officer's uniform with gold epaulets, topped by a tall beaver hat sprouting a green feather. An old saber acquired from a blacksmith clanked by his side. His feet were shod in navy boots that had been cut open at the sides to improve the fit.

Norton could not have chosen a better capital for his dominion. Gold-rush San Francisco was perhaps the most colorful, rambunctious, and irrepressible city on earth, brimming with adventurers and individualists of every kind. The population took Emperor Norton to its collective heart and held him there. He was given free meals and drinks wherever he went. His royal quarters—a room in a humble boardinghouse—were paid for by friends. When he levied taxes of twenty-five cents on shopkeepers, most of them cheerfully paid. He rode the municipal streetcars for free and traveled in complimentary train berths on his infrequent forays to cities in northern California. He issued Bonds of Empire bearing his image, each worth fifty cents, backed by his promise to repay the bearer the full amount, plus five percent, in twenty years. A public subscription provided him with new uniforms as the old ones wore out. Norton I became visible evidence of the city's good and tolerant heart.

In return, the emperor did his best to be a wise sovereign. His decrees included the abolition of Congress and, as a follow-up, the dissolution of the United States—although, when the Civil War broke out, he ordered Jefferson Davis and Abraham Lincoln to come to San Francisco so that he could repair the breach. He appointed himself

Emperor Joshua Norton, imperially dressed in a used army officer's uniform, pedals through the streets of San Francisco in 1869, the ninth year of his self-proclaimed twenty-year reign.

protector of Mexico—but withdrew in dismay when rebels executed his fellow emperor, Maximilian.

On a more mundane level, he gave speeches (largely unintelligible), inspected construction sites, checked streetcar schedules, and wandered the streets to show his imperial personage. Dignified, earnest, visibly concerned with the welfare of his subjects, he retained the affections of San Francisco for twenty years. When Emperor Norton I died in 1880, more than 10,000 people attended the funeral to pay their last respects. □

Runaway Train

"I have lived fast," wrote publicity-loving American financier George Francis Train (right) not long before his death in 1904. "I was born into a slow world, and I wished to oil the wheels and gear, so that the machine would spin faster and, withal, to better purposes." This was certainly an understatement: George Train lived at a positively headlong pace, which finally accelerated beyond his control.

Train was born in 1829, orphaned at the age of four, and raised by dour, strict grandparents. At sixteen, he joined a Boston-based shipping company owned by a cousin and soon displayed remarkable originality and acumen by pushing the design and construction of clipper ships. Rich but restless by his mid-twenties, he went to Australia and built up a successful shipping business there, then wandered across Asia, the Middle East, and Europe, hobnobbing with the powerful wherever he went, yet si-

multaneously embroiling himself so deeply in revolutionary movements that he periodically landed in jail.

By the 1860s, his life had become a truly bizarre mixture of business genius and compulsive attention seeking. He built streetcar systems in Europe and played a key role in promoting America's first transcontinental railroad. Then he decided that he should be president of the United States. He created a new political party for the run and—presumably to demonstrate his vigor—left the country for a round-the-world trip that took approximately eighty days. The feat inspired French novelist Jules Verne to cre-

ate Phileas Fogg, the hero of *Around the World in Eighty Days*. The absentee campaigning failed to work: Electoral records list not a single vote for Train.

A reporter's comment that "the Train of ideas sometimes lacks the coupling chains" seemed increasingly accurate. Learning that feminist Victoria Woodhull, one of his minor competitors for the presidency, had been jailed with others on charges of obscenity—they had exposed the secret love life of revered preacher Henry Ward Beecher—Train leaped into the fray. He published a paper containing three columns of sexually implicit quo- ◊

tations from the Bible. Arrested for obscenity himself, he was trotted off to New York's jail, the Tombs, where he was finally pronounced a lunatic and released. Although no one seriously believed that Train had gone mad, he began styling himself the Great American Crank. He traveled twice more around the world, bettering his eighty-day mark on both trips. But his writings went increasingly against the established order of things. His own preferences soon became clear: He announced that he was running for dictator of the United States and that the nation would get a new calendar based on his birth date.

As the years passed, he added many new touches to his crankdom. He chose to communicate mostly in writing as a way of "saving up my psychic powers," and he greeted people by shaking his own hand. He made his living with speaking tours across the land, urging such things as the invasion of Canada to audiences that dwindled with each tour. On one engagement in San Francisco, the Great American Crank encountered another memorable eccentric: Norton I, emperor of the United States and protector of Mexico *(pages 16-17)*. Wanting to head off Train's invasion, Norton offered to turn over Vancouver Island for $1,200. When Train rejected the offer, Norton published a notice banning the Crank from the empire forever.

Eventually reduced to utter poverty, Train spent his last years sitting on a favorite bench in a New York City park, feeding the pigeons and playing with children, whom he plied with tales, candy, and occasional trips to the circus. "To the children," he wrote in the dedication of his last book, "and to the children's children, in this and in all lands, who love and believe in me, because they know I love and believe in them." Few others still believed in George Francis Train; the once-brilliant entrepreneur and traveler had become something of a child himself. □

Designing Woman

When Boston grande dame Isabella Gardner built a temple to house the artworks she had collected during the second half of the nineteenth century, she chose a suitable seal for the building. It was a shield bearing an image of a phoenix rising from its own ashes—a symbol of immortality—and a motto that stated simply, *C'est mon plaisir:* "It's my pleasure." To her way of thinking, art was humankind's best chance at immortality and perfect pleasure. Being rich was nice, too.

Born Belle Stewart in New York in 1840, she enjoyed every comfort as a child, attended finishing school in Paris, then married Jack Gardner, a wealthy Bostonian. Some unhappy years followed as the new Mrs. Gardner suffocated in the stern atmosphere of Brahmin society, then lost a baby to illness, had a miscarriage, and learned that motherhood would thenceforth be denied her. Depressed, she re-

Isabella Stewart Gardner patronized such artists as John Singer Sargent, who painted her portrait *(above)*. Her fortune created Boston's Gardner Museum, centered on a dazzling interior courtyard *(right)* of her design.

treated to Europe for almost a year—and discovered an elixir in the form of museum going and hobnobbing with artists. She evidently discovered something else, as well: Eccentric behavior made a marvelous disguise.

Back in Boston, she was a new woman, matchlessly vivacious. She gave the most lavish parties, wore dresses and jewels that hovered near the outer edge of propriety, and conducted a salon that included such luminaries as Oliver Wendell Holmes, writer Henry James, and portraitist John Singer Sargent. Her life became her art, with every action calibrated for effect—she relished her spreading reputation for caprice and outrageousness. Once she rode about in her carriage with two lion cubs as companions. On another occasion, she displayed her piety during Lent by washing down the steps of a church while a curious crowd looked on. At a ladies' tea at her home, she displayed a near-naked prizefighter as a living work of art. When she collected a new male protégé, as she often did, Boston gossips whispered of affairs. Even at home, dramatic gestures were regular fare: If she found a flaw in the running of her household, she would fire all of her many servants, herding them toward the door with cries of "Out! Out!" Her husband invariably rehired them.

Beneath her cloak of startling behavior, however, Belle Gardner exercised a sharp intellect and keen eye for art. She accumulated an extraordinary collection of paintings by Raphael, Rembrandt, Vermeer, and other masters, usually acquiring them at bargain prices. After her husband's death in 1898, she devoted her energies, and every penny she could find, to designing and building a palazzo for her treasures—a structure called Fenway Court that mixed architectural elements from various countries and eras in a splendid stew. It was completed in 1903, and Gardner lived there until her death in 1924. She bequeathed the museum to the public, with one proviso: Not a single item was ever to be moved. A red line was painted under every art object to ensure that her idiosyncratic good taste remains forever in control there. □

India's Maharani of Cooch Behar was so careful of her guests' comfort that she would lie on their beds to adjust the lamps. She once sent a cook to Alfredo's in Rome to learn the secret of perfect lasagna. No one knows if he later prepared it, or where—her castle's three kitchens were dedicated to English and two types of Indian cuisine.

Glittering Glutton

In the turn-of-the-century era of high-living American millionaires, no one glittered more brightly than James Buchanan Brady—Diamond Jim, to all the world. This paragon of the Gilded Age was a hardheaded businessman who followed a simple creed: "If you're going to make money, you have to look like money." He looked like a Tiffany's window, and he made money like the U.S. Mint.

Brady was born into a working-class Irish family in New York City in 1856, began his career as a baggage handler for the New York Central Railroad, and displayed such intelligence and initiative that he was soon the right-hand man of the line's general manager. From that height, attained in his early twenties, he shifted into the business of selling railroad equipment, a role he performed with such élan that he rapidly became, in the view of his peers, America's greatest sales- ◊

Diamond Jim Brady struts his 2,500-gem Transportation Set, one of thirty diamond ensembles.

man. An opportunity to make and sell a new steel railroad undercarriage used in Britain—and to keep one-third of the take—swiftly blossomed into a large fortune. Work was his life, but he managed to link it with pleasure much of the time. Brady entertained potential customers in spectacular style at restaurants and nightclubs or in his New York mansion—reputedly redecorated every year at a cost of some $750,000.

When it came to keeping up appearances, he never missed a trick. In the city, he kept a stable of twelve gold-plated bicycles, and on his New Jersey farm, the cows were milked into gold-plated buckets. He had 200 custom-made suits and fifty hats. Diamonds, emeralds, rubies, and sapphires—almost all cannily bargained away from pawnbrokers across America—adorned his person whenever he appeared in public. They gleamed on his fingers and winked from his cuff links, shirt pins, buttons, watch chain, and belt. His favorite diamond ring and scarfpin, each set with a single stone, together totaled fifty-eight carats. But he believed in sharing the wealth: The bachelor bon vivant gave away an estimated two million dollars in baubles, mostly to the female companions who lent zest to his nights.

While he certainly enjoyed the fair sex, Diamond Jim's preeminent delight was eating—which, in his case, meant stuffing herculean amounts of food into his 250-pound form. He never touched wine, liquor, or coffee, but he did consume prodigious quantities of orange juice. Three dozen oysters would serve for a typical midmorning snack. An hour later, his hunger might be appeased with a lunch that consisted of two broiled lobsters, more oysters, deviled crabs, a large steak, most of a fruit pie, and a two-pound box of chocolates. Dinner was naturally a somewhat heartier affair: His oyster intake might rise to six dozen and the chocolates to six pounds, with a few ducks, a half-dozen venison chops, a saddle of lamb, and a dozen-egg omelet consumed in between. "Whenever I sit down to a meal," Jim Brady explained, "I make a point to leave just four inches between my stomach and the edge of the table. And then, when I can feel 'em rubbin' together pretty hard, I know I've had enough."

In fact, Brady never knew when he had had enough of anything. But the excesses of food, not extravagance, finally brought him down. In 1916, he experienced a severe, inoperable case of stomach ulcers, and his heart and kidneys began to misfire. He retired to a seaside hotel suite in Atlantic City, where in April 1917, at the age of sixty-one, he died in his sleep in the impersonal company of medics. None of Diamond Jim's generously treated friends was there at the end. □

Blighted Baron

In the forty-four years allotted to him, James A. Harden-Hickey, an American of wandering habits, lived with a sort of fatalistic passion that any nineteenth-century romantic would have admired. He was born in the cultural vortex of San Francisco in 1854, his father a wealthy Irish miner, his mother French. Wanting the best for the boy, they sent him to Paris to be educated. There, he was much impressed by the glamorous court of Napoleon III, with its chivalric sheen and such antique traditions as stag hunting—a perfect model, he thought, for a kingdom of his own.

At nineteen, he joined the French army but resigned when his father's death brought a small, but timely, infusion of funds. He married a countess and threw himself into a writing career, producing eleven novels written in French under the pseudonym Saint-Patrice—Saint Patrick. He also produced a stream of pamphlets defending Catholicism from critics, for which he earned the title of baron of the Catholic church, and he edited an outrageously satirical magazine whose chief cause was the restoration of the French royal family.

But Baron Harden-Hickey grew restive. He divorced his wife, rejected Catholicism (but not the title it had conferred), and, under the sway of the era's faddish mysticism, headed off to India for two years of religious investigations. En route, a storm forced his ship to put in at a tiny, uninhabited South Atlantic island called Trinidad, hundreds of miles south and east of the much larger Caribbean island of the same name. Responding to some deep royalist impulse, Harden-Hickey went ashore and claimed the speck of rock in his own name.

When he returned from his Eastern pilgrimage, Harden-Hickey married the American oil-and-steel heiress Anna Flagler. But, in part because her tycoon father kept tight reins on the family money, Harden-Hickey descended into a deep funk, resulting in the composition of a remarkable book entitled *Euthanasia: The Aesthetics of Suicide.* In this slender volume, he cited 400 favorable mentions of suicide "by the greatest thinkers ever produced"—most scholars believe that these were manufactured—and discussed fifty-one instruments and eighty-eight poisons suitable for killing oneself.

By the time the suicide manual was published in 1894, Harden-Hickey had declared his possession of Trinidad to governments around the world, crowned himself King

James I, and opened a chancellery in New York. He also began seeking settlers, issuing a prospectus that made clear that the government would be a military dictatorship, but offsetting this news with descriptions of the many alleged attractions of the island: "The surrounding sea swarms with fish, which are as yet wholly unsuspicious of the hook." Unfortunately for his plans, Britain decided that the island would be useful for a cable-laying project and seized it in January 1895, starting months of protests from Brazil. But neither nation paid the slightest heed to the claims of Harden-Hickey.

King James I expressed outrage. When the *New York Times* gave him sympathetic coverage, he awarded its editors the Cross of Trinidad and the promise of a pension. Then, abruptly, in January 1896, Great Britain withdrew from Trinidad, throwing the barren island to Brazil,

which claimed possession—and destroyed Harden-Hickey's case. Stunned, he brooded over his loss, and Britain's role in it. Offered an adventurer's help in securing a new kingdom—the Hawaiian island of Kauai—he declined, opting instead to plot an Ireland-based invasion of England. This campaign would require large sums of money, however, which his father-in-law prudently declined to supply.

When Harden-Hickey tried to raise funds by selling his own ranch in Mexico, he found the land unsalable. Despairing, he left his family in California but got only as far as El Paso, where he checked into a hotel. A week later, on February 9, 1898, Harden-Hickey went to his room early in the evening. The following noon, chambermaids discovered his body there, poisoned with morphine. King James I of Trinidad had followed his own bitter aesthetic to the end. □

Horse Flash

The millionaires who idled away summers in Newport, Rhode Island, during the declining decades of the nineteenth century took their sports seriously. That is, they threw money at these activities. They plied the surrounding waters in yachts the size of oceangoing vessels. They purchased racks of the finest English-made shotguns for trapshooting. And they built immense stables of brick and stone ("the size of railroad terminals," according to an observer) to support their equine diversions—chiefly fox hunting, polo, and coaching. Looking back on the era, one resident said, "Newport fairly reeked of horseflesh."

But one stalwart of the sporting scene was so enamored of his horses that he dispensed with conventional stables altogether and took his animals into his home. Oliver Hazard Perry Belmont *(left)*, heir to a great banking fortune, devoted the entire first floor of his house to lavishly equipped stalls, designed by the prominent architect Richard Morris Hunt. The animals had three separate sets of regalia for morning, afternoon, and evening. At night, they rested from their exertions on white linen sheets bearing the Belmont crest—embroidered in gold thread. Favorites in their ranks could even expect reverence after death: In the salon on the floor above were two especially beloved horses, stuffed by a taxidermist and carrying figures in knightly armor.

For all his affection for equines, however, Oliver was not the Belmont who established the famous racecourse that bears the family name. Belmont Park was the creation of his older brother, August, who owned the immortal racehorse Man O' War. □

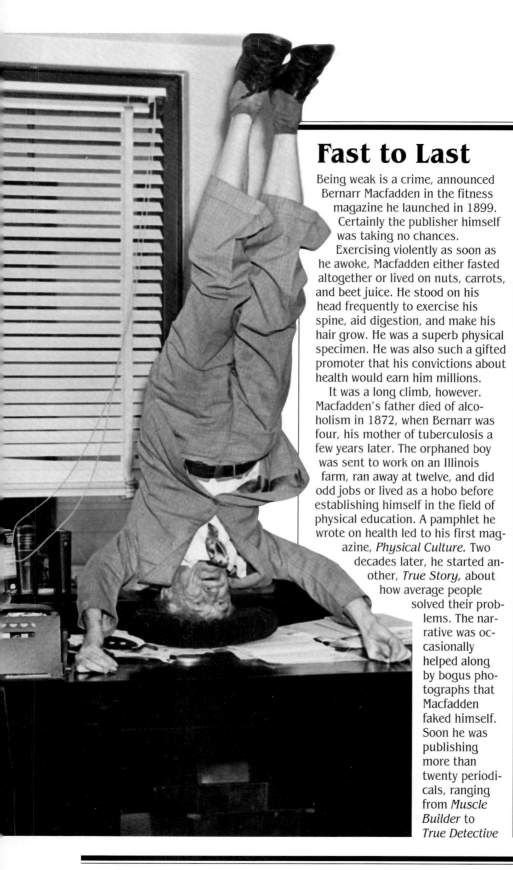

Fast to Last

Being weak is a crime, announced Bernarr Macfadden in the fitness magazine he launched in 1899. Certainly the publisher himself was taking no chances.

Exercising violently as soon as he awoke, Macfadden either fasted altogether or lived on nuts, carrots, and beet juice. He stood on his head frequently to exercise his spine, aid digestion, and make his hair grow. He was a superb physical specimen. He was also such a gifted promoter that his convictions about health would earn him millions.

It was a long climb, however. Macfadden's father died of alcoholism in 1872, when Bernarr was four, his mother of tuberculosis a few years later. The orphaned boy was sent to work on an Illinois farm, ran away at twelve, and did odd jobs or lived as a hobo before establishing himself in the field of physical education. A pamphlet he wrote on health led to his first magazine, *Physical Culture.* Two decades later, he started another, *True Story*, about how average people solved their problems. The narrative was occasionally helped along by bogus photographs that Macfadden faked himself. Soon he was publishing more than twenty periodicals, ranging from *Muscle Builder* to *True Detective*

Mysteries and *Fiction Lovers.* Macfadden's was a $30 million empire that wags said was based on "sex and raw carrots."

Sex was certainly part of it. Macfadden had four wives, but he was picky about his partners. His third wife was the winner of a contest he staged to select "Great Britain's Perfect Woman." Apparently, Macfadden intended the title to be permanent, since he divorced her when "she did not follow my instructions as to her own body. I wanted her to be an example of my work and a credit to me." Among the wifely duties evidently neglected by the formerly perfect woman were calisthenics at daybreak, followed by a ten-mile run.

Despite his own matrimonial misfires, Macfadden had much wisdom to offer in connubial matters. He recommended intercourse for procreation only (he himself fathered eight children) and having babies without doctors.

Marriage was by no means the only subject on which Macfadden held strong personal opinions. He insisted, for example, that cancers of every kind could be cured by eating grapes. Where money was concerned, Macfadden was believed to favor secret burial over banking; legend holds that some four million of his dollars remain buried in old ammunition chests across the United States.

It was his stated intention to live to the age of 120, and he gave it a good try, flying planes and making parachute jumps as an octogenarian. But at eighty-seven, he contracted jaundice and, to the considerable surprise of everyone who knew him, died. His illness had been fatally accelerated by a typical Macfadden cure: a three-day fast. □

Publisher and health guru Bernarr Macfadden practiced what he preached, including office headstands such as this one, performed for reporters around 1935.

Fish Hooks

During the glory days of Newport, Rhode Island, a dinner invitation from Mrs. Stuyvesant Fish *(left)* was not to be declined. At that seaside concentration of wealth, the Fishes were relatively small fry; but style and wit—sharp-edged, to be sure—more than made up the ground.

Mrs. Fish was born Marian Anthon, daughter of a socially prominent but not especially wealthy New York family. When she married the aristocratic Stuyvesant Fish in 1876, she immediately put his name and fortune to work establishing herself as a leader of society. With or without the benefit of her husband's presence, she entertained constantly at their New York home, their country place on the Hudson River, and their summer cottage in Newport. ("Cottages" in Newport are generally palace size.) Although Mamie, as she was known to her close friends, was uneducated and indeed almost illiterate, her mind was quick and her tongue famously tart. When another grande dame accused Mrs. Fish of saying she reminded her of a frog, the irrepressible matron instantly replied, "No, no, not a frog. A toad, my pet, a toad." Spotting an exceptionally dandified playboy at a soiree, Mrs. Fish inquired, "Who is that young man in a negligee?"

Her own parties flouted or even mocked the social conventions of her set. Rebelling against the stodgy three-hour dinners that were the norm, she introduced the fifty-minute dinner, in which courses were whisked away by footmen almost as soon as they were presented. Sometimes, according to some accounts, guests were required to speak in baby talk for the entire evening.

Once, competing with a neighbor who had secured a visiting Grand Duke Boris of Russia, she countered with a party at which the guest of honor was the czar—actually her friend and creative partner, playboy Harry Lehr. He also assisted on another occasion, when Newport society was invited to meet a certain Prince del Drago of Corsica. The prince turned out to be a monkey rigged out in evening clothes. The guests, as usual, were amused—one said that the monkey's manners were superior to those of some princes—but newspapers got wind of the affair and accused Mrs. Fish of holding up American society to ridicule. Some such motive did no doubt underlie her biting remarks and irreverence. Wrote a contemporary, "Her harsh gaiety had the bitter overtone of a grotesque disillusionment with herself and everyone else." Not even her court jester escaped the bite of Mamie. When Harry Lehr married, obviously for money, she guessed his favorite flower: the marigold. □

Family Ties

Haroldson Lafayette Hunt, the legendary Texas oilman, was a numbers whiz: a professional cardplayer who won his first oil well in a poker game in 1921; a wildcatter who parlayed that first gusher into holdings that earned one million dollars a week by the late 1940s; and the maestro of an ever-expanding international empire. That empire was worth several billion dollars by the time Hunt died in 1974 at the age of eighty-five.

Once said to be the richest man in America, Hunt was not a man of lavish tastes. Although his house in the suburbs of Dallas was an outsize duplicate of Mount Vernon, he tended to pass the evenings in a rocking chair on the front porch listening to country music. He drove around town in an ancient Dodge and wore cheap suits and a single, much-mended pair of shoes. He brought his lunch of carrots, apricots, and other faddish health foods to work in a brown bag or sponged sandwiches from his secretary. And he constantly reminded his children—staggeringly wealthy themselves—that a 100-watt light bulb consumes electricity at the rate of four cents an hour. Since he seemed never to carry enough cash, he had to borrow from employees. Somehow, he always seemed to forget to repay them.

Despite such tightwad ways and a refusal to give a single nickel to charity, he happily spent money on promulgating political rectitude. He bankrolled political programs that attacked what he saw as threats to the American way of life—the Supreme Court, unions, and the oil-depletion allowance, among them. He also wrote a novel, *Alpaca,* that envisioned citizens receiving voting power in proportion to the taxes they paid. Such a system, not coincidentally, would have made him one of the most powerful men in America as well as the richest.

But his most vivid legacy had less to do with money and power than with parenthood. His fifteen children came not from a single marriage, but from what amounted to three overlapping ones. Technically a bigamist and in effect a trigamist, Hunt evidently believed that one family was insufficient to propagate the vessel of his remarkable qualities—what he modestly called his genius gene. □

Pleasure Dome

William Randolph Hearst, heir to a mining fortune and the architect of a publishing empire during the early decades of this century, was well-equipped to indulge every whim. In an average year, his twenty or more newspapers alone brought in some $12 million, and his magazines, radio stations, and film companies contributed millions more. But he did not—biographers say because he could not—save a penny. "Every time Willie feels bad," his mother was quoted as saying, "he goes out and buys something." Mostly he bought grandeur.

Hearst owned several castles around the world, but none compared to his magnificent California estate, San Simeon, some 200 miles south of San Francisco. The tough press boss had cherished memories of family picnics in this place of rolling, grassy hills and rocky cliffs overlooking the Pacific. When it came time to build his monument to conspicuous consumption, he turned to San Simeon to raise one of the grandest and most extravagant edifices ever devised in America. Now a popular tourist attraction, the estate was immortalized as the fictional Xanadu of *Citizen Kane,* the film based on Hearst's incomparably spendthrift life.

Setting out to build San Simeon, he gave his project breathing space: fifty miles of ocean frontage and 250,000 acres of property in the surrounding hills. To decorate its vast interior, art dealers scoured the world for rare paintings, suits of armor,

For his eighty-third birthday, plain-living billionaire H. L. Hunt sits down to a feast of carrots, dried fruits, nuts, and juice, arranged on a newspaper-covered side table in his office.

Newspaper titan William Randolph Hearst *(inset)* spent fortunes on San Simeon *(left)*, an opulent 123-acre California compound filled with such treasures as a bed *(below)* owned at one time by seventeenth-century French cardinal Richelieu.

tapestries, statuary, silver, and other art treasures—some 20,000 items in all.

But piecemeal purchases did not satisfy Hearst's acquisitive impulse. He bought European villas, palaces, and monasteries—in whole or in part—and ordered them dismantled and shipped to one of his vast warehouses in New York or California. From there, some were relayed to his seaside estate, to be incorporated into the ineffably eclectic fabric of San Simeon; many remained in storage, never to be seen again in his lifetime.

No expenditure daunted the owner. He allocated $400,000 to the indoor saltwater swimming pool, which took Italian artisans three and a half years to complete. The outdoor pool—Neptune, as it was called—cost $430,000. The grounds were enlivened by wild animals, with the lions and tigers kept caged but the giraffes and kangaroos allowed to roam free. An army of gardeners ensured that San Simeon was a perpetual floral extravaganza. On one occasion, the garden crew was kept working through the night under a battery of portable lights so that guests would wake up on Easter morning to see thousands of Easter lilies blooming on the grounds.

In the end, even Hearst's pocketbook could not stand the strain: He lost control of much of his empire in the 1930s, although his holdings remained substantial. Invalided by heart trouble in 1947, when he was eighty-three, Hearst was forced to leave San Simeon for a Los Angeles bungalow, from which he continued to wield his waning power until his death in 1951.

Years earlier, at a lavish dinner, Hearst had received some sound advice from another expert moneymaker. Auto magnate Henry Ford, aware of his host's splurges on art, asked him straight out, "Have you any money?"

"I never have any money, Mr. Ford," said Hearst. "I always spend any money that I am to receive before I get it."

"That's a darned shame," said the great automaker. "You ought to get yourself two or three hundred million bucks and tuck it away." Instead, William Hearst went out and bought something. □

Spirited Performance

Few twentieth-century leaders did more to shape their country than Canada's William Lyon Mackenzie King. As prime minister for almost twenty-two years, he loosened the nation's ties to Britain and established its sovereign status; he helped knit the English- and French-speaking parts of the country together; he built a close relationship with the United States; and he fashioned a superb civil service. Intelligent, decisive, hardworking, and occasionally ruthless, the nondescript, lifelong bachelor seemed the most levelheaded of men—perhaps even a bit colorless. But after his death in 1950, the diaries he had scrupulously kept since 1893 revealed quite another side to him, a secret life richly populated with spirits of the dead.

King's feelings about the here and now were decidedly mixed. He once remarked, "I've always found I can control people better if I don't see much of them," and he seemed to prefer his own company to that of almost anyone else. He spent as much time as possible alone at Kingsmere, his country home outside Ottawa, a retreat stuffed eclectically with bric-a-brac. On the sprawling grounds around the main residence, King raised ancient-looking arches, walls, and temples, all constructed from the remains of abandoned Ottawa buildings—a bogus antiquity that reinforced the ties he felt with the spiritual realm of the past.

Beneath his brusque exterior, he was a man of deep—even maudlin—affections. He worshiped the memory of his mother, the daughter of a prominent Canadian politician. As a young man, he wrote in his diary, "I love her with all my heart and I would never feel a longing for the love of another if she were always with me, so pure so almost holy." After she died in 1917,

he had her portrait placed where he would see it whenever he looked up from his desk at his official residence in Ottawa; the parental shrine was kept perpetually lighted.

In time, he came to sense an association between his mother and his beloved dogs. Of an Irish terrier named Pat—the first of three terriers with that name—he wrote in his diary: "Dear little soul, he is almost human. I sometimes think he is a comforter dear mother has sent to me, he is filled with her spirit of patience, and tenderness & love." Upon Pat's death, which came as King shaped Canada's role in the deadly serious business of a second world war, the prime minister

Made from Ottawa rubble, the Abbey Ruins were among the "antiquities" built by Canada's spirit-minded prime minister Mackenzie King at Kingsmere, his estate.

wrote, "I kissed the little fellow as he lay there, told him of his having been faithful and true, of his having saved my soul, and being like God—thought of how I felt as I knelt at dear Mother's side in her last illness." Pat crossed to the spirit world, King surmised, bearing "messages of love to take to father, mother," and a large assortment of dead relatives.

King apparently found nothing amiss in entrusting Pat's spirit with messages, nor did he think it odd that he sometimes sought advice from people who, however smart, were also dead. At what he called his "little table" at Kingsmere, the prime minister asked for help from Renaissance masters Leonardo da Vinci and Lorenzo de' Medici on the matter of ruins and talked medicine with famed French chemist Louis Pasteur. In fact, King ranged widely through the spirit world for many years, usually in the privacy of his estate and in the company of a close female friend—a living one.

During the 1920s and 1930s, his interest in spiritualism had deepened. He became a frequent participant in séances, though taking care to conceal the practice. Apparently he was mindful that his dabbling with the dead might be less than reassuring to his constituents. At the séances, mediums used various techniques to make contact with departed beings—King's mother, his brother, his friends, his dogs. Alleged messages from the dead came in the form of voices heard by the mediums or automatic writing done in trances or coded knocking on the table. Most of the communing steered clear of the subject of politics. Recounting how he talked to the spirit of King's moth-

er, one medium said, "He wanted to know how she was, whom she had with her. He wanted to talk to her about family matters." He did, however, seek her advice about retiring from public office, and he also received some astral input from the spirit of Franklin Delano Roosevelt, who urged him to remain in office awhile longer. Somehow, King kept his very different temporal and spiritual lives completely separate.

On and off, his mystical outings continued throughout his life.

Although few Canadians knew of it—indeed, he might not have been so long in office otherwise—their longtime leader's need to speak with spirits was not so hard to understand: He was a desperately lonely man, more comfortable communing with shades than dealing with troublesome companions of flesh and blood. The voices of the dear departed were a comfort, King once said. They also could be generally counted on to say whatever he wanted to hear. □

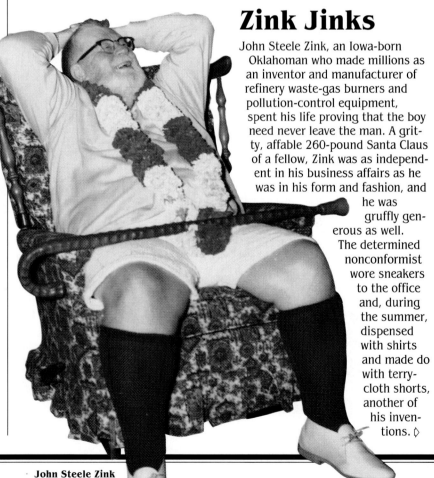

John Steele Zink models custom terry-cloth shorts and a birthday lei.

Zink Jinks

John Steele Zink, an Iowa-born Oklahoman who made millions as an inventor and manufacturer of refinery waste-gas burners and pollution-control equipment, spent his life proving that the boy need never leave the man. A gritty, affable 260-pound Santa Claus of a fellow, Zink was as independent in his business affairs as he was in his form and fashion, and he was gruffly generous as well. The determined nonconformist wore sneakers to the office and, during the summer, dispensed with shirts and made do with terry-cloth shorts, another of his inventions. ◊

Cold weather meant donning red long johns under the shorts. "If people judge me by my appearance," he liked to say, "I don't want to have anything to do with them." Zink kept his business—begun in 1928 and finally the largest industrial-burner manufacturer in the world—in the abandoned dairy farm that it first occupied in the 1930s. His own office was filled with bric-a-brac—and, always, a can of peanut brittle. Zink also liked peanut butter on his large steaks.

Renowned for his generous celebrations of his own birthdays, Zink could also enliven the more formal functions at the Rendezvous, as he called his ranch home on 10,000 acres near Tulsa. When Supreme Court Justice William Douglas came to dinner, for example, Zink brought table conversation back to life by releasing a raccoon for his "hounds"—actually, dachshunds—to chase around the dining room.

For many years, he joyfully greeted visitors to his office by firing a pistol round into a wooden pillar outside his office door, then asking the startled visitor to initial the bullet hole. He discontinued this custom when a slug ricocheted and lodged in the desk of his longtime secretary, Marie Jett, who duly fainted. For a dreadful moment, Zink believed he had killed his faithful assistant; he subsequently abandoned the ritual shots. But shooting continued to be an important part of life on the ranch, which served as host for national rifle competitions. Guests invited to take part in target practice received a considerable jolt when the targets—described by Zink as "brown sticks"—turned out to be sticks of dynamite. "There's never any doubt when you've scored a hit," he said.

Reluctantly drawn by his son's interest in formula one auto racing—and also determined to keep his son, Jack, on the sidelines as an owner and builder and not a driver—Zink entered cars in the Indianapolis 500 during the 1950s and 1960s, winning twice. His own personal brand of fun driving was to take the controls of bulldozers, graders, and other earthmoving equipment. He used these behemoths to crisscross his ranch with more than twenty miles of dirt roads to serve the extensive Boy Scout facilities he established there. For local travel, however, Zink preferred to ride reclining in a kitchen-equipped, air-conditioned bus.

Relegated to crutches and a wheelchair by arthritis in the mid-1960s, Zink may have begun to feel the chill of conformity toward the end of his life. The peanut butter departed his steaks; the bus was replaced by a black Cadillac. John Zink presented fewer and fewer surprises. "The only mistake I ever made was growing old," said Zink not long before he died in 1973 at the age of seventy-nine—a rare old man with no regrets. □

West Whim

Houston's James Marion West, Jr.—better known as Silver Dollar Jim—had money that was fairly respectable by Texas standards—perhaps $10 million worth of oil, cattle, and land by the time of his death in 1957. His prodigal spending habits, however, sometimes made even fellow potentates of the oil patch blink. His personal transportation needs, for instance, were met by a stable of forty cars, including eleven Cadillacs. To stay in touch with the world when at home, Silver Dollar Jim had twenty-four telephones in the house, another dozen in the garage, and several radio transmitters.

Beside his bed, murmuring day and night, was a bank of radio receivers, including a pair tuned to city and county radio frequencies. But West did more than listen to the police calls: Playing cop was his chief amusement, and whenever he could, he patrolled with police

Silver Dollar Jim West won his nickname by casting coins to crowds, but the wealthy oilman's first love was dispensing justice, replete with .45 automatic, broadbrimmed hat, and honorary Texas Ranger badge.

Egypt's light-fingered spendthrift King Farouk was photographed at the island spa of Capri shortly after his overthrow and exile by an army junta in 1952.

at night. At any nocturnal emergency—a break-in, a murder, or merely a car accident—West would strap on a revolver and race to the scene in a car specially equipped with tear-gas canisters, a shotgun, a .30-30 rifle, and a machine gun. Occasionally, he got a chance to exchange gunfire with malefactors—a treat curtailed when he accidentally shot a police officer in the foot.

But Silver Dollar Jim also liked to hand out money, perhaps out of generosity—and perhaps, critics suggest, to watch the less fortunate grovel for it. His pockets were designed to hold large numbers of silver dollars, which he would present by the fistful to waitresses and porters or fling to employees in an expansive moment or simply scatter in the street. He made sure that he always had sufficient coinage on hand for his impromptu prodigality. When he died, $290,000 in silver dollars was found at his house. An armored truck was summoned to tote this ready money to the bank; the job took seven trips. □

No thin-skinned politico, the nineteenth-century U.S. senator Thomas Hart Benton of Missouri followed the hard regime of a Roman gladiator: Twice each day, a servant scrubbed him with a coarse horsehair brush—but not all of the robust senator at one time. Morning scrubs covered the powerful torso; the lower body got its rubs in the afternoon.

Klepto King

When the sixteen-year-old boy called Farouk became king of Egypt on the death of his father, King Fuad I, in 1936, he spoke to his subjects in a radio address. "I start my new life with a good heart and a strong will," King Farouk said. "I promise to devote my life and my being to your good, to bend all my efforts to create your happiness." No modern monarch had ever addressed the people of Egypt directly, and in their own language, and the crowds quickly embraced the attractive young king. It was an auspicious beginning.

Unfortunately, Farouk had not been trained to devote his life to anyone's happiness except his own. He had spent his youth sequestered—and greatly insulated from life—either in the royal compounds at Cairo or Alexandria or on an English estate. The young monarch brought very little wisdom and no real-world experience to the throne of Egypt. Born to what was then the world's oldest extant throne, Farouk was almost incalculably wealthy. He had five palaces, two oceangoing yachts, a hundred cars, a squadron of aircraft, and thousands of acres of valuable farmland.

All the wealth merely catered to Farouk's weaknesses, since he was as dangerously impulsive as he was rich: He was always seeking new thrills. He painted his cars a bright red so that police would know not to stop him when he was speeding, and he shot at the tires of any car that unwisely attempted to

pass him. Visiting the spas and ski resorts of Europe, Farouk frittered away his days playing pinball machines or shopping.

Acquisitiveness became the central activity of his life. He collected everything and was said to have incomparable assemblages of precious watches, coins, stamps, medals, ◊

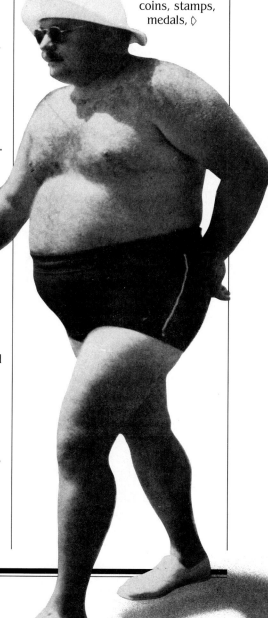

jeweled boxes, and paperweights. He also collected women, at home and across Europe. His excesses seemed those of tremendous wealth and immaturity, except for one: The young ruler was more than acquisitive—he was a thief.

As the years passed, he found that stolen objects had a luster that was absent in purchased ones. He stole whatever he fancied, even from friends and fellow rulers. In the early days of World War II, the Axis-leaning Farouk and his servants robbed confiscated German houses in Cairo, looted the best guns from a collection made for the local home guard, and, according to one account, siphoned gold from Italian bank vaults seized by the Egyptian government. He pilfered a jeweled dagger from the visiting emir of Yemen. When the father of the shah of Iran died in South Africa and the body passed through Cairo en route to a state burial, Farouk secretly had it stripped of a ceremonial sword and medals. His minions scouted homes to which he was invited, to identify objects for him to steal.

Farouk also became a skilled pickpocket; he claimed he had released a criminal from prison specifically to teach him the craft. Once, British prime minister Winston Churchill sat down at Farouk's table and discovered that his watch—a famous one given to his ancestor, the duke of Marlborough, by Queen Anne—was missing. Farouk denied taking the timepiece but left the table, returning soon afterward with the watch. He explained with a chuckle that he had picked off the real thief. Very few people took the explanation seriously: Farouk's concern for the truth was so slight that he bought

trophies commemorating imaginary sporting victories.

Given such behavior and his compulsive womanizing and gambling, it was perhaps inevitable that King Farouk would be overthrown. Egyptian army officers led by General Mohammed Naguib and Colonel Gamal Abdel Nasser sent him into exile in 1952, then decided to auction off the contents of his Cairo palace. An inventory taken before the sale revealed his runaway lust for possessions—not just mountains of watches and rare coins and stamps and jewels, but also hundreds of matchbox tops, vast (and worthless) aggregations of razor-blade packets, endless oddities such as a gold holder for pop bottles, paintings and photographs and sculptures of nudes by the score, pornography of every conceivable type, a pile of American comic books, and such personal articles as a thousand neckties and seventy-five pairs of binoculars. One journalist described it as "the world's biggest and most expensive accumulation of junk."

Farouk, who had smuggled crates of gold from the country, became a citizen of Monaco and took up residence in Rome, where he was attended by a staff of forty. He traveled the circuit of international watering places, sought solace with girlfriends, and periodically issued condemnations of the Egyptian government. He ballooned up to 280 pounds, suffered from various ailments, and tended to grow tearful when talking about old times. But his new times did not last very long. He had a stroke while dining with a girlfriend in a nightclub near Rome in the early hours of March 18, 1965. He died, an exiled boy-pharaoh, at the age of forty-five. □

Emperor of Everything

No one ever accused Homer A. Tomlinson of aiming low. Son of the leader of the Church of God, a Pentecostal sect known commonly as the Holy Rollers, he founded a similar church himself in 1943. But that was the least of his exploits. He traveled the world proclaiming that a new era of peace and goodwill had arrived, repeatedly ran for president of the United States, and capped his political efforts by crowning himself king of the world. The Bible anticipated the appearance of a global sovereign, he said, and he felt sure that the scriptural foreshadowings referred to him.

Tomlinson was born in Indiana in 1892 but spent most of his life in New York City, where he formed an advertising agency in 1916. After a few years as an adman, he entered the ministry of his father's church, then went off on his own when he failed to succeed to the leadership. He generously reckoned his flock at somewhere between 50 million and 100 million, although other observers put the number at a maximum of 3,000.

In 1952, claiming to have been "hailed almost as a new Messiah" during extensive international travels, Tomlinson ran for president as the candidate of the Theocratic Party, advocating the union of church and state, the abolition of taxes in favor of tithing, and the creation of two new cabinet posts: secretary of righteousness and secretary of the Holy Bible. The nation declined to award him the presidency—and would decline again in 1960 and 1964.

But it hardly mattered, since his

Standing by his distinctive folding aluminum throne, Homer Tomlinson crowns himself king of the world in England in this simple ceremony at London's Hyde Park on October 5, 1967.

was a personal friend of President Franklin D. Roosevelt. His cheerful outlook and easy reworking of reality sustained him until his death in 1968, although he knew that doubt remained. In his later years, Tomlinson told a reporter, "My wife helped me make the crown, but she don't much think I'm a king." No doubt there are others. □

Casley like a Fox

Sometimes, revolution is the only effective reply to tyranny. That, at least, was the reasoning of a West Australian farmer by the name of Leonard Casley, who founded his own country in 1970 after the Australian government set a wheat quota lower than the amount of grain already growing on his land.

Although the provocation was not the usual stuff of independence movements, Casley's sense of grievance ruled out halfway measures. In addition to declaring his 18,500-acre farm a sovereign state—the Province of Hutt River—he made himself a prince and created a homespun government led by his wife, Princess Shirley, and a cabinet comprising their three sons: Postmaster General Ian, Foreign Minister Wayne, Treasurer Richard. He then began printing his own currency and stamps and created a flag, a coat of arms, and an anthem.

His show of eccentric defiance did nothing to solve his wheat problem, but it did win him a huge harvest of publicity. As one reporter put it, "Anyone who takes on the ◊

real job was to be king of the world. Beginning in 1955, he traveled "a million miles" to spread the news of his monarchy, briefly landing in 101 countries for a coronation ceremony, sometimes carried out at the local airport. The coronation rite consisted of Tomlinson's donning blue silk robes, holding an inflatable plastic globe as a symbol of his domain, seating himself on a six-dollar folding chair, and placing on his head a gold-painted iron crown.

His reign, Tomlinson has reported, did wonders for humankind. He claimed to have fended off revolutions, averted a war between Israel and the Arabs, ended droughts, and launched a period of general well-being. His 1958 coronation in Moscow's Red Square "melted the iron curtain," he announced. Bemused Soviet newspapers, however, unable to grasp that a king had appeared in their midst and wrought instant peace, referred to Tomlinson as "an American actor."

By his own account, Tomlinson had been at the center of events for a long time: For example, he had been with the Wright brothers when they invented the airplane, and he taxation department in Australia easily finds many admiring listeners." Tourists by the tens of thousands traveled to the Province of Hutt River, flying in from Perth, 370 miles to the south, and landing on a grassy strip after cattle had been shooed away. They found T-shirts and other national mementos for sale at a souvenir store in the capital (population: thirty), and with luck, they had a visit with the royal proprietor. His customary attire for such occasions was a dress uniform of white tie and tails, with a venerable British naval sword at his hip.

To keep the tourists coming, Prince Leonard assiduously stoked the publicity furnace with new shows of sovereign feistiness. He talked about declaring war on Australia. He announced plans to found an airline, create a shipping register, and annex Antarctica. He traveled through Australia to promote his principality, doling out knighthoods at receptions. But by the 1990s, the tourist traffic was down to a trickle, and Hutt River was no closer to real sovereignty. After contesting his claims, the nettled Australian government chose a better weapon to deal with the secessionist: It simply ignored him. But the self-styled prince continued to be hopeful about the future of his little independency. After all, he boasted, it was recognized by Greece, Lebanon, and the Vatican. Those governments deny the claim. □

Flanked by Foreign Minister Wayne *(top, left)* **and Postmaster General Ian** *(right),* **Prince Leonard and Princess Shirley pose for a portrait of Australia's only royal family—the rulers of Hutt River, which issues its own, mainly decorative, stamps** *(above).*

MISERS AND MISANTHROPES

Society's quintessential eccentrics are not, perhaps, the flamboyant nonconformists or the artists tacking erratically against cultural winds, but the lonely, tragic hoarders and haters of the world. Usually propelled by base instincts—fear and loathing, meanness and greed—they are compelled to acquire, only to be possessed by their possessions. Or they are disposed to isolate themselves, shrinking from contact with their fellow beings. Fear is their hallmark; they are eternally afraid of an uncertain future, afraid of other people, afraid, in a way, of light.

Some are miserly stereotypes: ragged ancients crouched spiderlike over caches of gold. Others may be socially prominent but still guided by the secret miser's stunted soul: They lurk behind position and money, walled off from any meaningful human contact. Sometimes, there is not even the semblance of sociability. Misanthropes, driven by an inner voice that only they can hear, simply vanish from the everyday human scene into the clutter of a fortress home—until there comes at last the terse, pitying newspaper obituary, a final flare that momentarily illuminates the murky underworld of eccentricity.

Innocent Bystander

With the riches of seventeenth-century Rome hers to command, Donna Olimpia Maidalchini knew no limits to avarice. The powerful adviser of Pope Innocent X, Donna Olimpia amassed a fortune by selling influence and offices to the ambitious and stealing from the powerless—even, in the end, from Pope Innocent himself.

Donna Olimpia was the wife of Pamfilio Pamphili, a prominent Roman magistrate. Soon after her marriage, however, she transferred her attentions to her husband's brother, Giambattista. Despite his priestly calling, Giambattista was weak-willed and moody. The clever, power-hungry Donna Olimpia soon installed herself as his closest confidante; many in scandal-ridden Rome believed that she was his mistress as well.

From the moment her brother-in-law was made a cardinal, according to one contemporary account, Donna Olimpia began scheming for his election as pope. A consummate politician, she moved easily among the various Vatican factions and coached her cardinal on behavior suitable to a pope-in-waiting. The payoff came in 1644, following the death of Pope Urban VIII, when a stalemated college of cardinals compromised on Pamphili, who, at the age of seventy, took the name of Innocent X.

The aging pope was by now largely under the sway of Donna Olimpia, who at fifty was rejuvenated by access to the power and wealth of the Vatican. She had long been the one to whom petitioners of the cardinal presented their cases—and their fees. With the pope's favors to dispense, her income rose sharply.

(And, in one area at least, her expenses decreased. She stopped distributing alms to the poor, an uncharacteristic practice she had undertaken solely to smooth Giambattista's way to the papacy.)

Every office that the pope bestowed reportedly went to the highest bidder, with Donna Olimpia collecting the proceeds. Some bishoprics stood vacant for as long as five years, because no one could meet the minimum tariff: one year's revenue for an office that lasted three years, or twelve years' income for a lifetime position. One would-be bishop persuaded his brothers to sell their estate in order to help raise 20,000 crowns. Named to the bishopric, he died before he was ordained. And Donna Olimpia, far from refunding the fee to the ruined family, doubled her profit by reselling the office.

Not even Innocent was safe from her greed. Familiar with his chambers, she visited him there on his deathbed. What consolation she brought to his last hours is unknown, but she allegedly departed with two coffers of gold from under the bed.

Pope Innocent died in January of 1655, after ten years on the papal throne. By then, his sister-in-law had siphoned away his wealth, leaving him impoverished. Beseeched to provide for his funeral, Donna Olimpia declined, describing herself as "a poor widow." She refused even to buy a wood-and-lead coffin for the man who had made her rich, causing him to be buried, according to one contemporary account, "in the most simple manner imaginable."

After her benefactor's death, Donna Olimpia turned her influence to electing another pope. The effort failed, and the new pope, Alexander VII, ordered papers drawn up with the idea of bringing her to trial for receiving church property and selling benefices. In the end, Donna Olimpia was banished from Rome to a village a few miles from Orvieto. There, less than three years after Innocent's death, she died in the plague that ravaged Europe. She left no friends, but she did leave an immense fortune of two million gold crowns. According to one historian of the day, this cache was soon raided: The new pope reclaimed a million of the dead widow's crowns, which he reportedly dispersed among *his* relatives. As one outspoken cardinal put it: "The money of Donna Olimpia had passed out of the hands of one thief into the hands of many." □

The implacably greedy Donna Olimpia Maidalchini glowers eternally from this marble likeness by seventeenth-century sculptor Alessandro Algardi.

"Herbes and Roots," says Roger Crab, seventeenth-century hermit and fiber faddist, in a drawing from an 1813 volume about notable English characters.

Hermit Crab

During the 1650s, Roger Crab was an occasional inhabitant of the punishment stocks at Ickenham, Middlesex, where he insisted on defying authorities by working through the Sabbath—what he sarcastically called "the Priests' Market Day." It was not his only departure from the conventions of the time.

During and after England's civil war, when religion was a fighting matter, Crab had little use for any church. He served seven years in the parliamentary army, once suffering a serious head wound in which his skull, he reported, was "cloven to the braine." Perhaps the grievous wound amplified his eccentric behavior. In any event, he continued with his cantankerous politics, which placed him briefly under a death sentence and eventually cost him two years in prison.

Leaving the army around 1649, Crab set up a hat shop in Chesham, where he lived comfortably until about 1651. Then, uneasy in the role of prosperous merchant, he decided to follow the advice of Jesus to "sell whatsoever thou hast, and give to the poor, and thou shalt have treasure in heaven." He kept just enough to lease a small plot of land at Ickenham, where he built a rude shack.

Crab dressed himself in sackcloth and contrived to live on just three farthings (less than a penny) a week. His ascetic ways grew from his conviction that true happiness required the soul to rule the body. He became a vegetarian, eating what he grew as well as the wild produce of neighboring fields—a roughage-ridden diet that weakened the old man, as Crab called his body, but made it "more humble."

Humility did not prevent Crab from extolling his severe lifestyle in an autobiographical pamphlet entitled *The English Hermite, or, Wonder of this Age.* And despite his remove from society, Crab continued to attack its ills, particularly his favorite enemies, churches and clergy. In time, his devotion and abstinence won him a small reputation as a prophet, and he lived out his days free of conflict with the authorities. His harsh, high-fiber regime sustained him until his death at the age of fifty-nine. □

Gnome of the Brave

Benjamin Lay moved into a cavelike cottage near Philadelphia in 1732 to avoid the sinful world. A number of people in that world would have been happy to see the last of him, but they reckoned without Lay's fiery temperament. Although he lived in his grotto for years, he regularly sallied forth to carry on the battle against wickedness.

Lay was unconventional in many ways. He was about four and a half feet tall, with sharp features and a hunched back. Born in England to Quaker parents about 1681, he had apprenticed as a glove maker, then became a sailor in his early twenties. His voyaging allowed a treasured trip to the Holy Land, but Lay was scandalized by the behavior of sailors and quit the sea after seven years to marry and settle in London. He promptly involved himself in religious disputes that led to his expulsion from two meetings of the Society of Friends.

About 1731, Lay and his wife, Sarah, immigrated to the small Caribbean island of Barbados, where Lay established himself as a merchant—and where he formed his virulent, lifelong aversion to the brutality he saw around him. When a wild pig ravaged his garden, Lay furiously killed the animal and strung it up. But soon the gentle little man had second thoughts about his violent reaction, and he resolved never again to eat or wear any product that involved the killing of an animal. He was likewise deeply touched by the plight of the African slaves traded and harshly treated in Barbados, arousing the passion that would rule the rest of his life. ◊

Artist William Williams's long-lost portrait of diminutive gadfly Benjamin Lay turned up at a 1977 auction in a four dollar lot of picture frames.

He soon won a reputation for benevolence that drew hundreds of slaves to his home every Sabbath, where he preached to them and handed out food. But the rising hostility of the Barbados planters soon drove the Lays out, and they arrived in Philadelphia in 1732.

Lay was no more welcome among American Quakers than he had been among the English. While many Friends could agree with his beliefs, few could put up with his methods. Lay disrupted worship with long harangues against slavery, and he once stopped a meeting cold when he graphically illustrated the violence of the institution by stabbing open a bladder filled with red berry juice, spraying the congregation with symbolic blood. He would not eat in a house where slaves were kept, and he wrote books that decried slaveholding as "Filthy Leprosy and Apostacy." One time, in order to teach some neighbors the anguish felt by their slave girl's parents, Lay briefly kidnapped the neighbors' six-year-old son.

The Lays lived for nearly ten years in the cavelike structure not far from Philadelphia, until ill health forced them to move. Sarah died the following year. Lay subsequently moved to a natural grotto, on a friend's farm, where he kept his 200-volume library and frequently retired to read or write. In Lay's declining years, the world began to catch up with his advanced thinking, and he became a minor hero to right-thinking Quakers. In 1759, the gnomelike eighty-year-old received the news for which he had waited a lifetime: The Society of Friends had voted to expel all members who did not free their slaves. Lay shouted thanksgiving, then fell back. "I can now die in peace," he murmured. Within a month, he did. □

Tight Genes

John Meggot (*opposite page*) was a rather ordinary young English gentleman, well educated in the classics, but possessing little knowledge of business or commerce. His ruling passions were good horses and gambling—fit pursuits for a young man of wealth and rank in eighteenth-century England. He was heir to two fortunes. The first, nearly £100,000, had been left by his father, an eminent brewer who died when the lad was only four. The second, about £250,000, was that of his maternal uncle, Sir Harvey Elwes, a wealthy Suffolk landowner.

Unfortunately for Meggot, he stood to inherit more than riches and position. The Elwes side of his family had a peculiar—and destructive—attitude toward money. Despite her husband's legacy, Mrs. Meggot had reportedly starved herself to death. And Sir Harvey was a tightwad of the first order; he pared the expenses of his family estates to £100 per year. It was as if a miser's withered spirit lived in the wealthy family's genes.

After completing his education in London's Westminster School and Geneva, Meggot began paying visits to his uncle in 1735. Sir Harvey deplored wasting money on clothes.

(His own, often fifty years out of date, came from an ancestral trunk in his attic.) So the nephew always stopped to change at an inn en route. His tattered coat, darned stockings, and shoes with rusty iron buckles won the uncle's approval. Meggot further pleased his uncle by eating sparingly; Sir Harvey never learned that the younger man diminished his hearty appetite by dining secretly with friends before taking supper with his uncle. Soon the London dandy was spending several ingratiating weeks each year in this imposture—which, slowly but irresistibly, began to shape the man.

Middle-aged when he inherited

his uncle's estate in 1763, Meggot had begun living in earnest the miserly role he had formerly only affected. He still gambled regularly at cards, winning or losing thousands of pounds at a sitting; but now petty savings had become urgently important to him. After a night of gambling, for example, Meggot would walk miles to market to meet cattle being driven there from one of his farms. Only a few hours removed from the sumptuous gambling rooms, he would stand in the mud arguing with a carcass butcher over a shilling.

A clause in his uncle's will required Meggot to take the name Elwes, which seems to have set a kind of seal on his penurious ways. For some years, the new John Elwes maintained a few old indulgences, most notably a kennel of foxhounds and a stable of hunting horses, considered the best in the kingdom. But frugality reigned even here; Elwes's huntsman was required to do the work of three ordinary men. Nevertheless Elwes frequently denounced the man as "an idle dog" who wanted to be paid for doing nothing. Wags among the neighbors said that the dogs were savage hunters because it was the only way they got to eat.

Eventually, Elwes gave up even the vestigial pleasures of the hunt, turning all his efforts to saving money. He frequently ate rotting meat to postpone a visit to the butcher, where he had whole sheep slaughtered for his larder, to be eaten bit by bit until the entire carcass was consumed—even, as one writer put it, "meat that moved in his plate." He thought nothing of walking through the heaviest London rains to avoid spending a shilling on a coach. He kept no house of his own in the city, passing his nights instead in whichever of his many rental properties was unoccupied. He never allowed his shoes to be cleaned, lest they wear out sooner, and he took to wearing coats from the same attic chest that had supplied his uncle's wardrobe. When traveling, Elwes fed himself from a pocketful of hard-boiled eggs or moldy crusts of bread.

Despite the niggardliness of the private man, the public Elwes had a reputation for courtesy, honesty, and occasional generosity. His servants, though embarrassed by his more extreme economies, were on the whole well treated and loyal.

Elwes was a respected magistrate and even served three terms in Parliament. When political leaders first asked him to stand for office, he put forth only one condition: that the venture cost him nothing. As it turned out, the cost was satisfactorily small. His sole campaign expense was supper that cost eighteen pence at a pub.

When political upheaval engendered by the American Revolution threatened a contested election, Elwes left public service rather than spend money on a campaign he would probably have won. This evidently ruined his chance for a peerage, which seemed to be good news to Elwes: The honor would have carried the expensive obligation of maintaining a carriage and several servants—probably better dressed than their master. Returning to his country homes, he amused himself by picking over his fields, gleaning stray corn left on the ground by his tenant farmers.

Apparently, the Elwes strain of cheapness was not propagated to the next generation. Elwes had two illegitimate sons by a housekeeper, and they eventually took over the management of his properties from the increasingly unreliable old man. Perhaps immune to the miser gene, they were solicitous of their father in his declining years.

But the aging miser had begun to disintegrate. Tortured by imagined thefts, his memory in tatters, Elwes died in 1789, aged over eighty. His last words to his younger son were that he hoped he had "left him what he wished"—an estate, bequeathed mostly to the two sons, of more than £800,000. □

Hermits R Us

In eighteenth-century Britain, hermits became something of a fad among the gentry. It was not that aristocrats wanted to become recluses themselves—they merely wanted to acquire hermits of their own. Wealthy country gentlemen, who lived opulent lives from the proceeds of their land and other holdings, were especially intrigued by these peculiar people—mostly men—who actively shunned wealth, pleasure, and human company. Such people were as exotic and unlikely as unicorns. It became fashionable to have a hermit living miserably somewhere on one's grounds, among such romantic relics as ruined walls, false cliffs, and replicas of Greek temples and medieval abbeys. Unable to find a genuine hermit, but much taken with the idea of having one to deco-

rate the hermitage that he had constructed, Charles Hamilton, master of Painshill, in Surrey, tried to hire someone for the job.

Hamilton advertised for a hermit to occupy the determinedly uncomfortable retreat he had built atop a steep mound on his estate. The successful applicant would live for seven years in a spare cell partly supported by gnarled tree roots. There he would be provided with a Bible, spectacles, a mat, a hassock for a pillow, an hourglass, and food and water. He would wear a heavy robe; allow his hair, beard, and nails to flourish uncut; and never leave the grounds or speak even one word with the servant who brought his food. At the end of the seven years, the hermit would receive a token of Hamilton's esteem: £700, in those days a generous wage for seven years' work.

Hermits are born, however, not

bought. The man Hamilton hired lasted only three weeks before giving in to loneliness and a fondness for beer. He had no successor.

Still, some gentlemen had more success than Hamilton. A Lancashire squire offered fifty pounds a year for life to anyone who would live for seven years underground, without human contact, clipped nails, a haircut, or a shave. One candidate lasted four years, living in a large underground apartment.

Despite its obvious drawbacks, the job of ornamental hermit, as the isolated employees were called, apparently was not wholly without allure. In an 1810 newspaper, this advertisement appeared: "A young man, who wishes to retire from the world and live as a hermit, in some convenient spot in England, is willing to engage with any nobleman or gentleman who may be desirous of having one." □

Dancers Cheap to Cheap

Lying naked on Harrow Weald Common under the warm sun, Daniel Dancer *(below)* might have been mistaken for a hedonist. In fact, Dancer's inclinations were in just the opposite direction: This world-class pinchpenny bathed only on sunny days, to avoid the expense of towels, and saved on soap by scrubbing with sand.

Daniel Dancer had no need for such parsimony. The oldest among three sons and a daughter of a prosperous Middlesex farmer, the miserly twenty-year-old inherited property worth £3,000 per year in 1736—a fortune in his day. And, in fact, he was frugal only with himself and his family. On the road with a friend—despite infrequent bathing and changing of clothes, he did have a few pals—he would sleep with the horses at an inn but cheerfully pay £15 to cover his companion's expenses.

Dancer spared everything at home. He lived with his sister in a run-down outbuilding that eventually deteriorated into a hovel. Kin in spirit as well as blood, the two made but one cooking fire each week. Every Sunday they boiled a chunk of beef and fourteen hard dumplings, which they would slowly consume, ignoring the gathering odor of spoiled meat. Once, when Dancer came upon the rotting carcass of a diseased sheep, he took it back home to be made into mutton pies, which the parsimonious pair ate with gusto.

The meager fare never improved, even as the sister lay dying. "If you don't like it," Dancer is said to have scolded, "you may go without it." Urged by concerned neighbors to summon a doctor, he decided that it would be wicked to waste money trying to counteract Providence with medicine. He declared that his sister "may as well die now as at any future period."

The dying woman proposed to leave her own property, about £2,000, to Lady Maria Tempest, a solicitous neighbor who nursed her during her final illness. But Miss Dancer expired before she could sign a will, and her brother moved quickly to take possession. When Dancer's two brothers sued for their rightful, equal portions, Dancer responded with a claim against the estate: £30 per year for board for thirty years, with the last two years billed at £100 each because, he claimed, his sister had done nothing during that period of time except eat and lie in bed. Dancer received £1,040 of the estate, with the remainder apportioned equally among him and his brothers.

Dancer's house was half-filled with sticks stolen from his neighbors' hedges, which fueled his infrequent fires. He was reluctant to waste even these, however. Once Lady Tempest sent him a dish of trout stewed in claret, which congealed in the cold of a frosty night. Unable to eat the meal cold from fear of toothache, but unwilling to light a fire to warm it, Dancer solved the problem by putting the dish between two pewter plates and sitting on it until his body warmth spread to the food.

The only affection old Dancer ever showed was for a dog he called Bob: He went so far as to buy milk for the animal. But even here, his fondness for money dominated. After Bob was accused of chasing sheep, Dancer worried that he might someday have to pay compensation to a farmer. To put an end to such risk, he took Bob to a blacksmith and had the animal's teeth broken off short. Thereafter, Dancer continued to feed the unfortunate dog a pint of milk a day, augmented with bones that he found and broke into pieces small enough for Bob to swallow.

The bones were only some of the small treasures Dancer picked up along the roads. He regularly filled his pockets with cattle dung, which he added to a pile in his shed and used to fertilize his fields—and more. After he died in 1794, at the age of seventy-eight, his neighbors began to investigate long-standing tales that the old skinflint had harbored hidden cash. And indeed they found the loot—hundreds of guineas stashed in jugs and teapots, stuffed into chairs, and shoved up the chimney. The largest hoard—£2,500—was hidden in a place that few burglars would want to look for it: under Dancer's little mountain of manure. □

The Man Who Came to Dinner

Judged by his appearance, Thomas Cooke might have been anything—except a miser. A well-turned-out, portly merchant who boasted openly of his fortune, Cooke exuded promise of legacies to come—especially for those whose dining tables he regularly shared. But few of his hosts saw any reward for favors rendered: Cooke was a kind of raider, a pirate of parsimony running under the flag of wealth.

Cooke was born near Windsor, England, around 1726, the son of an itinerant fiddler who played at fairs and alehouses. Raised by his aged grandmother, the lad went out on his own as soon as he was old enough to work in a factory.

There Cooke showed the first signs of a lifelong obsession with saving money on meals: He refused to join the mess that other boys put together by pooling a small part of their weekly earnings. Instead, he limited himself each day to a halfpenny loaf of bread and an apple, washed down with water from the brook that ran by the factory.

His youthful economy allowed Cooke to hire a schoolboy to tutor him in reading, writing, and basic arithmetic. He parlayed that learning and plenty of ambition into a position with the Board of Excise, the British tax collection agency.

His job included inspecting factories, a large paper mill near Tottenham among them. After the master of the mill died, and management of the facility passed to the widow, Cooke began to discover a number of irregularities—tax offenses that carried ruinous fines. Instead of reporting the offenses to the Excise, however, Cooke offered the widow two choices: She could marry him and make him lord of her considerable holdings; or she could let him report the infractions and be beggared by the penalties. The unfortunate widow chose Cooke over penury—or thought she did.

Once married, the fiddler's son was a wealthy man, intent on getting wealthier. When his lease on the Tottenham mill lapsed, he bought a large sugar-refining concern in nearby Puddle Dock and became a prosperous sugar baker. But Cooke was not concerned merely with earning more money: He turned the devious intelligence that had won his fortune to schemes to avoid spending it.

Cooke's chief strategem was never to be home at mealtimes, so that customers and friends would be unable to dine at his expense. Instead, he turned the tables, choosing traders who valued his business and dropping in just at the family's dinner hour. When asked to stay, he typically pretended reluctance, then gave in to the slightest persuasion.

At such a meal, he would drop broad hints about his great wealth, express his gratitude for the hospitality, then carefully write down the names of the children. Parents who imagined their family mentioned in his will cultivated his friendship. So Cooke was not only a regular dinner guest, but also frequently a recipient of presents of all kinds of food. He kept the worst for his household and sold the rest.

When acquaintances failed him, Cooke exploited the kindness of strangers. He might feign a fit in the street before a selected house. The occupants, moved by the apparent distress of this respectable man, would offer a glass of wine, then another; soon they would find themselves on Cooke's list of mealtime destinations.

As for the unfortunate wife whose wealth had made him rich, Cooke denied her any luxuries beyond a short ration of table beer. He treated her so badly that her death was said to be of a broken heart. The greedy widower then paid court to other rich widows, but he was stymied by his insistence that a wife sign all her property over to him and disinherit her children.

Finally, Cooke retired from business to a rented house with a small garden that he planted in cabbage, his favorite food. His health declined, but not his avarice; few doctors who treated him ever received their full fees. Cooke's passing in his mideighties went largely unmourned, but not unnoticed: At his burial, a jeering crowd threw cabbage stalks on his coffin as it descended into the grave.

Most of the long-suffering families that had catered to Thomas Cooke's appetite and hoped to inherit his wealth were disappointed. His will left the bulk of his estate, valued at more than £127,000, to almshouses and charity groups—the sole act of generosity in a long, mean lifetime. □

The miserly Thomas Cooke is the picture of wealth in this early nineteenth-century caricature.

Master of Welbeck Abbey (below), the reclusive fifth duke of Portland created a subterranean world with a network of tunnels (left), a giant ballroom, and stately halls illuminated by skylights.

Burrowed Time

When William J. C. Bentinck-Scott decided he wanted to avoid all human contact, he did not move into a cave; he more or less created one. Like a shy, burrowing animal, Bentinck-Scott, who became the fifth duke of Portland in 1854, began deploying his resources to hide himself from the eyes of the world.

In his youth, Bentinck-Scott was by all accounts a normal member of the British aristocracy, even serving as a member of Parliament for a few years. When he acceded to the dukedom, however, he began to withdraw from society, as his mother had before him. He retired to a few sparsely furnished rooms in vast Welbeck Abbey in Nottinghamshire. Bentinck-Scott then issued orders that none of his servants or tenants was to speak to him or acknowledge him in any way whatsoever; a laborer who tipped his hat to the duke would be dismissed immediately. Communications were conducted through a pair of letter boxes on the door to his room—one for incoming messages, the other for outgoing ones.

When he was ill, the doctor could come only to the door; questions and answers were relayed by the valet, the only person authorized to feel the ducal pulse.

As his reclusive bent intensified, the duke developed a passion for burrowing. Some said it was a generous man's way of employing out-of-work laborers in lean times; others, that working invisibly underground kept his projects from seeming ostentatious. Whatever the motivation, the grandest expression of his subterranean passion was a tunnel, a mile and a quarter long. It connected Welbeck Abbey with the train station in the nearby village. When the duke traveled to London, he rode through the tunnel in a carriage that was then lifted onto a reserved train car; no prying eyes ever penetrated the carriage's tightly drawn green silk blinds. In town, he was said to throw coins from the carriage to children, although no urchin ever saw his face.

Portland kept hundreds of laborers working on a network of tunnels that eventually totaled fifteen miles in length. One tunnel connected the house with a huge underground stable filled with horses that no one ever rode. Another led to the kitchen, where there was always a chicken roasting on a spit, so that one would be ready whenever the duke rang for it. A heated car running on rails carried the food through a tunnel to the house.

The molelike noble also built an immense suite of subterranean rooms, including an enormous library, a billiard room, and the largest ballroom in the country, big enough for 2,000 people. For his household staff, he built a spacious skating rink, and he insisted that they use it. If he chanced upon a housemaid sweeping the stairs instead of skating, he would chase her out to the rink whether she wanted to go or not.

In his last years, the duke emerged from his mansion only at night, following a lamp held by a silent servant woman who stayed forty yards ahead. When he died at the age of seventy-nine, he had held his title for more than twenty years and had spent hundreds of thousands of pounds on improvements—mostly subterranean ones—to Welbeck Abbey. But no visitors played billiards or attended balls in his cavernous house while he lived. The estate, one contemporary wrote, was "vast, splendid and utterly comfortless: One could imagine no more awful and ghastly fate than waking up one day and finding oneself Duke of Portland and master of Welbeck." □

Starman

David Wilbur was a valuable re-source for the farmers and fish-ermen of Westerly, Rhode Island, often providing accurate weather forecasts—no small feat in the early nineteenth cen-tury. But getting a report from him was a tricky business, nec-essarily conducted at a distance, for Wilbur was deathly afraid of any contact with other humans. The only questions he would an-swer were about the weather.

Wilbur left his family home when he was about twenty, after the death of his father. Taking to the forests, he lived on wild berries and fruit during the summer and stored up grain and nuts for the win-ter, when he also ate roots and whatever game he could trap. He slept by a large rock in a swamp, with an old door for a roof and flax for a pillow. In the worst weather, he might take shelter in a barn; but he rarely entered a house.

By day, Wilbur watched the clouds and checked the winds; by night, he watched the stars. Though completely uned-ucated, he obviously made something of his observations, and neighbors took to calling him "the astronomer."

Wilbur's only attempts at ini-tiating communication were the numbers and peculiar signs and figures he frequently scratched on pumpkins in fields. Although several residents tried to deci-pher these strange markings, none succeeded; if they held meaning, Wilbur took it with him when he died in 1848, aged about seventy. In death he final-ly left the woods to rejoin his fellows, in a small farm bur-ial ground. □

Sage of Wall Street

A poor country boy who worked his way to the top of Wall Street in the robber baron era, Russell Sage was as well known for pinching pennies as for making mil-lions. He could reputedly get hold of more capital faster than any other fi-nancier of his day, and he claimed to have more cash on hand than any bank. But he habitually chose the public trolley over a fine carriage or car; and even for that lowly transit, he found it hard to produce the ten-cent fare if he could cadge a ride instead. A miser lived within the millionaire.

Sage was born in a small settle-ment in central New York State in 1816 and spent his childhood on the family farm. His full load of chores taught him the meaning of hard work. He took instruction in thrift from his father, who advised, "Any man can earn a dollar, but it takes a wise man to save it."

Sage's first commercial venture was as a boy-of-all-work in a grocery store run by an older brother in Troy, New York. There at the age of twelve, Sage determined to succeed in whatever he did. Late in life he was fond of recalling that he saved the first dollar he ever earned and that he was never a penny short or a minute late in paying what he owed.

He invested his first savings in night school, where he learned bookkeeping and a smattering of history. But by the time he was fif-teen, he had already saved enough from his wage of four dollars a week to buy two vacant lots across the street from the store. He al-so became a shrewd horse trader, putting his profits into more land and a cargo boat that he used to carry horses to New York City.

Sage soon had his own store. He then moved into wholesaling and branched out into the growing rail-road business. At twenty-two, he owned $25,000 in cash, land, and two boats—a sizable chunk of capi-tal then. By his midthirties, he was a leading citizen of Troy, deeply in-volved in politics at the local and national level. After two terms in Congress, however, he decided his future lay in business. Politics, said Sage, "did not pay."

It was a well-timed decision. Sage arrived on Wall Street at the begin-ning of the Civil War and quickly de-veloped close ties with such leg-endary financiers as Jay Gould and Cyrus Field. Noted for his shrewd, conservative investment style, he was not a creative capitalist who set up railroads or transatlantic cables. But he was a reliable investor in such ventures, and he almost al-ways won a handsome return on his

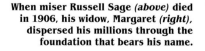

When miser Russell Sage *(above)* died in 1906, his widow, Margaret *(right)*, dispersed his millions through the foundation that bears his name.

investment. He ended up on the boards of more than twenty railroad and steamship companies. By 1884, when he suffered his only major loss on Wall Street, he covered obligations of more than four million dollars, as the *New York Times* wrote, "without a murmur."

His great fortune did little, however, to change the habits of his frugal youth. Although he lived in an expensive house in town and maintained a comfortable country house as well, Sage filled them with broken-down furniture that he had owned for years. He dressed in twelve-dollar suits and routinely carried a small lunch basket to work rather than pay restaurant prices.

In an era of public fascination with the lavish lifestyles of rich capitalists, Sage became famous for his difference. Oddly enough, his peculiar blend of great wealth and legendary stinginess seemed to single him out as a target for strangers seeking financial help. Sometimes threats accompanied the requests. In 1891, one petitioner confronted Sage in his office with a note demanding $1,200,000. When Sage waved him away, the visitor promptly detonated a dynamite bomb—blowing himself to bits. The blast also killed Sage's typist and injured five other clerks and colleagues. But the seventy-four-year-old financier survived with only bruises and superficial cuts—and a lawsuit from visiting Wall Street clerk William R. Laidlaw, who was injured by the blast. Laidlaw sued when Sage refused to cover his hospital bills, claiming that the millionaire had used him as a shield. The clerk was granted several awards before Sage's customary luck prevailed: A New York court of appeals found the financier to be blameless.

The experience confirmed Sage's already strong inclination to avoid charitable works. He even objected when he saw a newspaper picture of his second wife, a Troy schoolteacher he married in 1869, feeding peanuts to park squirrels. Surely, he admonished her, bread crumbs otherwise wasted in the kitchen would do as well. Margaret Sage quietly went along; although she devoted herself to charitable work, she declared that her husband's money was his to dispose of as he saw fit.

He ultimately disposed of his estimated $70 million by leaving it to her—minus a few small bequests and a $22,000 outlay for a six-ton casket. Neurotically afraid that his body would be kidnapped and held for ransom, Sage arranged to be interred in a copper envelope, which was placed inside a mahogany coffin enclosed in an outer sarcophagus of case-hardened steel and rigged with electrical alarms.

After her husband's death, Margaret Sage, who had quietly followed her own counsel for nearly forty years, put her legacy to work to help the less fortunate. Her largest gift established the Russell Sage Foundation. "I am almost eighty years old," said the widow when she announced the foundation, "and I am just beginning to live." With a single act, she transformed the accumulated wealth of her miserly millionaire into a gold mine for generous good works and made his name, once despised, a virtual synonym for charity. □

R ussell Sage was the favorite millionaire of kindred spirit Hetty Green (pages 46-48), who revered money perhaps even more than he did. Contemptuous of the way that Sage's widow gave away his wealth, Hetty also felt a touch of envy: For a short period of time, it was Margaret Sage, not Hetty Green, who was the richest woman on earth.

Lovely Ida Mayfield Wood, shown here in the 1860s, vanished in 1907. She reappeared almost a quarter-century later, a wealthy recluse with a secret history.

Belle Belied

No one had heard of Ida Mayfield Wood in years. A leading socialite in New York society from the 1860s to the turn of the century, she had been a beautiful Louisiana belle, the radiant daughter of a distinguished judge. She married Ben Wood, newspaper publisher, politician, gambler, and brother of a one-time New York mayor. In 1907, Ida, by then a widow, had anticipated an imminent financial panic and had withdrawn all the money—upwards of half a million dollars—from her bank account, carrying it away in a net bag. And then, as suddenly as she had appeared on the New York scene half a century earlier, the seventyish southern belle vanished.

In March 1931, a doctor called to a suite at New York's Herald Square Hotel found Ida living there with her sister, Mary, who was dying of cancer. The sisters had lived in those same rooms for twenty-four years. Mary had seldom left the suite; Ida, never. The only person to enter the suite was a night elevator operator who brought food every few days from a nearby delicatessen. Ida always tipped him a dime and told him it was the last of her money. With Mary fatally ill, however, Ida had finally allowed a doctor into their rooms, and soon the news of her reclusive existence was out.

In response to questions about her life—and her fortune—the vinegary little ninety-three-year-old waved stock certificates and talked portentously of $385,000 in cash. The suite was jammed with trunks stuffed with every valentine, dance card, and ball gown that Ida had ever possessed, along with cartons of yellowing menus, correspondence, and notes jotted down on ragged scraps of paper in her distinctive hand. While the intruders marveled at the rodent's nest that she had created, Ida crouched in her rocker, smoking one of her long, thin Havana cigars.

In September of 1931, she was declared incompetent to handle her affairs, but she resolutely refused to relinquish any valuables, noting, "I made money and I kept it. So many people whom everyone considers quite competent can't do that." In fact, she had preserved her wealth through both the panic of 1907 and 1929's Wall Street crash. In October of 1931, she was moved from her squalid rooms to an identical suite on another floor. It took the efforts of two nurses, a doctor, and two private detectives to effect the transfer, with the tiny nonagenarian kicking, biting, and scratching every inch of the way. "You're only doing this so you can go through my things and steal my money," she cried. "But you'll never find anything. I've hidden it too carefully."

But not carefully enough. Within an hour the cluttered suite yielded a crumbling shoebox with $247,000 in large bills. A gorgeous necklace of diamonds and emeralds, later sold for $37,000, was found in a box of moldy crackers Ida had kept by her bed. But she carried the real trove with her. The day after the move, a nurse examined a strange lump under Ida's skirt. It turned out to be a makeshift money belt stuffed with half a million dollars in $10,000 bills.

Newspapers provided a tumultuous chronicle of Ida's affairs as events unfolded through the year, with the doughty widow inviting reporters in to hear her side of the story. But, feisty though she was, the sudden return to the world proved more than she could bear. She contracted pneumonia and died in March 1932—just a year after her rediscovery by the public. And, characteristically, her death merely deepened the central mystery of Ida Mayfield Wood.

Scores of Louisiana Mayfields, her putative heirs, descended on New York to stake their claim to her fortune—but all were disappointed. Among the hundreds of annotated scraps, officials had discovered a piece that would unlock the puzzle of Ida Wood. "Father arrived in California August 6, 1862," it read. "Died Nov. 9th at 10 a.m., 1864. Buried November 10th in Mount Calvary Cemetery, California." Father, it turned out, was not the distinguished—but fictional—Louisiana jurist, but one Thomas Walsh, described by one reporter as "a wretched Irishman." The New York public administrator established that Ida Mayfield Wood had been a fiction, the false identity assumed by Ellen Walsh. Born in Oldham, Lancashire, the daughter of an itinerant Irish textile vendor, she had arrived with her family in Massachusetts about 1845. Her early life was suffused with memories of hardship, insecurity, and poverty. Even after the family settled in rural Massachusetts, times were hard. The adolescent Ellen apparently took work as a domestic servant—and took charge.

Determined to change her luck, the beautiful Miss Walsh set out on her own in 1857, assuming a new identity and setting her cap for Ben Wood, who fell deeply in love with her. She never divulged her secret, and when she brought her sisters, brother, and mother to New York, all went by the name of Mayfield. Even at the end, as Ida (or Ellen) talked with nurses about her family, her mind meandering across whole eras of her life, she kept the fictitious names straight. But after years of legal wrangling, her estate finally went to Walsh family members—ten grandchildren of two aunts and an uncle—in shares of $84,490.92. None of the heirs had ever met their resourceful relative, and only one had even been aware of her existence. □

In 1951, charitable Harvard men paid classmate Harry Chapin Smith's way to their fiftieth reunion. The apparently penniless Smith roamed New York City streets looking for junk—but he also had several safe-deposit boxes. Opened after Smith's death later in 1951, they revealed that he had parlayed a $4,000 inheritance into a cool $400,000.

No Will of Her Own

Henrietta Schaefer Garrett's life was part Cinderella story. A poor child of German immigrant parents in Philadelphia, she loved and married a wealthy older man, and she lived with him happily—but not ever after. Henrietta's life with Walter Garrett was idyllic, despite a rocky reception from Philadelphia's social set, who considered her an unworthy match for the heir to a formidable fortune from the thriving snuff industry. For his part, Garrett was so devoted to his wife, eighteen years his junior, that he severed his old social and business connections in order to make her life more congenial. But after twenty-three good years, Garrett died in 1895, leaving his widow six million dollars—and insupportable grief. Shattered by the loss of her husband, Henrietta withdrew from the world.

From the day her husband was buried, she rarely left their mansion, which she maintained exactly as he had known it. As time passed, and as times changed, she refused to install such modern conveniences as a telephone and electric lighting. Her brother, a bank clerk, lived with her until his death in 1913; thereafter, she became a complete recluse, going out only once in the last fifteen years of her life.

Henrietta deprived herself of companionship, but not of comfort. She kept a number of servants, and she regularly placed expensive orders with dressmakers and hat shops for stylish ensembles that she very rarely wore outside the house. She gave lavishly to charity, bought season tickets for the

Philadelphia Orchestra—which she never attended—and sent presents to needy friends.

Desperately afraid of death, Henrietta had always refused even to talk of a proper will, despite her husband's pleas. He had worked long and hard to accumulate the fortune, Garrett told her, and he hoped Henrietta would keep it out of the hands of "scalawags."

But when Henrietta died intestate in 1930, at the age of eighty-

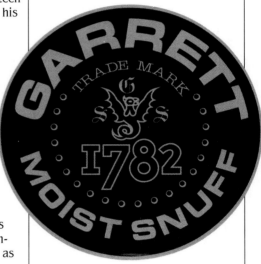

one, the scalawags descended in droves on her estate, by this time swollen to more than $15 million. By 1937, there were more than 26,000 claimants. Honest misconceptions as well as false wills and perjured testimony took so long to sort out that the estate was not finally settled for decades. In the end, $3 million went to cover legal costs, $4 million went to the U.S. government, and $8 million went to distant relatives. In Garrett's view, perhaps, the scalawags had won. □

America's oldest continuously used trademark logo (above) still identifies the 1782 origin of Garrett Snuff, which was the source of Henrietta Schaefer Garrett's heirless fortune.

End of the Line

Augustus Van Horne Stuyvesant, Jr., had many memories to ponder in his Fifth Avenue limestone chateau. The fodder for reminiscence included not only his own eight decades of life, but also the illustrious past of his family, descended from Peter Stuyvesant, the last Dutch governor of New Amsterdam, the city that became New York. Augustus was of the eighth generation directly descended from the near-legendary peg-legged Dutchman, but the family had begun to recede from public view. According to social historian Cleveland Amory, the sixth generation had turned toward quiet scholarship; subsequent generations were quieter

yet. But the generation of Augustus was the last—when the octogenarian bachelor passed on, he would take his family with him.

The last Stuyvesant had carried his family's growing reclusivity to its extreme point. His last twenty-five years were spent in extraordinary seclusion, living behind three locked bronze doors. He had no family or social life and scant business affairs. His only recreation was a daily one-hour stroll through the streets near his home.

He was a tall, dapper aristocrat, courteous and terribly shy, and cursed with a speech impediment that made him sound like a child. After the 1938 death of Anne, the younger of two sisters who had spent their lives with him, his sole contact with outsiders became a weekly church service. He even went days at a time without seeing his servants; they left his food in a sitting room, and he came out of his bedroom long enough to eat.

Stuyvesant's English butler, Ernest Vernon, worked for the old man for thirty-three years, never taking a vacation. "We were perfect strangers," he later told reporters. "No one ever passed the time of day with Mr. Stuyvesant."

And no one passed the time with any Mr. Stuyvesant again. On August 11, 1953, aged eighty-three, Augustus Van Horne Stuyvesant, Jr., died after a short illness. Three days later, on a rainy Friday, he was buried at the Church of St. Mark's-in-the-Bouwerie in the marble vault built by his Dutch ancestor in 1660, where more than eighty Stuyvesant descendants were interred. Nearly three centuries after it received the first Stuyvesant, the mausoleum received the last—and its bronze doors were sealed forever. □

Augustus Van Horne Stuyvesant, Jr., the last direct descendant of the seventeenth-century New York governor Peter Stuyvesant, poses with sister Anne beneath the stern gaze of his peg-legged ancestor.

The Color of Money

"My father taught me never to owe anyone anything," said Hetty Green, "not even a kindness." To the end of her days, the richest woman in America did her best to live up to that bitter credo.

She was born Henrietta Howland Robinson in 1834, heiress to two fortunes made on whaling from the port of New Bedford, Massachusetts. Her Quaker family reared Hetty to believe in plain living and profitable investments; as the only child in her generation, she was groomed to manage the family affairs. As soon as she could puzzle out numerals on her own, her father set her to reading stock-market reports to him. He carefully explained all his business transactions and expected Hetty to keep strict accounts of her own expenses. By the time she was eight years old, Hetty had begun saving and keeping accounts on her own.

The fledgling businesswoman attended a Boston finishing school, but her rough language and rebellious spirit frequently outstripped her social graces, such as they were. Although she was an attractive young woman, suitors came and went, always rejected as fortune hunters—which many no doubt were. Hetty's mother, frail and inaccessible beneath the heavy hand of the senior Robinson, died in 1860, leaving her twenty-five-year-old daughter some real estate. Soon afterward, Robinson moved to New York, but Hetty stayed in New Bedford with her mother's spinster sister, Sylvia Ann Howland. Hetty nagged and scolded her aunt over petty issues of domestic economy

Photographed at the age of seventy-eight in her customary soiled black costume, Hetty Green was called the Witch of Wall Street.

until the aging Sylvia fled her home for the nearby family farm. Only when Hetty was assured that the bulk of Sylvia's two-million-dollar estate would pass to her did she finally join her father in New York—perhaps as a way of keeping him from remarrying.

In New York, she met Edward Green, a wealthy Vermont trader recently returned from building a fortune in the Philippines. Although Hetty was suspicious of his open-handedness, she was pleased at last to be courted by a man with his own fortune. Romance took a backseat, however, when her father and aunt died two weeks apart in 1865—murdered, Hetty believed, in a nameless conspiracy. From her father she inherited $1 million in cash and real estate, and a trust fund of some $4.5 million. Sylvia left Hetty a trust fund of about $1 million, enough to provide an annual income of nearly $70,000 for life. But Sylvia had bequeathed more than half her fortune to a variety of relatives, friends, servants, and charities. Infuriated, Hetty soon produced a document that she claimed was Sylvia's last will, signed in her presence; not surprisingly, it named Hetty as the sole heir. She brought a lawsuit claiming the entire estate, beginning a long contest that would make Hetty Robinson notorious before the matter was dropped—one of the few business fights that Hetty ever lost.

The suit was still pending when Hetty married Edward Green in 1867, after allegedly getting him to sign an agreement that she would not be liable for his debts. The couple soon sailed for England, where Green paid their considerable living expenses while Hetty wheeled and dealed in London's financial mar-kets. The couple spent eight years in England, and their children, Ned and Sylvia, were born there.

Hetty was devoted to the children, but not even they could overcome her obsession with money. Eight years after the family returned to New York, Ned injured his knee in a sledding accident, and Hetty tried to avoid doctors' fees by treating him herself. When the injury worsened, she dressed herself in rags and took the boy to a charity hospital. Although she understood the seriousness of the situation, and eventually had the boy treated by numerous doctors, her initial parsimonious reflex took its toll. A number of years after the original injury, Ned's leg was amputated—at his father's expense.

By that time, Hetty was no longer living with Green, who had lost most of his fortune through poor investments while she was building her own to more than $25 million. Although she gave him some aid, his failures repelled her. She moved out, but she did not divorce him. She did, however, abandon Green's high style of living, which had always made her uncomfortable. Once known as the Queen of Wall Street, she now became the Witch of Wall Street, clad in a shabby dress so old and worn it acquired an odd, greenish hue. To save money, she washed only its hem. When Green died in 1902, she added a widow's veil to her costume and wore it for years afterward. She kept no office—her business was conducted from her vault in the Chemical National Bank—and no permanent residence, staying instead in a series of dingy apartments and boarding-houses around Manhattan's fringes. For lunch, she dug into her handbag for scraps of food or heated oatmeal on a radiator.

Hetty's huge collection of securities reposed in boxes and trunks, which she occasionally stacked on a wagon to haul from one New York bank to another. Rarely carrying more than a few dollar bills in a handbag, she often traveled by public stage with cash and negotiable bonds worth hundreds of thousands of dollars stashed in secret pockets. When a nervous banker suggested a private carriage might be safer, Hetty replied, "Perhaps you can afford to ride in a carriage—I cannot." Because one of her main business activities was usury—some critics labeled her a mere pawnbroker—she often had the satisfaction of lending such spendthrifts money on their way down.

The children suffered under constrictive budgets. Ned proved an excellent businessman, but even at the age of twenty-five, when he was running one of his mother's railroads in Texas, the six-foot-four, 300-pounder was reduced to pleading for an increase in his meager allowance to attend the Columbian Exposition in Chicago. Ned even- ◊

tually rejected Hetty's miserly way of life, squandering money on women, cars, boats, costly collectibles, and a baseball team. But their mutual affection was undimmed, and Ned honored his pledge not to marry until he reached his forties.

Hetty's daughter, Sylvia, was another story. Hetty taught her little business and only grudgingly paid for the necessities of her social life—although, uncharacteristically, she staged a sumptuous coming-out banquet. She disapproved suitors one by one as fortune hunters, although she finally allowed Sylvia to marry after a prospective groom appeared with a fortune of his own. The match was to millionaire Matthew Astor Wilks, aged sixty-three; Sylvia was thirty-eight.

Two years after Sylvia's marriage, Hetty's health began to fail. She summoned her son from Texas to be near her; but she only occasionally stayed at his home, preferring a tiny flat she rented in Hoboken. In 1916, visiting a friend, Hetty got into a heated argument with the cook, whom she accused of squandering money by using whole milk instead of skim in a recipe. Midtirade, Hetty suffered a stroke from which she never recovered. She moved into Ned's

apartment, where, after a series of strokes, she died on July 3, 1916.

Her will hewed to her conviction that money should stay in the family: Most of her estimated $100 million went to Ned and Sylvia, who treated it according to their different natures. Always profligate, Ned now became a legendary high liver; he promptly married the woman who had been his companion for twenty years, and he spent money at the dizzying annual rate of $3 million. Even so, his own estate was valued at $50 million at the time of his death in 1936.

In keeping with the Green family tradition, almost all of Ned's money went to Sylvia, with only a small life income granted to his wife; her effort to annul a prenuptial waiver of her claim to his estate failed in the courts. Sylvia now had a fortune of nearly $200 million—which she, being neither a Hetty nor a Ned, put to no use whatever. Although she lived in greater style than her mother, she spent little and kept millions of dollars in checking accounts, earning nothing. Her husband had died in 1926, and the childless Sylvia lived on alone, shuttling between a run-down city apartment and four decaying country estates. Spared the full-blown miser's soul, she nevertheless shared Hetty's persistent fear that others plotted against her. Sylvia died of cancer in 1951 at the age of eighty, frightened and alone.

Even so, Sylvia's last will

and testament was an act of real courage. Like someone throwing handfuls of money from a tall building, she broadcast the Green fortune into the world, some of it to people—including very distant relatives—she had never met; the bulk of it she carefully apportioned among charities, churches, and universities. Thus, the wealth that Hetty Green had so tenaciously kept within her family was, as one reporter put it, given to strangers—to give to strangers. □

Secret Powers

Surrounded by wealth from birth, Mary Bullock Powers grew up in New York City. Seemingly rich in everything but self-confidence, she was, in fact, the unloved issue of a bad marriage. She lived in a world choked with bitterness and empty of emotional comfort. Her domineering mother kept Mary and her younger brother, Ellis, secluded. When classes ended each day at the Gardner School for young ladies, Mary immediately hurried home. So shy was she that she would hide in a closet to avoid visitors.

When her mother died in 1911, Mary was a lonely spinster of thirty-five, living with Ellis in the family suite at New York's Buckingham Hotel. Despite the fortune they now controlled, brother and sister were unable to live anywhere else. They relinquished the familiar rooms only when the Buckingham was torn down in 1922.

Mary and Ellis took a seven-room, thirty-dollar-a-day suite in the Hotel Seymour near bustling Times Square.

Unable to shift gears with only one leg, Ned Green, Hetty's spendthrift son and heir, had this electrical car built for trips around his estate.

Ellis died in 1925, and Mary, never outgoing, became ever more reclusive. She even gave up her rare visits to a nearby bank in which she kept a million-dollar checking account. In 1927, she bolted the door to her suite. Keeping to her bedroom and connecting bath, she never again left her rooms except for an occasional wraithlike nighttime walk in the adjacent corridor.

Her callers were few: Her banker and lawyer made rare business visits; her doctor paid an annual call; and the hotel manager presented her accounts quarterly. In the last years of her life, she received visits from a cousin she had known and liked since childhood, Hollis Powers Gale. He often brought menus from other hotels, at Mary's request, so that the miserly recluse could compare the Seymour's charges for her single, simple daily meal.

When the Seymour remodeled its rooms in 1940, Mary refused to let workers into hers, which remained untouched. Only when she fell ill in 1948 was her suite finally invaded. The doctor found her lying in squalor, amid insect-infested furniture and walls worn down to the bricks. Hairpins had rusted into her hair, unwashed for fifteen years. The appalled physician had Mary moved to a clean room, where she died a few weeks later.

Perhaps afraid to let anyone see her sign her name lest the witness later forge it, Mary Powers had left no will. Lonely and friendless for seventy-two years, in death she was suddenly cherished: More than 200 people laid claim to her five-million-dollar fortune. After more than a year of litigation, the entire estate was awarded to her closest kin, Hollis Gale, the only person who had ever befriended her. □

Dead of Winter

Stephen Senior ended his days in the weather-beaten hovel where he had lived alone for more than forty years. The bitter New Jersey January of 1924 proved too much for the ailing old man; he was found frozen to death by a helper who worked at Senior's two-cow dairy.

The dairy had once been Senior's pride and joy, stocked with pedigreed cows. But even after the dairy's early success, Senior continued peddling milk from a cart he pushed door-to-door. When competition cut into his trade, however, he quickly capitulated. He sold off most of his cows, continuing to serve only a few longstanding customers from the crumbling dairy, and became a recluse.

Senior was a well-known character around the city of Perth Amboy, stretching his apparently meager means by buying old bread and almost-spoiled foods for next to nothing. To heat his shack, he scrounged for coal along railroad tracks and picked up discarded wooden boxes at grocery stores. His final winter was unusually cold, however, and the sixty-five-year-old Senior, partially bedridden, soon faced a coal shortage. When a coal dealer told him that a few bushels of coal would cost almost a dollar, Senior drove the merchant away with a barrage of wooden blocks—which he hastened to retrieve for his stove. Three days later, he was found dead.

Officials who examined the shack discovered signs that Senior had tried valiantly to keep the fierce winds at bay. He had used anything he could find to seal cracks in the flimsy walls, stuffing them with newspapers and rags—and paper money amounting to thousands of dollars. A further search of Senior's property turned up a fortune of more than half a million dollars in cash and investments.

The man who had seemed to be an impoverished hermit, officials found, had invested almost every penny his dairy earned in real estate. He owned a square block in the heart of Perth Amboy's business district, which brought him a handsome rent. Exaggerated thrift had compelled him to build his miserable home on unclaimed property, to preserve the income from his own real estate—or die trying. □

Bleak House

When Ella Wendel took her poodle, Toby, out for a romp in the yard—a vacant rectangle of prime Manhattan real estate—it was one of the day's few pleasures for both of them. For although she was one of the richest women in New York, Ella was imbued with her family's passion for privacy. She seldom left her mansion at Fifth Avenue and Thirty-Ninth Street; and apart from a small number of servants, Toby was her sole companion.

Ella was the last of the seven Wendel sisters who inherited huge family real estate holdings accumulated over more than a century. The founder of the fortune, John Gottlieb Wendel, had been in the fur business with the legendary millionaire John Jacob Astor. Investing his profits in land, Wendel enjoined his descendants to buy nothing but choice New York real estate—and never to sell it. He left his properties to his only child, John Daniel Wendel. The son assiduously built the family fortune until his death in 1876, the same year that saw the tragic death of one of his seven daughters, Henrietta. His children enjoyed the privileges of wealth, traveling abroad and spending summers at the family beach house and spring and fall at a country home. The family took a reclusive turn, however, when control of the fortune passed to the children, six surviving sisters and their autocratic brother, John G. Wendel.

John dominated his sisters, insisting that none should marry because doing so would disperse the property, putting it under names other than Wendel. The sisters were sequestered in the family's brick-and-brownstone mansion, where

the passing decades brought little change. Even as skyscrapers sprouted around the house, it stood as it had been built in 1856, without electricity or telephone, shuttered against the outside world. Gaslight, they said, was easier on one's eyes. The sisters dressed in the styles of their teens, hand-sewing their drab clothes and wearing them until they were shabby.

Apart from seasonal visits to the other family estates, the sisters were seldom away from home. They left the conduct of the family affairs to their brother, who carried the titles to all the Wendel property in his own name. John remained a man of the world, a scholar who spoke several languages and attracted women of all ages. Faithful to the Wendel credo that he himself had established, however, he was a bachelor to the end of his days.

Two sisters tried in their own ways to escape. The first was Georgiana. Attractive, witty Miss Georgie fled the Fifth Avenue house in the 1890s, traveling frequently to Europe, where she tried a variety of health fads. John, offended by her increasingly eccentric behavior, committed her to a lunatic asylum in 1900. Georgie won her release after a series of court battles, but her mind continued to deteriorate and

The last of the mysterious, wealthy Wendels, Ella takes the sun with one of a series of dogs named Toby in a Fifth Avenue lot that was kept vacant so the Tobys could exercise.

she spent her last years in and out of sanitariums.

Rebecca Wendel followed another path to freedom. In 1903, she married Luther Swope, a kindly private tutor, after a courtship of many years. Miss Beckie waited until she was sixty to depart from the family's bosom, so there was no danger of children to disperse the Wendel wealth. Rumors of opposition notwithstanding, her brother appears to have given his blessing, along with a fine New York residence, to the newlyweds. Rebecca lived happily with Swope for twenty-two years, and even after his death, she did not move back into the Wendel mansion.

Accustomed to attrition—Augusta died in 1912, John and Josephine in 1914—life for the four surviving Wendels changed little with each loss. The adventurous Beckie took over the management of the family properties, handling the holdings even though she was not living in the family home. According to close friends, the other sisters were happy in their quiet, anachronistic way but increasingly isolated by the death of acquaintances. The turn-of-the-century world they knew survived only in the bleak house on Fifth Avenue. Nevertheless, they talked cheerfully of trips and early suitors; and there was much to do around the four-story home. Ella apparently felt that her spinster's life was not so bad, compared to that of some of her married friends. And there was nothing at all miserly about the Wendels' reclusive existence. When informed that living in the Fifth Avenue mansion cost a thousand dollars a day, Mary Wendel was not impressed. "Well, it's home," she stated, "and we don't need the money."

Although viewed by the public as the eccentric denizens of New York City's "Mystery House," the Wendel women stayed active, continuing to travel and keeping close tabs on current events. Georgie was in an asylum, and Mary and Ella stayed in the mansion, receiving fewer and fewer visitors with each passing year. Inexorably, the fruitless Wendel tree gave up its aging branches: Mary died in 1922, Georgiana in 1929, Beckie in 1930.

One by one the rooms were closed; when only Ella remained, she used just her bedroom, the book-lined library, the dining room, and the million-dollar side yard where she walked Toby, last in a long line of dogs with that name. Famous as the last Wendel sister— the recluse who was also New York City's largest property owner—she found outings in Manhattan increasingly oppressive.

Sometimes, when strangers accosted her on the street, she would pretend that she did not speak English. Finally, she ceased venturing out in New York altogether and spent only four months in the city. She passed the rest of the year at her beloved family estate in rural Irvington, New York.

The Wendel family died with Ella in 1931, and the fortune guarded so closely for so long was finally dispersed. After a few bequests to friends and servants, Ella left the bulk of the estate to Methodist seminaries and hospitals—including one that had tended to one of her Tobys when no veterinarian was available. Oddly, the final Toby, the chubby white poodle who outlived his mistress by two and a half years, was not mentioned in Ella's $100 million will; he ended his days in the care of strangers. □

Garden of Ice

Karp Osipovich Lykov *(below)* was an Old Believer, who in the twentieth century still rejected changes in Russian society and religion wrought three centuries earlier by Czar Peter the Great. For generations, the Old Believers had roamed the Siberian wilderness. Lykov followed their example, teaching his followers to worship God and distrust men. In the 1920s, he led them farther into the hostile, uninhabited forests, fleeing revolutions and war. The wandering ended in the early 1940s on a rough site in southern Siberia's Sayan Mountains, 200 miles from the nearest town. By then, of Lykov's followers, only his family remained.

For nearly four decades, the Lykovs saw no other humans. Karp Osipovich built a crude hut for his wife, two daughters, and two sons; planted potatoes, onions, and turnips; and hunted game and fished. The family went barefoot in warm weather and wore homemade boots in winter; their clothes were patched homespun burlap and skins. The mother died in the 1950s; and as the children grew to adulthood, they learned of civilization only from frayed prayer books and their father's apocalyptic ◊

preaching. Somehow they survived the rigors of their rugged paradise, where winter temperatures plunged to minus fifty degrees Fahrenheit, with not even a kitchen match from the outside world.

In 1978, the Lykovs—the father, now in his seventies, and his four middle-aged children—were discovered by Soviet geologists prospecting for iron ore. Speaking to strangers for the first time in four decades, the father's reluctant first words were: "Well, come in, now that you're here." His daughters, Natalya and Agafya, cried, "This is for our sins; this is for our sins." Soon the two sons, Savin and Dmitri, appeared, bearded and rumpled like their father. The visitors found Karp Osipovich still preoccupied with the policies of Peter the Great. He knew that World War I had occurred, but he had missed World War II. "What do you mean, a second one, and again the Germans?" exclaimed Karp to a visiting reporter. "It is that cursed Peter and his plotting with the Germans."

Whatever the divine implications of their renewed contact with the world, the Lykovs seem to have suffered from it. Having lived for decades in the wilderness, they began to sicken and die after exposure to outsiders. By early 1982, both sons and one daughter, Natalya, were dead. But even as his youngest son, forty-three-year-old Dmitri, lay dying of pneumonia, Lykov rejected outside aid, possibly with his usual refrain: "This is not permitted us." The unshakable Old Believer and his remaining daughter, Agafya, returned to the forest in 1982 to live out their lives—for them, reckoned from the expulsion of Adam and Eve from Eden, the year 7490. □

For more than forty years, Russian Old Believer Karp Lykov and his family lived in this Siberian hovel.

Pages from the catalog of Sussex auctioneers R. H. Ellis & Sons illustrate David Mason's determined inclination to acquire anything and everything.

Thing King

David Reginald George Mason was a sucker for fancy advertising. He pored over magazines and newspapers, eagerly pulling out his checkbook when he came across an offer that intrigued him—anything from books to clocks, cameras to hand-carved chess pieces; everything, from everywhere.

Mason was heir to a fortune from a department store in Manchester, England. He never worked, spending his time on sports, hobbies, and travel. Married once and divorced in 1934, he lived alone until his death in 1974 at the age of seventy-seven. Acquaintances knew him as a lonely, unhappy man, so secretive that few dared to drop by to see him. He always interrupted his winter of skiing in Switzerland to come home for Christmas, but he spent the holiday alone because, as a cousin related, "he was not the kind of person you could invite to spend the festive season with you."

Largely eschewing contact with other people, Mason had evidently filled his life with things. His large Edwardian house was packed with a bewildering variety of collections. His dining room shone with silverware and fine china. One upstairs room contained more than 100 pieces of photographic equipment, including bulky antique cameras as well as the latest in Japanese technology. Other rooms held model railroads and gear for skiing, shooting, golf, croquet, archery, and motorcycling. A safe in the garage overflowed with coins, as did the kitchen oven. The press likened Mason's place to "an Aladdin's cave."

After Mason's death, the contents of the house brought £36,000 at auction. Curiosity seekers thronged the sales, and some buyers walked off with real bargains—reproductions of intricate seventeenth- and eighteenth-century clocks; sets of signed, limited-edition books; even a knitting machine—one of many objects that David Mason, in his frenzy to collect, had never even bothered to unwrap. □

Slaughter on Fifth Avenue

The call that came to the New York police on the morning of March 21, 1947, concerned a familiar house. Over the years there had been many calls about strange doings at 2078 Fifth Avenue, home to the city's most famous recluses, Homer and Langley Collyer. But this one was the most ominous: The caller reported that there was a dead body in the house.

It took the police only minutes to converge on the four-story brick-and-brownstone building, in a once-fashionable section of Harlem. The doors were locked, the lower windows either shuttered behind rusty iron grates or boarded up behind shattered panes. Unlike previous occasions, no one answered their knocks. Chopping a hole through the front door, they found a hallway completely blocked by trash. Finally, a patrolman climbed a ladder, entered a second-story window, and began picking his way through another mass of refuse. After a few minutes, he found the body of an old man, sitting in a tattered bathrobe on the littered floor.

It was Homer Collyer, the sixty-five-year-old elder of the pair. Blind and paralyzed, the one-time admiralty lawyer had not left the house for years, relying on his brother, Langley—four years his junior—for all his needs. But Langley, a personable former engineer and concert pianist, was nowhere to be found.

The Collyers had never quite been able to leave the house on Fifth Avenue. They had lived there with their parents, who raised the two boys with gentle care. Stunned when, in 1909, their beloved mother separated from their father, a wealthy Manhattan obstetrician, the brothers seem to have been shattered by her death in 1929. Both men abandoned their careers and were seen less and less outside the house. Homer lost his sight in 1933 and became paralyzed about 1940, but he never saw a doctor; Langley treated his brother's blindness by feeding him as many as a hundred oranges a week. "Remember," he once said, explaining his prescription, "we are the sons of a doctor."

The brothers stopped paying taxes and bills and made no objection when their utilities were cut off for nonpayment. Langley, remembered as the timid brother, became an energetic provider. He cooked meals on a kerosene stove, carried water from a ⬠

Reclusive Langley Collyer *(left)* testifies against a burglar in 1946, accompanied by a stack of newspapers picked up on his way to the hearing. Believing that the sight of his blind and paralyzed brother, Homer, would one day be restored, Langley hoarded newspapers, which, with other debris, choked the rooms *(above)* of their Fifth Avenue home.

park four blocks away, and roved the nighttime streets in search of food and other supplies—and various castoff objects, which he added like a pack rat to their growing collection of everything. His rare outside contacts included the neighborhood druggist, whose shop stayed open until midnight, and a persistent newspaper reporter. They found him courteous, cultured, and willing to answer their questions—but also prone to breaking off conversations abruptly to dart off on his errands. A deepening mystery to their neighbors, the Collyers were the stuff of legend: Within their boarded brownstone, some said, they lived in splendor, with millions of dollars stashed on the premises. In fact, they lived like vermin, and they were not secret millionaires; at the end, they had about $100,000 in the bank.

Fearful of intruders—there had been several burglaries over the years—Langley had built barricades of junk in front of doors and windows. He had also booby-trapped the house with mountains of debris, pierced by narrow crawl ways that he traversed like a mole. When police and sanitation workers began to clear the house, they removed 120 tons of refuse in the three weeks it took to work from the basement to the upper floors.

The catalog of discoveries was diverse. The house contained fourteen grand pianos, most of a Model T Ford, a seven-foot segment of a tree, 3,000 books, sewing machines and dressmakers' dummies, unopened mail, a number of guns and swords, pictures of pinup girls from 1910, and several tickets to a 1905 church excursion. Dominating everything were vast stacks of newspapers that Langley had saved for Homer to read when he eventually recovered his sight. And still there was no sign of the younger Collyer brother.

Then, on April 8, sifting through the huge heaps of trash that still remained on the second floor, officials discovered what had become of Langley. Crawling through a tunnel to feed his brother, he had sprung one of his own booby traps and been suffocated by debris. His trapped body, gnawed by rats and in decay, lay just ten feet from the spot where police had found Homer several weeks earlier. Waiting day after day for Langley to bring him food, Homer had finally starved to death. □

Rubble Rouser

Clinton Bolin had always paid his rent on time with five- and ten-dollar bills; so when he failed to appear with his money in April 1975, his landlady decided to check the Long Beach, California, apartment where he had lived for four months. She found that Bolin had disappeared—but not his rock collection.

It was no ordinary assemblage of mineral specimens. In fact, the apartment was stacked from floor to ceiling, wall to wall, with neatly wrapped packages of stones and concrete slabs. Closets, kitchen cabinets, and the bathtub were all filled; only a narrow crawl way led to the toilet and to the couch where Bolin had apparently slept. Most of the packages weighed 100 pounds or more, and all were labeled with the word *Me* and the name of a European country. The collection weighed about thirty tons in all, enough to buckle the floor of the

Even hoarders ordinarily part with their garbage, but not one California family. Besides keeping their own, they also took home other people's garbage. In 1988, they were evicted for not clearing their rat-ridden bungalow of twenty-five tons of garbage. Only three years earlier, they had been forced out of another garbage-jammed house.

apartment, which had to be repaired after it was cleared.

Long Beach residents remembered seeing the slightly built Bolin rummaging through trash bins at construction sites and stuffing concrete into gunnysacks. Not one person, however, had seen him carrying anything like this into the apartment. And no one knew much about him, although one newspaper reporter learned of a mail carrier attempting to deliver a welfare check after Bolin had left.

In subsequent weeks, Clinton Bolin checked into and out of three Long Beach motels, leaving similar batches of packaged rubble in each. Then Bolin simply disappeared; where he went, and whether he is still collecting rocks—and why—remains a mystery. □

A Long Beach, California, apartment-house manager, Sue Power, ponders the rock collection abandoned by former roomer Clinton Bolin.

To Fetch a Thief

Indianapolis fire-fighters and police summoned to the scene of a suspicious fire in the spring of 1977 stumbled on the pathetic end of a strange life. Marjorie Jackson lay dead on her kitchen floor, apparently killed by burglars. But a search of the house showed that the thieves had left plenty behind—more than five million dollars, stuffed in closets, drawers, suitcases, and garbage cans.

The police already knew something about Marjorie Jackson, who had inherited a fortune when her husband, heir to a grocery chain, died in 1970. Only a year earlier, the wealthy widow had lost more than $800,000 in a burglary—but refused to testify against the perpetrators, reasoning that it "must have been God's will."

Ironically, Jackson had become a magnet for miscreants in a failed effort to protect her wealth. In early 1976, she had discovered that her banker had embezzled $700,000 from one of her investment accounts. Determined not to be robbed further, she began siphoning her money from the bank in the form of hard cash. Over a period of about five months, she carried $9 million home from the bank in a battered suitcase, ignoring warnings that news of these huge withdrawals would attract thieves.

Jackson had already withdrawn from society. After her husband's death, she lived alone on a three-and-a-half-acre estate, where accumulating weeds and debris created the impression that the house was empty. When the police came to investigate complaints about the condition of the property, Jackson ordered them to leave.

Having baited the place with millions of dollars, however, Jackson was no longer protected by such seclusion: It became her enemy. Over the course of five days in May of 1977, her house was raided three times. In the second sweep, the two burglars shot her; returning for a third bite at her fortune, they torched the house in order to conceal the murder. They were apprehended, with four accomplices, within two weeks; more than three and a half million dollars in loot was recovered.

The partially burned house was so cluttered that police had trouble determining what had been stolen. In addition to the vast cache of money, they turned up fifty loaves of bread, 150 pounds of coffee, 200 dozen cookies, and an array of cakes decorated with religious inscriptions. Thousands of packages, wrapped in aluminum foil, bore greeting cards with notations such as *To God, from Marjorie.* One contained fifteen new washcloths.

Jackson willed her estate to a half sister she had not spoken with for years. Her private possessions were disposed of at auction, where, as buyers hoped to discover hidden troves of money, even used clothing and bedding fetched outlandish prices. This last grab at Marjorie Jackson's fortune, however, was a disappointment for everyone except the auctioneers: There was no more cash to be found. □

Investigating the murder of heiress Marjorie Jackson *(above)*, Indianapolis police discovered some five million dollars in cash hidden in her home.

True Britt

Although he lived alone in a succession of handmade forest hovels for twenty years, Bill Britt was not much of a recluse. The tall, wind-burned iconoclast was actually a gregarious sort, welcoming visitors and courting publicity in his long fight against eviction from his domain, a makeshift shelter on public land in one of Boston's most exclusive residential areas.

Nevertheless, Britt came to be known in the mid-1980s as the Chestnut Hill Hermit, a fervent advocate of individual rights and closeness to nature. He came by his flair for publicity honestly, having worked as a marketing executive before a bitter divorce and the loss of his family led him to abandon the world of jobs and houses. Britt made his new home on five ◊

After one of many confrontations with the Boston city government, hermit Bill Britt *(left)* talks things over with police officer Bob Connors in 1987.

wooded acres overlooking a reservoir and adjacent to a cemetery. Using whatever lumber, cardboard, cloth, and plastic sheeting he could find, he assembled a succession of jerry-built structures he called wigwams. For food he rummaged through the garbage cans behind restaurants and groceries. His only income was the few dollars in deposit money that he received each week for aluminum cans he gathered and hauled to a nearby market in an onion sack.

Years of outdoor living took their toll on Britt, leaving him with few teeth and legally blind from an insulin disorder. But none of that hindered his opposition to government officials who tried to get him to move from the public land he occupied. They regularly tore down his hovels and hauled away his possessions; just as regularly, Britt rebuilt and moved back in.

When his confrontations with the authorities went to court, Britt began to woo the press. He memorized the names and phone numbers of many reporters and proved an irresistibly colorful subject—a white-bearded wild man with fingerless gloves and a lobster-claw tie clip, defending his simple way of life against a heartless bureaucracy. An unexpected result of the publicity was a reunion with two of his long-lost children—a son and a daughter. While the son had some reservations about his eccentric parent, the daughter began to visit regularly with bundles of food.

The spring of 1987 brought multiple disasters to Britt. While he was in New York building his celebrity on a national television show, a suspicious grass fire consumed his latest shelter. Two months later, the government finally won in court, and Britt's belongings were removed from the reservoir grounds. Undaunted, he set up a new wigwam in the adjacent cemetery. There, he froze to death in February 1988. But his death earned him an eternal reprieve: His ashes were sprinkled in the woods where he had fought to stay. □

WIZARDS OF ODD

The world, perhaps sensing that the urge to create is also a compulsion to diverge, has adjusted to the oddness of the creative and has even joined in celebrating their nonconformity. They are viewed as the wizards among us—the artists, musicians, scientists, inventors, and industrialists who are set apart by their uniqueness. They make discoveries or have profound insights or follow with brilliance some inner imperative to perform. Or they just blaze a notably bizarre trajectory through life.

Some boldly shatter the icons of dress and protocol just as they splinter the temples of science and art. They are the best of their type—and the determined worst as well. There are secret misers among them, public figures born to be hermits, hyperactive doers and the utterly inert, great thinkers frightened of their household help, and towering figures who illuminate human experience even as they spend their lives in hiding. Intellects capable of wonderfully apt designs may be incurably infected with a bad—but fixed—idea that gives all they undertake an eccentric wobble. And, now and then, their peculiar conduct spins an illusion: One's seeming oddness may be merely the cheery incandescence of a full and well-directed life, mistaken by outsiders for eccentricity.

Shy Person

Henry Cavendish was one of the greatest scientists in British history—and very likely the shyest. His agonizing diffidence—indeed, his nervousness at any human contact—kept him from publishing most of his experimental findings, so that the real breadth of his contribution remained a secret until after his death.

The reclusive savant was born in 1731 into one of England's wealthiest and most distinguished families, with an aristocratic, moneyed root system stretching back to the reign of Edward III. Although his branch was not the richest one in the Cavendish line, Henry's father, Lord Charles Cavendish, was brother to the third duke of Devonshire and a distinguished scientist in his own right. Henry's mother died when the boy was only two years old, and the family was not close.

After attending Cambridge University, the budding scientist returned to his father's home, where he lived and assisted the elder Cavendish for the next thirty years. In all that time, Henry made his way with what was said to be a niggardly allowance; historians are not sure whether Lord Charles was poor or merely parsimonious.

Eventually the son, like the father, was elected to the Royal Society, Britain's early equivalent of a national academy of sciences. The society's Thursday night dinners were virtually the only events he attended—perhaps because his shyness was aggravated by embarrassment over a lack of funds: His father met the five-shilling cost of his son's weekly dinner out, but with not a pence extra.

With the death of his father in 1783, however, Cavendish came into his inheritance; a subsequent bequest from an aunt made him suddenly immensely rich. But by that time, his reclusive habits were too deeply ingrained for him to enjoy wealth. Instead, he turned his life entirely toward science. In an era of first-rate experimenters, Cavendish became one of the best—although he kept it quiet.

"Everything is ordered by measure, number, and weight," was one of Cavendish's mottoes. He followed it to become one of the Enlightenment's greatest scientific analysts. He was the first to identify the element hydrogen, and he discovered that water was not, as then believed, an element in itself, but a compound of hydrogen and oxygen. He did pioneering work with condensers and uncovered the rules of electrical resistance more than half a century before they were quantified by German scientist Georg Simon Ohm. At sixty-seven, he used measurements of gravity to calculate the mean density of the planet; his figure: 5.448 grams per cubic centimeter. (The figure used today is 5.52.) Cavendish outlined the molecular basis of heat long before the theory was publicized by his great contemporary Joseph Black. But such groundbreaking work was largely consigned to notebooks that remained hidden during Cavendish's lifetime.

Cavendish did not mind the anonymity. Fame was the last thing he wanted, for social intercourse of any kind terrified him. At Royal Society gatherings he hardly ever spoke; the tall, gaunt bachelor had a slight, but evidently discomfiting, stammer. When he talked at all, it was only on technical matters. Recognized and praised as a great scientist by a foreign visitor to the society, Cavendish fled into mortified silence. Newcomers were warned to talk to the great scientist without looking at him. When someone violated the rule at one function, Cavendish rushed out of the place, tumbled into a cab, and sped toward home.

There he was even more reclusive. He ordered dinner by leaving notes on a hall table—uncomplicated menus, consisting always of mutton. His shyness intensified around women, and female servants were ordered to stay out of his sight or be fired. Once, after running into a female servant on the stairs, he had a second staircase built so that it would never happen again.

The great scientist's style of dress was as bizarre as his behavior.

This only known portrait of shy savant Henry Cavendish was sketched surreptitiously at a Royal Society dinner by colleague William Alexander.

He wore shabby clothes that were fifty years behind the style, topped with a long-passé tricornered hat. He would not sit for portraits, and the only likeness of him ever done from life was a watercolor sketch, composed from some distance, surreptitiously. Yet Cavendish was no misanthrope. Whenever he was asked for charitable contributions, he would look up the largest previous donation and match it. Clever fund-raisers soon cooked their books accordingly.

Secretive about his life, Cavendish supposedly sought privacy even in the final moments of it. Lying in bed when the time came, he ordered his manservant out of the room. He had something to think about, Cavendish said, and did not want to be disturbed. Alone, the seventy-eight-year-old genius gave up his timid ghost.

After his death, Cavendish was revealed to be more than a great scientist who had hidden much of his best work from the world—he was also the largest holder of bank shares in Britain. Caring nothing about wealth, he had let his inherited fortune grow like an untended garden, through good times and bad, to a value of some £750,000. Most of his wealth went to a nephew, Lord George Cavendish, whom the older man had allowed to visit him for half an hour every year. But £15,000 went to Sir Charles Blagden, secretary of the Royal Society, whose conversations the great scientist had suffered and, somehow, secretly enjoyed.

The bequests to virtual strangers were a sad but fitting legacy for the man. "He did not love;" wrote a colleague remembering Cavendish, "he did not hate; he did not hope; he did not fear." □

Claymates

During the heyday of British sculpture in the late-eighteenth-century, effigies of cherubs, fawns, pagan deities, and Georgian celebrities were everywhere. It was the perfect, florid setting for Joseph Nollekens, who became one of England's most prolific and successful sculptors. Never regarded as a great artist, the well-paid, workmanlike second-rater might have vanished from the history of British art. But in John Thomas Smith's 1828 *Nollekens and His Times*—called by one historian "the most candid, pitiless, and uncomplimentary biography in the English language"—the aged artisan was immortalized, not as an artist, but as a repulsively eccentric pinchpenny.

Nollekens came naturally to his skinflint ways. Born in London in 1737, he was the son of a miser so mean that his house was attacked by an angry mob during the Rebellion of 1745, partly because he was a Catholic and partly because the rioters expected to find a cache of money. Young Joseph was apprenticed to a local sculptor and won prizes with some early figures. Then, as a budding sculptor, he traveled to Rome, where he modeled famed actor David Garrick and author Laurence Sterne, among others. Nollekens also put his talents to work at faking Roman antiquities and smuggling luxury goods home in hollowed-out busts.

While plying this dubious trade in Italy, he began to display the symptoms of parsimony. He developed a taste for cheap but dreadful food

cooked by a housekeeper who used scrapings of gristle and fat she found on a butcher's floor. "I never tasted a better dish," declared Nollekens years afterward, "than my Roman cuttings." When he returned to London, Nollekens found a wife of a higher class but an even meaner spirit than he. The couple would sit in the dark at home rather than use candles, and they would put out any scant fires they lit for guests as soon as the company left. Nolly, as his wife called him, brought home the excess lather from a barbershop shave to use as bath soap.

Marriage did not improve Nollekens's taste in food, which ran to flour fried in rancid butter. Nonetheless, he managed to draw commissions from scores of the greatest luminaries of his age, including the duke of Wellington, Samuel Johnson, William Pitt, and even George III. The great buildings of London displayed his plaster statues, and Nollekens's monuments adorned a host of cathedrals, including Westminster Abbey.

What his famous subjects probably never knew was that their very poses were determined less by the requirements of art than by the ◊

Miserly sculptor Joseph Nollekens often used discarded marble for such objects as this bust of George III.

sculptor's stingy quirks. Nollekens hated to pay much for marble, so he would buy pieces that other artists had rejected as too small. To fit his commissions to the stone, he ordered sitters to pose with their head cocked backwards, looking over their shoulder. A model—what his wife called an "abandoned" woman—who posed nude for his Venus statues fared worse yet, posing eight hours at a time, coldly naked, with nothing to eat or drink, for a miserly two shillings.

For all his pathological thrift, Nollekens could be a friendly, social man, with inexplicable bursts of generosity. He was careful to reward his servants, becoming more liberal with them after his wife's death in 1817. And he was capable of spontaneous kindness. The story was told that, on his way back to London from Rome as a young man, he had discovered an uncle living in poverty in Paris and undertook to support him with a small stipend. But such openhandedness was the exception, and the sculptor's more characteristic tightfistedness was to prove his undoing.

In 1779, Nollekens took on the son of his chief assistant as a studio boy. The apprentice grew to manhood in Nollekens's employ, avidly soaking up what he could about the celebrities who visited the studio. When the sculptor died in 1823, the younger man waited in vain for the large inheritance that he had been led to expect. The money was there—some £200,000 had been squirreled away—but only £100 of it was earmarked for the disappointed protégé. In spite of that—or perhaps because of it—John Thomas Smith, Nollekens's "pitiless" biographer, made his former employer immortal. □

Stuffed Shrimp

Few thinkers have been so fiercely consistent in pursuing social and legal reform as British philosopher Jeremy Bentham. The influence of his utilitarian ideal—the greatest good for the greatest number of people—shaped the constitutions of the New World, enraged despots, and inspired liberal revolutionaries during the late eighteenth and early nineteenth centuries. Yet the man considered one of the most important minds in British history was more comfortable with animals than with his fellow humans, and he was so innocent of the world that one friend observed, "All his life, he was a philosopher and a child."

The child had been an incredibly precocious one. At age three, Bentham had read a history of England; at five, he could read Latin and Greek. He entered Oxford University at twelve and was graduated at fifteen. His mind was powerful, but his body was puny. He crept up stairs one at a time, and when seven, he could not dance because his legs lacked the strength to stand on tiptoe. Bentham's innate social discomfort was exacerbated

by a domineering father, who liked to trot out his frail prodigy for friends. He embarrassed the lad until, as Bentham put it later, the child was "ready to faint—to sink into the earth with agony." His shyness, especially in the shadow of the parent he always addressed as Honored Sir, became pathological.

Following his father's wishes, Bentham became an attorney, but only reluctantly. "I went to the bar," he wrote later, "as a bear to the stake." And then, remarkably, the fragile young barrister went his own way. He rejected the entire British legal system as arbitrary and un-

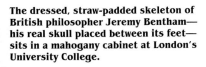

The dressed, straw-padded skeleton of British philosopher Jeremy Bentham—his real skull placed between its feet—sits in a mahogany cabinet at London's University College.

just, and began to construct a scientific substitute based on the rationalism of the Enlightenment.

For the next fifty years, Bentham squirreled himself away at home, obsessed with his grand reform based on the famed principle of utility—that the purpose of all things should be to augment human happiness and reduce suffering. It did not bother him that utilitarianism would also drain life of its aesthetic delights; he believed that poetry was simply prose that failed to cover the page. Each day, Bentham wrote ten to fifteen pages of closely argued manuscript, most of which never saw light of day: He rarely tried to publish anything. Rats ate some of his work, dust gathered on the rest. One reason for the waste was that he hardly ever finished anything. Time and again, he would be struck by a thought just as a project was nearing completion and suddenly start another one, never returning to the first. Bentham composed one philosophical unfinished symphony after another.

Word of his revolutionary ideas began to spread only when a Belgian admirer finally published five volumes of Bentham's work in French, causing excitement in Europe and the New World. For many years, the philosopher was better known and more highly venerated in France, Germany, and the Americas than in his native England. But gradually, his views took hold in his homeland, liberalizing British society and inspiring various humanizing changes, especially in criminal law and prison reform. Ironically, even while he was making society more humane, his morbid shyness and lifelong seclusion crippled his personal understanding of human nature. He innocently believed that if one exposed iniquity, an intelligent public would get rid of it and that those in power "only wanted to know what was good in order to embrace it."

For all his concern with human happiness, Bentham was morbidly antisocial. He could barely tolerate more than one visitor at a time, and he found meeting people for the first time excruciating. To minimize the agony, he would dictate the precise locale where an introduction could take place, to the very room or exact stairway. His correspondence suffered: Bentham would write letters to other Enlightenment sages such as Voltaire, then shrink from mailing them. Marriage was impossible, although he once fell in love; he was far too timorous to pursue the matter.

Inherently warm-hearted, Bentham compensated for his shyness by loving animals, especially cats—and mice. He tamed little rodents in his workshops, though sometimes regretting that the time he spent stroking the friendly vermin had not gone to philosophy. Bentham once trained a pig to follow him like a dog, and he bestowed pet names on such inanimate companions as his walking stick, Dapple, and his teapot, Dick.

These private sentimentalities contrasted sharply with his ruthlessly utilitarian views on certain formal, emotional displays, among them funerals. Burial was a waste of time and money, he felt. Corpses should serve a more constructive purpose. Rather than plant trees along stately drives, he argued, people of means should plant their embalmed ancestors, upright and aboveground, where they could act as their own memorials.

In the end, Bentham arranged something similar for himself. Under the terms of his will, his body was dissected before a gathering of friends at London's University College, which he had helped to found. Then his skeleton was padded out with straw, dressed, and placed on display at the institution in a mahogany cabinet. The dissection was so thorough that his head had to be replaced by a wax copy, although the actual head was mummified and placed between his feet in the enclosure. There he remained forever after, nattily attired in his best clothes and straw hat, walking stick in hand—an enduring, if useless, monument to utilitarianism. □

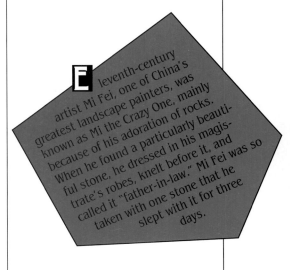

Eleventh-century artist Mi Fei, one of China's greatest landscape painters, was known as Mi the Crazy One, mainly because of his adoration of rocks. When he found a particularly beautiful stone, he dressed in his magistrate's robes, knelt before it, and called it "father-in-law." Mi Fei was so taken with one stone that he slept with it for three days.

Basic Oglish

During the 1930s and 1940s, Charles Kay Ogden was considered one of Britain's most brilliant linguists. He was editor of several distinguished journals and coauthor of a best-selling book on words. His creation of a radically simplified form of English was an international success, hailed by Prime Minister Winston Churchill. As solitary as he was brilliant, however, Ogden so undercut his achievements with bizarre behavior that he is almost unknown nowadays.

His aversion to the limelight was established early. Born in 1889, the son of a schoolmaster, he came down with rheumatic fever at age sixteen and had to be kept in a dark room for two years. Later, when he attended Cambridge University, he was a full-blown "claustrophiliac." He loved being shut in. He insisted fresh air was harmful and kept all his windows closed. He indulged a nonsmoking habit by affecting a fake cigarette with a bulb at the end that glowed red when he inhaled. In his London flat, an ozone machine produced "healthful" particles.

Og, as friends called him, was a manic collector of everything from music boxes to shoes, but he especially loved masks. In arguments—and interviews—he would put one on and encourage his interlocutors to do the same. This, he insisted, would keep the focus on logic and off personalities. An insomniac, Ogden would stalk the streets of London and Cambridge at night, knocking on the door of any friend who stayed up late. Toward the end of his life, he kept his coffin on display in his London front hall, perhaps in emulation of one of his heroes, the philosopher Jeremy Bentham *(pages 64-65).* Legend has it that for Bentham's centennial, Ogden organized a change of underwear for his idol's remains, on display at University College in London. Somehow, Ogden had even been lucky enough to acquire, and he wore, one of Bentham's rings.

If he admired Bentham, however, he did not share the great man's hopeful view of humanity. Where Bentham had envisioned a public intelligent enough to solve its own problems, Ogden believed most people were too stupid to understand much at all. To help out this race of dolts, he created his great linguistic lifework: Basic English, a language stripped of all but eighteen of its verbs and pared down to 850 simple words. It was a tool of empire, a tongue the whole world could learn and understand. He opened the Orthological Institute in London to train Basic English teachers, who by 1935 were working in thirty countries around the world. With Winston Churchill's backing, the British government began to underwrite Ogden's work in 1943; and for a time, it appeared that Basic English would sweep the entire planet—and make its inventor a wealthy man.

But the determined eccentric was never comfortable with officialdom, and he made himself a laughing-stock among British journalists as he popped in and out of his house during interviews, each time sporting a new mask. After a series of abortive starts, the government paid Ogden £23,000 to cover his alleged losses and took over the Basic English business. By the early 1950s, Ogden had abandoned his creation, and the streamlined patois, widely perceived by then as an instrument of imperialism, slid into obscurity. So did its creator. When the man of masks died of cancer in 1957, a friend mused sadly, "What a lot of poking about among his mysteries must be going on." □

Photographed in his cluttered rooms around 1943, reclusive scholar Charles K. Ogden wears a mask from his large collection.

Robert "Romeo" Coates performs his popular—and ludicrous—death scene in a contemporary drawing.

Shakespeared

In the early 1800s, Robert Coates realized his one burning ambition: He became a star. For six years, thousands of theatergoers in Regency England flocked to see him play a love-doomed Romeo or a lascivious Lothario, and to discover that Coates was indeed in a class by himself—by all accounts, he was the worst actor in the history of the English stage.

Critics thought him ungainly and passive, and complained of his idiocy onstage. His dramatic posturings were ridiculous—designed, some said, to show off what he felt were exceedingly handsome legs. He often forgot his lines and would then talk aloud to himself about what they ought to be. Whatever he came up with, he seemed to think, was better than anything Shakespeare originally wrote. He loved to play Romeo dressed in a sky-blue cape, long, curled wig, and top hat. When it came time in the play to die, he would sweep the stage with a silk handkerchief, remove his hat, and slowly lie down. If the applause was loud enough, he would get up and do it again.

It undoubtedly helped Coates's career that he was independently wealthy, since he often had to bribe theater managers to get a part. He was born on the island of Antigua in 1772, the son of a rich plantation owner, and was brought up in England. When his father died, Coates inherited an allowance of £40,000 per year, a large collection of diamonds that he wore at every opportunity—and a ban on ever managing the family estates.

No one knows exactly when Coates's acting mania first struck, although he had evidently acted in amateur theater at home. His first performance in England came in 1810, when he finally wangled an appearance as Romeo on the stage at Bath. Coates was jeered and hissed, objects were thrown, and he stopped his performance and threatened to fight the hecklers. The curtain came down when Romeo grabbed a crowbar, intending to open Juliet's tomb—a maneuver distinctly absent from the script. The audience's scorn would have been a nightmare for most actors, but Coates found in it a kind of triumph. The very badness of his acting exerted a strange fascination, and he set off on his career as Romeo Coates, often playing to packed houses.

Eventually, the thundering thespian made the leap to London's famed Haymarket Theatre, bringing with him his distinctive, odious allure. Sometimes his fellow actors would demand police protection from the audience before they would go onstage—no idle request, since Coates himself was often threatened with lynching. One actress who played Juliet to his overwhelming Romeo had hysterics and clung to the scenery, refusing to move. Several audience members were so convulsed with laughter that they had to be treated by doctors. In 1811, Coates added a second character to his repertoire, the arch-seducer Lothario in Nicholas Rowe's *The Fair Penitent.* For this role, he wore a diamond-sprinkled silver suit, a pink silk stole, a gold sword, and a hat bedecked with ostrich plumes. The effect, all agreed, was deliciously dreadful.

Coates reached the apotheosis of his bizarre fame when his terrible performances were satirized in another West End theatrical production. By then, Coates considered his celebrity complete. Glittering with diamonds, he rode through the streets of London in a sky-blue, clam-shaped carriage drawn by two white horses and emblazoned with a heraldic rooster and the motto While I Live, I'll Crow.

But the end of the crowing was in sight. Economic setbacks in the West Indies undercut his princely allowance; soon Coates could no longer afford to maintain his theatrical delusion. In 1816, he withdrew from the stage and retired across the English Channel to Boulogne until his fortunes restored him to the fashionable life of London. In 1848, while he was crossing a street to retrieve his opera glasses, the preposterous, septuagenarian Romeo was struck by a passing carriage—a cheaper version of his own flashy conveyance of years past—and killed. □

A stuffed cock-of-the-rock on his finger and a preserved cat's head at his side, taxidermist-naturalist Charles Waterton poses for an 1824 portrait by Charles W. Peale.

Curiously Refreshing

"Our pleasure in ourselves would suffer sadly if Charles Waterton were not called eccentric," one biographer begins, "for few of us are so full of life, love, curiosity, and plain joy that we dare consider him normal." Born in 1782 of wealthy parents, and of a British Catholic lineage that included Saint Thomas More, Waterton was a lifelong dynamo of interests, especially in nature—but nature seen straight; he was not much for formal classifications and Latin names. In 1812, the young Yorkshireman traveled to the almost untouched wilderness of British Guiana in order to oversee his family's holdings there, and he became enthralled by the mysteries of the jungle.

He evidently feared nothing. He is said to have immobilized a large boa constrictor by tying it up in his suspenders and, with the help of his native companions, once rode a tethered ten-and-a-half-foot caiman. A believer in the healthful effects of bleeding—he bled himself regularly—he tried in vain to induce vampire bats to take blood from his exposed big toe. He was contemptuous of heights. On an 1817 visit to Italy, he scaled Rome's Castle of St. Angelo and the spire of St. Peter's Cathedral, where he planted his gloves on the lightning rod. The pope was not amused. Learning of the pontiff's ire, the faithful Waterton climbed back up and retrieved the souvenir.

He made four journeys to South America in all, developing his distinctive brand of naturalism as he went. Much of what he found there went against the views of more conventional, England-bound scholars—what Waterton called "closet naturalists." For example, his first encounter with a sloth led him to the prevailing conclusion that it was a poor thing indeed. "His looks, his gestures, and his cries all conspire to entreat you to take pity on him," he wrote of the sluggish tree dweller, which he relegated to the bottom of the heap among quadrupeds. But, after keeping a sloth for a few months, he amended his view, noting that "it is but fair to surmise that it just enjoys life as much as any other animal."

Waterton's account of such things appeared in his 1825 book, *Wanderings in South America,* which enthralled readers with tales of his exploits on the little-known continent. But his experience there also won him scientific esteem for his experiments with curare, which he properly identified not as a deadly poison but as a muscle-relaxing drug: Curare can kill, but only when the dosage is sufficient to immobilize the muscles involved in breathing. Waterton proved this by "killing" a donkey with curare, then giving it artificial respiration to keep it breathing until the drug's effects wore off. The lucky creature is said to have lived another twenty-five years at the naturalist's beloved Yorkshire estate, Walton Hall.

It was to Walton Hall, to its great house on an island in a serene lake, that Waterton retreated in 1826. Building a high wall around it, he made his home into England's first wild-bird refuge, which he protected by removing the predatory badgers and foxes. Several years after his return home, Waterton, on a trip to Belgium, met and married Anne Edmonstone, the seventeen-year-old granddaughter of an Indian princess; he had known her British father in Guiana. When his young wife died in childbirth less than a year later, he was heartbroken, and his life remained rather solitary thereafter.

On their honeymoon, he had taken his bride to study the great stuffed-animal collections of Paris, for taxidermy was another of his passions. But ordinary preservation of specimens was too mundane for his tastes. Instead, the Catholic naturalist created an animal collection of his own by turning dead beasts into effigies of famed Protestants. Waterton also created an imaginary animal called a Nondescript by contorting the features of a red howler monkey until they resembled those of a human being.

Waterton also seemed to find the

line between human and animal difficult to draw in his own case. After his wife died, he never slept in a bed again, preferring the floor. He would hide under tables and playfully attack guests like a dog, nipping at their ankles. Sometimes he would greet his visitors by bounding out of doors on all fours, barking. In his eighties, he was still climbing trees, according to one biographer, "like an adolescent gorilla." When a wild orangutan arrived at the London Zoo, Waterton hurried there to meet it and insisted on entering its cage. Warning that he would be torn limb from limb, the keepers admitted him. Waterton and the fierce primate liked each other upon first sight, however, and they quickly embraced and kissed.

Not until 1865 did Squire Waterton's legendary agility fail him. In the spring of that year, the eighty-two-year-old tripped and fell heavily against a log, causing injuries that eventually killed him. Waterton's funeral procession was a flotilla of boats on the lake surrounding Walton Hall—an eccentric end for what one writer called "a very agreeable kind of eccentricity." □

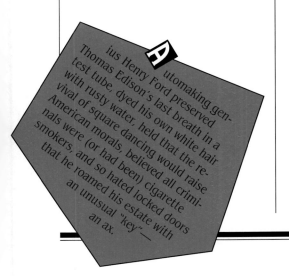

ius Henry Ford preserved
Thomas Edison's last breath in a
test tube, dyed his own white hair
with rusty water, held that the re-
vival of square dancing would raise
American morals, believed all criminals were (or had been) cigarette
smokers, and so hated locked doors
that he roamed his estate with
an unusual "key"—
an ax.
utomaking gen-

Calorie Counter

Richard Kirwan was the archetypal Irish savant, a brilliant eighteenth-century polymath who became the second president of the prestigious Irish Academy. He was renowned for his salon conversation—and for some strange theories about the personal conservation of heat.

Born in 1733 at Cregg Castle in County Galway, the comfortably well-to-do scholar studied abroad for twenty years before setting up household in Dublin in 1788. By then, he had made an international name for himself for studies in mineralogy, logic, music, philology, meteorology, and law, among other things; he had won Britain's Copley medal for chemistry and been made a Fellow of the Royal Society.

A widower for twelve years before his return to Ireland, Kirwan always dined alone. He suffered from dysphagia—chronic difficulty in swallowing—and he did not want others to see the convulsive movements he made while eating the milk and ham that constituted his entire diet. But he was not reclusive in the least. After the table was cleared, he became a social lion, holding separate soirees for ladies and gentlemen every Thursday and Friday. Guests were invited for 6:00 p.m. At seven, the door knocker was removed to bar late-comers. Conversation and music lasted until nine, when everyone was expected to leave. Those who did not take the

hint were shown the door by Kirwan himself, by then in stockinged feet.

Kirwan had an obsessive hatred of flies and would pay servants a bounty for each one they slew. He also had a deathly fear of catching a cold, and he believed he could avoid that common contagion by storing heat. Summer or winter, he presided over his soirees in front of a roaring fire, and he always wore a hat indoors to retain every calorie of body heat. When he left home for a stroll—often in the company of large dogs and a shoulder-tamed eagle—he would first stoke himself before the fire, then pace briskly, keeping his mouth shut tight to prevent heat loss. His trusted manservant, Pope, who later shared Kirwan's grave, slept in the master's room and woke him every few hours to pour hot tea down his throat—and sometimes, inadvertently, into his hair, eyes, and nose—to sustain the inner fires through the night. Despite all his efforts, however, Kirwan finally died at seventy-nine, in 1812—of complications from a cold. □

Cold-conscious Irishman Richard Kirwan was painted by eighteenth-century artist Hugh Hamilton.

Heart Throb

England's eighteenth-century Industrial Revolution was followed by a revolution in nineteenth-century social thinking, led, in part, by Herbert Spencer. A civil engineer, an ardent advocate of evolution before Charles Darwin, and a pioneer in the budding disciplines of sociology and psychology, Spencer appeared to be preoccupied with science and society. In fact, Spencer's main preoccupation was himself—specifically, his pulse. Pulse taking was something that Spencer, a bulky, genial man with fragile nerves, undertook often and with great ceremony. At home—he lived in a boardinghouse for twenty-six years—he would command all conversation to cease while he checked his heartbeat. Often, Spencer enforced silence by donning a pair of velvet earplugs. If he happened to be traveling when the urge struck, he would command his carriage driver to stop—in the middle of the street—while the vital measurement was taken. If Spencer did not like the result, the carriage would be ordered to speed home.

The practice dated from heart trouble following an energetic visit to the Swiss Alps in 1854. From that time on, Spencer spiraled into a determined invalidism that left him increasingly world-weary, trivia ridden, and alone. Even the excitement of reading a novel became too much for him. In 1897, he severed his ties to the rooming house and began to live once more on his own. But his worrisome heart ticked on until 1903. When the eighty-three-year-old sage finally succumbed to his infirmities, he was wrapped in a terrible dreariness and, as always, in himself: One of Herbert Spencer's final contributions to humanity's quest for knowledge was a history of his teeth. □

Brilliant hypochondriac Herbert Spencer was caricatured for Britain's *Vanity Fair* in 1879 by Sir F. Carruthers Gould.

Muse Amiss

There may have been worse poets in history than Scotsman William "Topaz" McGonagall *(right)*, but there cannot have been too many. Nearly a century after his death in 1902, McGonagall's sense of rhyme and rhythm can still cause stunned disbelief, as in his famed ode to a bridge over Scotland's river Tay that collapsed in 1879:

Beautiful Railway Bridge of the Silv'ry Tay!
Alas! I am very sorry to say
That ninety lives have been taken away
On the last Sabbath day of 1879,
Which will be remember'd for a very long time.

Born in Edinburgh in 1830, McGonagall grew up and made his living as a weaver in Dundee. There, as he described it later, in June 1877, the self-trained forty-seven-year-old became invincibly convinced that he was intended to be a poet—a fortuitous revelation, as the town's jute mills had entered a long period of chronic unemployment. A kindly clergyman published a few of his verses, and McGonagall was launched in a new career of shattered meter and tortured rhyme. He celebrated bat-

*Faithfully Yours
William McGonagall
poet, and Tragedian.*

tles and royals, mourned shipwrecks and the wages of Demon Rum. His only means of support were scanty proceeds from broadsheet editions of his poems and small fees received for public readings, usually arranged so that scoffers could pelt him with eggs and vegetables. In fact, McGonagall's Dundee audiences were so rude to him that he was forced to leave the town:

> Welcome! thrice welcome! to the year 1893 (sang McGonagall in parting),
> For it is the year that I intend to leave Dundee,
> Owing to the treatment I receive,
> Which does my heart sadly grieve.
> Every morning when I go out
> The ignorant rabble they do shout
> "There goes Mad McGonagall"
> In derisive shouts, as loud as they can bawl,
> And lift stones and snowballs, throws them at me.
> And such actions are shameful to be heard in the City of Dundee.

Returning to Edinburgh, the man who called himself Sir William McGonagall, Poet and Tragedian, found a wildly enthusiastic audience among university students, who greeted him as a kind of literary geek, to be celebrated with irony, false honors, and the usual shower of garbage. Over time, McGonagall became a kind of national joke. He had hundreds of imitators, but none of them could match the natural awfulness of the man known in his own time as the "greatest bad verse writer of his age."

Except for his strange confidence in his talent, McGonagall was a soft-spoken, unassuming man who endured great poverty for the sake of his art. When he died in 1902, aged seventy-two and abjectly poor, few mourned his passing. But McGonagall may have laughed last after all. His poems have enjoyed more than twenty printings, sold an estimated half million copies, and found a seriously admiring audience in Eastern Europe and the Far East—attracted, perhaps, by the translation. □

Gothic Airs

In the early nineteenth century, Charles Maturin was all the rage as a Gothic novelist and playwright. His works, dripping with murder and even cannibalism, influenced such literary luminaries as Charles-Pierre Baudelaire and Honoré de Balzac and were praised by the likes of Sir Walter Scott and Lord Byron. When it came to unleashing his own passion, however, the Irish Protestant clergyman had a peculiar taste of his own: old-fashioned ballroom dancing.

At the height of his success, Maturin kept a lavish house in Dublin. The ceilings were painted with clouds and eagles, the walls with scenes from his novels. There, he indulged his terpsichorean passion with morning quadrille parties, two or three times a week, keeping the curtains and shutters closed to preserve the illusion of darkness while he and his cocelebrants danced in stately squares. At night, he would venture out to real ballrooms for more of the same. How he remembered where to ◊

Gothic novelist, cleric, and dance fan Charles Maturin strikes a romantic pose for this 1819 engraving.

go was something of a mystery, since the novelist was monumentally absent-minded. He occasionally made social calls in a dressing gown and slippers, and occasionally he showed up at the sites of parties twenty-four hours late. Maturin hated to talk when he sensed his muse approaching, and he would paste a wafer to his forehead as a sign that he did not want to be disturbed.

As his popularity waned, Maturin slipped into poverty; the dancing extravagances ended. But to the end of his brief life—he died in 1824 at the age of forty-two—he tried to keep his wife dressed in the most sumptuous clothes—his own belle of an eternal, but no longer visible, ball. □

Playing the Numbers

Modern forensic science owes much to Sir Francis Galton *(below)*; so do meteorology, mathematics, and genetics. The distinguished British scientist and explorer was brilliant beyond all question—and as quirky as they come. He was, for instance, obsessed with the notion that almost anything could be counted, correlated, and made into some sort of pattern. Until his death in 1911,

Galton was an inveterate quantifier.

Born near Birmingham in 1822, Galton, a younger cousin of Charles Darwin, dabbled cleverly in nearly everything. He deciphered the weather pattern known as the anticyclone, promoted fingerprinting and composite illustrations to identify criminals, and perfected a form of calculus. Galton also carried out some groundbreaking studies in the field of eugenics, the science of selective breeding. He traveled widely, and his book entitled *The Art of Travel; or Shifts and Contrivances Available in Wild Countries* found quite a large audience for such entries as "Revolting Food, that May Save the Lives of Starving Men." Like several other great thinkers, Galton believed that his head needed special protection. He invented a Universal Patent Ventilating Hat, basically a top hat with a mov-

able lid that he raised by squeezing a rubber bulb. This, Galton was convinced, would allow his overheated cranium to breathe. It was a bit weird, he admitted, but better than "falling into a fit upon the floor."

But taking measurements was his obsession. He invented a registrator, a strange device with five interconnecting dials that he claimed would produce anthropological statistics of any kind. He demonstrated one of the gadgets in compiling an unpublished beauty map of Britain, recording the incidence of attractive, nondescript, and ugly women he saw on the streets of various towns. (London had the best rating, Aberdeen the worst.)

At a meeting of the Royal Geographical Society, he compiled a boredom index based on the average rate of fidgets among the audience. Attentive audiences, he observed, sat upright and maintained about the same distance between heads; but bored groups were a choppy sea of heads waving back and forth at a frequency one might use to quantify the degree of ennui. Galton even devised a fiendishly elaborate mathematical formula for calculating the quality of his morning and evening tea, and he filled notebooks with the result. But not all his explorations were so fruitful: Once, while in an infirmary, he resolved to sample everything in the *Pharmacopoeia,* in alphabetical order. He made it only to *C*—for *castor oil,* whose purgative effects distressed him beyond further experimentation.

Apparently, however, such bizarre researches left no long-term ill effects. Active almost until the end of his life, Galton finally succumbed to respiratory problems at the age of eighty-nine. □

Animal Crackers

If Francis Trevelyan Buckland were alive today, he would be known as a food freak. The term did not exist, of course, during his nineteenth-century heyday, when the distinguished zoologist and government inspector became one of Britain's most accomplished and best-beloved scientific popularizers. Among other achievements, he founded the Buckland Museum of Economic Fish Culture, and his efforts to upgrade and protect Britain's salmon fisheries were far ahead of their time. But he was best known for his attempts to vary the boring British diet with interesting recipes from the wild.

Buckland was convinced that, in the wake of massive crop failures, Britons were not getting an adequate amount of food. Not only were vegetables and grains scarce, but the two staple meats—beef and mutton—were in short supply. In 1860, he founded an organization to remedy the situation: the Society for the Acclimatization of Animals in the United Kingdom. Its sole purpose was to alleviate food shortages by introducing new species into Great Britain and teaching the British how to eat them.

There was more at stake than pâté de foie gras and pheasant. At Acclimatization dinner parties, he served truly new concoctions: rhinoceros pie, panther chops, mice on hot toast, slug soup, boiled and fried slices of porpoise head. For Buckland, almost nothing was inedible, and he was inclined to try anything that came to hand. Still, everyone has his limits. He found earwigs bitter, and he could not take stewed mole and bluebottle flies. He abhorred horsemeat and doubted that it had "the slightest chance of success in this country."

Buckland came by his culinary convictions honestly: He ate similar stuff as a child at home. His father, William Buckland, was Britain's first professor of geology, a man who liked an exotic cut of meat or two and would sometimes serve his guests crocodile steaks, roast joint of bear, or a ragout of hedgehog. The father also encouraged the son to keep curious pets, such as alligators.

All of this may have helped to nudge the son toward odd tastes in food and companions. He was genuinely attracted to physical oddities—giants, dwarfs, and sideshow freaks— and was fond of circus people in general. He also favored the company of taxidermists and rat catchers, possibly as a way of gaining experience needed at home: He customarily kept a considerable menagerie of his own. Coming downstairs in the Buckland residence at night, a relative once tripped on a dead baby hippo. It was ev-idently part of the permanent Buckland collection, which also included a live bear.

Buckland liked to take exotic species with him when he traveled, and they sometimes got away from him. On one train trip, a bunch of red slugs escaped and began crawling across a sleeping fellow passenger, who happily did not wake up before Buckland debarked, leaving the slimy creatures to do their worst.

When the great naturalist died in 1880, he evidently expected the afterlife to be something like the one just completed. "I think," he said at the end, "I shall see a great many curious animals." □

Photographed in Scotland in 1870, omnivorous naturalist Francis Buckland holds a graduated pole that was used for inspecting salmon rivers.

Dramatic Flair

British wit Oscar Wilde called her the Incomparable One. Others called her the Divine. And true enough, everyone but crusty playwright George Bernard Shaw considered her the greatest tragic actress in the world and the most forceful French personality since Joan of Arc, whom she often played to vast acclaim. Sarah Bernhardt, whose modesty was never her strong suit, could only agree. On her first visit to the United States, she was told that her wild reception exceeded that given to Dom Pedro of Brazil. "Yes," Bernhardt replied, "but he was only an emperor." She signed letters to her grandchildren simply: Great.

The illegitimate daughter of a Jewish-Dutch courtesan, Bernhardt was the first international stage star. She was also a carefully cultivated agglomeration of quirks, phobias, strange impulses, and postures. "She is not an individual," observed French critic Jules Lemaître, "but a complex of individuals."

Whatever her idiosyncrasies, however, Bernhardt the actress was an unmatched emotional presence. She had a voice of mesmerizing power, attached to a thin, frail frame that could shake with ravenous desires or excruciating mortal pangs: Dying was her undisputed specialty. Her pale, hollow-cheeked, cat-eyed face, framed in unruly red hair, was better than beautiful; it was riveting. Close friends said they had no idea whether she was good looking or not, and her myriad lovers never seemed to care. No one did.

Onstage and off, she was a consummate performer who knew how to mold her personal eccentricities into her image as the Magnificent Lunatic. Remarked Victorien Sardou, the playwright-impresario who made her a global attraction, "If there's anything more remarkable than watching Sarah act, it's watching her live."

All the world was aware, for example, of her death obsession, and of the small rosewood-and-satin coffin she kept in her room: Bernhardt liked to be photographed in it. But the obsession was real enough, and so was the actress's fascination with slaughter in general. She watched from a closed carriage, panting, while two of her lovers dueled over her. In towering temper, she came close to crippling other suitors herself: She pushed one from a second-story window and horsewhipped another. Four times, Bernhardt, who bitterly opposed capital punishment in public, secretly wangled her way into executions. Once she visited the Chicago stockyards to watch the bloodshed. Yet her passion for animals, especially big cats, was highly publicized and wholly unfeigned. At various times she owned pumas, cheetahs, and ocelots, giving them all free run of her many homes. There was even a tame lion, but awful odor limited his tenure. In London, Bernhardt turned a cheetah and a wolfhound loose at a garden party to watch the result. In Paris, novelist Alexandre Dumas once paid a call on the great actress, heard a crunching noise, and discovered a puma eating his straw hat.

Bernhardt's fondness for fauna extended to reptiles—but not too far. When Ali-Gaga, an alligator that she brought back from Louisiana, snapped up a pet dog, she sadly had the gator shot. She once wore a live chameleon as a lapel decoration. The only animal that never fared well with Bernhardt was the cuddly chinchilla, which appeared only in the fur coats she wore in all seasons, even summer.

For a woman who was, after all, only a working professional, the Divine Sarah was royally extravagant. She habitually spent more than twice what she earned on houses, servants, furniture, rugs, and art objects, not to mention the bizarre pets. There were also sumptuous dinner parties and entertainments, which she held almost daily for what was known as her Court. (The Court was not without its real royals, among them the prince of Wales, the future Edward VII of England.) Her homes were jungles of exotic clutter. Tremendous sums were invested in her costumes, both her own clothes and those she wore onstage. Silks were woven to her specifications, furs and laces ordered with abandon, semiprecious stones sewn on without regard to cost. Some of her contracts

promised to pick up almost every other cost but made her responsible for the costume bill. Even when an injury caused her to lose a leg to surgery at the age of seventy, Bernhardt found an occasion for extravagance. Scorning crutches, she insisted on a white-and-gold sedan chair, with retainers to carry her where she wanted to go.

Even more than her incandescent ambition, the constant need for more money was the force that drove Bernhardt to abandon the French stage for tours of England, North and South America, and even Australia. Foreign audiences seemed to love her more, and they paid better. Imbued with a classical French love for gold and a mistrust of banks, she insisted when possible on payment in gold coins. She carried them with her constantly, in a bag when they were few and in a metal-bound chest when they were many. An incompetent underling once spilled the entire contents of one chest into a Paris street. Bernhardt, who was fanatically loyal to those who served her, never fired the man. And the legend grew that, for all her pomp and pretense, her heart was as great as her talent.

The seventy-eight-year-old Divine died on March 25, 1923. Before she was buried, 30,000 people walked past her funeral bier, and tens of thousands more followed the casket through Paris to Père Lachaise Cemetery. Her final resting place was as simple as she had been complex, a plain mausoleum marked with a single word: *Bernhardt.* Even today, that says it all. □

Florence, Nightingale

There has never been another Carnegie Hall performance quite like it. On October 25, 1944, crowds thronged and scalpers charged an outrageous twenty dollars per ticket for an unforgettable night of opera. Thousands were turned away from the performance. Inside the hall, a plump seventy-five-year-old woman draped in a Spanish shawl held the stage, tossing rosebuds at her cheering, laughing audience. She sang the concert aria "Clavelitos"— rather, according to some members of the audience, she quavered and squawked, moaned and bellowed. Sometimes her coloratura voice simply disappeared. The audience loved it all. The show was an Everest of song for Florence Foster Jenkins, who, never troubled by self-doubt, took acclaim in her stride—and never seemed to brood about being called the worst opera singer in history.

The Carnegie Hall performance capped a thirty-two-year career for Jenkins, all of it simply awful. During most of those years, her singing—usually at charitable events, often while footing her own bills—was the subject of unparalleled critical scorn. Yet the First Lady of the Sliding Scale, as she was sometimes known, had also built up a gently perverse fan club that included such musical luminaries as tenor Enrico Caruso, who regarded Jenkins's efforts with bemused affection.

As far as she was concerned, her singing merely fulfilled a lifelong ambition. The daughter of a wealthy Wilkes Barre, Pennsylvania, banker, she had pleaded at age seventeen ◊

Always vivid, the Divine Sarah Bernhardt designed this elaborate, bejeweled costume for her Byzantine empress role in *Théodora* during the 1884 theater season in Paris.

RCA Victor released this Florence Foster Jenkins album in 1954, ten years after her death.

to go abroad to pursue a singing career. Her strait-laced father refused. Jenkins set out on her own, endured a short marriage that ended in divorce, and scraped out a living as a pianist and music teacher. When her father died in 1909, the aspiring middle-aged nightingale came into a large inheritance and decided to try to breathe life into her stillborn career.

Her first concert, in 1912, was a disaster to everyone but her, as were all that followed. But, somehow, laughter never turned to outright derision. She was socially well connected in Newport, Sarasota Springs, Boston, and Washington, and always handed on the concert proceeds to needy causes. In Manhattan, she founded the Verdi Club as a vehicle for her ambitions and gave annual recitals. Those who came to listen usually howled with laughter. The indomitable Madame Jenkins attributed the vulgar noise to "hoodlums" hired by rival singers, who were driven, she believed, by professional jealousy. Among the phonograph recordings of her work, only two remain, including her incomparable rendition of the "Queen of the Night" aria

from Mozart's *Magic Flute*—a famously demanding work even for the greatest voices. Jenkins, however, sang the piece once, unrehearsed, and pronounced the result too good to be improved upon. Eventually, reviewing Jenkins's work became a kind of literary competition among critics, an Olympics of artful invective that reached its apex on her night at Carnegie Hall. "It would be a presumption to speak of the artist's achievements in technical terms," wrote Robert Bagar cryptically in the *New York World-Telegram*, "for there can be none where freedom of expression is rampant." Said *Time* magazine: "Mrs. Jenkins' night-queenly swoops and hoots, her wild wallowings in descending trill, her repeated staccato notes like a cuckoo in its cups, are innocently uproarious to hear." The *Bulletin*, equally oblique, declared, "Mme. Jenkins' vocal art is something for which there is no known parallel." One reporter, less kind, observed that "she hit only a few notes; the rest were promissory," and that she had "screeched new highs." Still, to the star, it was a grand, long-deferred triumph.

Only a month after her Carnegie Hall success, the frail, melancholy trill of Florence Foster Jenkins was silenced by death. Her irrefutable epitaph: "Some may say that I couldn't sing, but no one can say that I didn't sing." She had chosen the words years earlier, perhaps aware that the soaring voice she seemed to hear was never heard by other people. □

Charmed

Poorly trained, Enrico Caruso *(right)*, the great Neapolitan tenor, triumphed through the sheer natural splendor of his operatic voice. As a child, his survival was equally miraculous. The son of a factory worker, he was the first of eighteen offspring to survive beyond infancy, and only his mother's coaxing won him a place in a choir school—and eventually in history. But even when his greatness was recognized and secure, fame was not enough to erase the scars of early hardships.

As one quirky vestige of his youth, Caruso had an uncontrollable passion for bookkeeping. He kept track of every single cent or centesimo that he spent in his life, jotting it down meticulously in a little black diary. When Caruso died in 1921, he left hundreds of the books behind, a memoir of fiscal apprehension, kept by one of the world's wealthiest performers.

His life was forever hemmed in by peasant fears and superstitions. As a child, he had worried constantly that Mount Vesuvius might erupt—a phobia that overtook him when he visited San Francisco in 1906, in time for the great earthquake. As an adult, he would never cross a large body of water without an astrologer's approval, nor would he travel at all on Tuesdays or Fridays, which he considered full of evil. He would not wear a new suit on Friday, and he changed his clothes completely each time he entered his apartment. To protect his golden throat, he resorted to a variety of quackish old wives' remedies, among them chewing garlic and spraying his vocal passages with caustic ether. Such practices would have been disastrous for a lesser

constitution, and they were not kind to his.

Above all, Caruso feared the evil eye, the random curse that might strike him down anywhere, and the vengeful spirits of the afterlife. When the great tenor finally suc-cumbed to pneumonia in 1921, a variety of charms and amulets were found under his pillow. Not intend-ed to save him from death, they were meant to deter the evil demons that might await a super-stitious singer's jittery spirit. □

No Account

Philadelphia's William Claude Du-kenfield, better known as W. C. Fields, the tomato-nosed, cantan-kerous, pool-playing, bibulous film star, had a Horatio Alger existence. A child runaway at eleven, he lived in packing crates and stole food from back porches, where sharp-toothed watchdogs gave him a life-long phobia of canines. He moved up to pool shark, then vaudeville juggler, be-fore his cur-mudgeonly comic tal-ents earned him a place in the Ziegfeld Follies and Hollywood. But those harsh early years would impart a parsimony that lasted Fields a life-time—and more.

The famous comedian had a pro-found and vocal mistrust of banks, at least where large sums of money were concerned. Instead of concen-trating his wealth in any one dubi-ous institution, Fields spread it around. Forever afraid that he would be stranded somewhere with-out money, he opened bank ac-counts everywhere that he went. Hundreds of them went under ficti-tious names: Figley E. Whitesides, Aristotle Hoop, Elmer Mergatroid-Haines, among a host of others. He tried to keep track of all his scat-tered accounts in note-books, but many of the books nevertheless were lost. Fields may have had another powerful mo-tive for squirreling money away: his soured marriage to Harriet Hughes, which produced his only son, William Claude, Jr. For years after their separation, the estranged cou-ple quarreled viciously, usually about money; Fields bemoaned the ruinous payments that he was forced to send his spouse.

Whatever his reasons for amass-ing stashes, the consequences of his lifelong hoarding began to emerge after Fields died in 1946, at the age of sixty-six. He left behind $700,000, a fortune in those days, most of which went to charity. But, according to some estimates, the funds that were found were only about half the funds that really ex-isted. The rest probably had been lost in accounts, under pseudonyms invented and then forgotten, all over the world. □

W. C. Fields, as Cuthbert J. Twillie in the 1940 film *My Little Chicka-dee,* slings some mis-chief with his youthful sidekick Jack Searle.

Hairrealism

Surrealist painter Salvador Dali's entire life could be described as an act of calculated eccentricity—epitomized, in a way, by his famed bristling mustache, waxed upward into trembling exclamation points that nodded staccato agreement to his every utterance. The spiked hair was intended mainly as an attention-getting device. But Dali *(below)*, who lied and bragged about everything, often compared it to insect antennae—the sort sported by the flies and ants featured in many of his obsessive paintings.

As the world grew more high-tech, however, he abandoned his insect metaphor for something more contemporary. "My mustache is my radar," he said. "It pulls ideas out of space. Great painters need a luxuriant mustache like mine. The points have to be just under the eyes to get the right perspective."

In a moment of veiled candor, however, Dali once said that the hardened hairs were actually used to "perforate dollars"— perhaps an allusion to how his determined peculiarity teamed with his talent to reap money. But the mustache may have had deeper spiritual roots than he knew. After the death of his wife, Gala, who was also the brains behind his commercial success, his satanic spikes turned saggy and gray. □

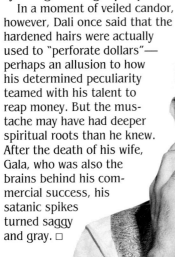

Wrap Artist

The no man's land between profound art and maverick eccentricity is inherently fuzzy, the two sides shading imperceptibly into each other. But rarely has the line been more blurred than in the case of the Bulgarian-born artist named Christo Javacheff, better known simply as Christo. This artist's strange, monumental works have mystified audiences from Australia to Paris: huge, swathed "environments," usually made of colorful plastic, that enfold some famous natural or man-made feature.

Born in Gabrovo in 1935, Christo studied art in Sofia and Vienna, then moved to Paris in 1958, where he found his niche: wrapping as art. He began by wrapping small objects, then escalated to such grander works as *Stacked Oil Bar-*

Planned for ten years, Christo's *The Pont Neuf Wrapped* straddled the Seine for a period of two weeks in 1985.

rels and *Dockside Packages* in Cologne; more wrapped oil barrels in France; and *Wrapping a Girl,* a 1962 project in London. In 1964, he became a resident of New York City and raised his sights to larger and larger packages. He stunned the world in 1969 by wrapping one-million square feet of Australian coast in erosion-control fabric and thirty-six miles of rope. Three years later, he created *Valley Curtain* on Grand Hogback Mountain near Rifle, Colorado: an orange curtain roughly a quarter of a mile long and up to 365 feet high. The year 1976 brought the astonishing *Running Fence:* twenty-four miles of woven nylon fabric, 18 feet high, in California. In 1983, Christo finished enclosing some small islands in Miami's Biscayne Bay in six-and-a-half-million square feet of pink polypropylene; in 1985, the famous Pont Neuf in Paris was enclosed in gold polyamide.

The artist's largest effort planted 1,340 blue umbrellas in a Tokyo-area rice field and 1,760 yellow ones on a hillside north of Los Angeles, California, in October 1991. But *The Umbrellas* came down after a tragic accident. On October 26, high winds tossed one of the quarter-ton, twenty-eight-foot parasols into a crowd of California spectators, killing one woman. Five days later, across the Pacific Ocean, a Japanese crane operator working to remove an umbrella was electrocuted by a power line. □

Hidden Gould

Unorthodox talent does not always demand an unorthodox personal life. But the self-absorbed genius of Canada's Glenn Gould *(right),* one of the twentieth century's greatest and most iconoclastic pianists, generated strange quirks by the dozens. Before he died of a massive stroke in 1982 at age fifty, the reclusive Gould had established himself as one of the most puzzling concert musicians the modern world has ever known.

Gould, born and raised in Toronto, was a prodigy whose off-center playing style—hunched virtually at eye level over the keys, on a wooden bench his father had cut down for him—underscored his unusual talent. He also hummed or sang with his performances, a practice that later drove his recording engineers to distraction. Gould established himself as an interpretive genius with his first smash recording of Johann Sebastian Bach's *Goldberg Variations* in 1955. He pushed and stretched the interpretation of Bach and other musical giants in daring and unheard-of ways—to the point that New York Philharmonic conductor Leonard Bernstein in 1962 publicly dissociated himself from a Gould performance of Brahms that Bernstein was about to lead.

Gould's personal habits quirkily mirrored his professional ones. He was an inveterate insomniac who never rose before noon, and he did much of his recording work after midnight. A lifelong bachelor, he talked incessantly or sang to friends in late-night telephone calls, and he delighted in creating imaginary personalities for himself on the phone. Sir Nigel Twitt-Thornwaite, dean of British conductors, was one; Her-

bert von Hochmeister, sage of the Arctic, was another. In his later years, Gould had a recording studio built in a Toronto hotel, where he could order dinner at 4:00 a.m.

The peculiar pianist never cared what he looked like in concert; he would show up in rumpled formal wear with gloves on his hands, the fingers cut off to allow him to play. Sometimes he would play in bare or stockinged feet. Keeping himself warm seemed to be a constant problem. Before every performance, Gould would soak his hands in warm water or warm them in front of a propane heater. In later years, he dressed more eccentrically yet, wearing mittens, shirts, vests, sweaters, coats, and scarves even in summer. Gould had a phobia about shaking hands—possibly due to fear of injury—and once sued Steinway after a piano salesman gripped his hand too vigorously.

The great pianist dreaded flying and drove everywhere, even to the Canadian Arctic, in hair-raising fashion, often with his right leg curled up on the car seat and his left foot on the accelerator. He cared almost nothing for food. "Greens are damnation," he once declared, and he lived mostly on such things as custard, milkshakes, and scrambled eggs. Yet he was ◊

also a hypochondriac; he would end a telephone call if the other party had a cold. His doctors prescribed myriad medications. Gould gulped Valium incessantly and may have been addicted to the tranquilizer.

For all his antisocial habits, however, Gould was described by his friends as a warm, generous person—if notably mercurial in his friendship. He could, and did, drop longtime professional acquaintances as if they had never existed. The truth was that the reclusive genius was closest to the people he most admired and could never meet—such creators as Bach, Joseph Haydn, and Paul Hindemith, whose music Gould understood in a unique, intimate way.

But Gould tired of sharing his gift. In 1964, when only thirty-two, he abruptly retired from all concert performances. Audiences got in the way of art, he declared. Thenceforth, he confined himself to working with musicians in recording sessions, taping and splicing his work to achieve what he felt was the best possible performance. And once he conducted a full chamber orchestra in a formal performance—without an audience. □

Lunnacy

Mild-mannered, former Yorkshire art teacher Wilfred Makepeace Lunn has become an international figure, not for what he teaches, but for what he builds. In his spare time, the brilliant Lunn is an inventor of perfectly useless, often pyrotechnic, things.

Founder of the Huddersfield Novelty Suicide Company, now defunct, Lunn took to "blowing himself up" onstage in the mid-1970s by attaching explosives to his head, which was encased in a thick helmet. He gave up these noisy simulations, he said, when he discovered that he had become somewhat punch-drunk: If a car backfired nearby, he found himself suddenly lying in the gutter.

Especially fond of bicycles, Lunn began to fashion exotic miniature variations of them in 1965. He was the first person recorded to have put a bicycle in a bottle. But most of his vehicles and accessories evoke the impossibly complex devices created by American cartoonist Rube Goldberg and are prized by private collectors. The nonhumane duck catcher, for example, wiggles a rubber worm in front of the bicycle rider. If a duck should swoop down to eat the bait, two spiked disks slam together to crush the fowl. (Its humane counterpart traps the bird without hurting it.) His Fat Child and Reluctant Obese Pensioner Exerciser consists of a three-wheeler with a circle of inward pointing spikes extending from the front at about waist level. The person needing exercise is placed in the circle; as the rider pedals, the victim either does roadwork or is impaled.

But all is not bicycles with Lunn. His inventions include the Halitosis High-Breathing Hat, which funnels away the breath of the offending wearer, and the Incontinence Sock, which has an umbrella attachment to the opening, to protect the wearer's footgear from any embarrassing downpour.

Lunn gave up teaching years ago, but he continues to live with his family in the Yorkshire town of Marsh and give lectures, mainly to children, on such things as fireworks. Sporting a broad, spiky mustache, he describes his inventions with such utter seriousness that he is sometimes known as the Deadpan Man of Marsh.

The child of deaf parents, Lunn debuted many of his inventions on "Vision On," a British children's television program for the hearing-impaired. There, he demonstrated such creations as his Exploding Christmas Tree, which could be seasonally reloaded and used again. Also displayed: a Steaming Teapot, a Walking Submarine, and Europe's largest Lark Lure—everything, it seemed, but a better mousetrap. Still, Lunn's young audience, and the world, have made a quiet pathway to his door. □

At his Wiz Bizard Cafe in 1991, Wilfred Lunn displays two new inventions: a tongued mechanical ice cream cone that licks back and a submarine designed to pick up underwater litter.

Street Beat

For a quarter century, Louis T. Hardin was a fixture on Manhattan streets—a homeless, blind eccentric in a Viking costume who sang jazz-poetry, played a drum, and went by the name of Moondog. He was odd—but only marginally so by Manhattan standards—and New Yorkers were comfortably accustomed to seeing him around. Then, one day in 1974, he vanished from the sidewalks. Moondog, most people believed, had died. In fact, he had been lured to Germany for a radio concert, and he decided to stay on there as a self-styled European. In 1991, seventy-five-year-old Hardin was still living in the German village of Oer-Erkenschwick— and he was acclaimed as one of the world's

extraordinary musical composers.

Hardin was born in 1916 in Maryville, Kansas, and grew up in Wyoming. He was blinded at age sixteen by an exploding dynamite cap. He attended an Iowa school for the blind, where he received a solid musical grounding and where composing became a lifelong passion. In 1943, he gravitated to New York City where he adopted the name Moondog and was taken in by officials of the New York

Philharmonic. They allowed him to attend rehearsals, where he honed his composing skills.

But Moondog was drawn to more than music: He also felt the fatigued attraction of the Beat Generation. He began dressing in Viking costume, complete with beard, horned helmet, spear, and homemade robe, and he moved onto the Manhattan streets, singing and declaiming poetry and selling copies of his music. Despite his vagrant bohemian existence, however, Moondog began to acquire a musical reputation, recording his work on the Mars, Prestige, and CBS record labels. That was when Europe, and destiny, beckoned.

In Germany, he met Ilona Goebel, a geology student who took him off the streets and into her family. She later became his manager. Moondog gave up the Viking look and became a full-time performer-composer. Since 1984, he has written more than forty jazz symphonies. Comfortable listening only to his own music, Moondog has adjudged the work of other composers, including the classical giants, full of unspecified "mistakes."

In 1988, Moondog returned to the United States for a celebratory concert and performance of his Symphony No. 50 by the Brooklyn Philharmonic. Back in Germany, the Viking of Cool continued to work as he always had—like a machine, according to Ilona Goebel, with ideas flying at him too rapidly for him to take them down in Braille. He also toured across Europe, conducting orchestras with his characteristic lack of orthodoxy. Eschewing a baton, Moondog sat at the bass drum, where the players could watch him, beating time while he listened to his work unfold. □

Blind, spear-bearing street musician Moondog, shown on a Manhattan sidewalk in 1971, became a world-famous composer-conductor.

Seascapes

Some artists will go to any length to pursue their art. Jamy Verheylewegen *(above)* goes to any depth—well, to thirty feet or so. That is where the native Belgian says he can "finally give free rein to my creative imagination." In scuba gear weighted down with thirty pounds of extra lead, using special canvas on a weighted easel, he paints seascapes from the seafloor. He has created hundreds of paintings since he took up his briny medium in 1983, won medals, and been enshrined in the *Guinness Book of Records.* Professional as he is, however, Verheylewegen re-creates waving meadows of sea grass and coral towers like an amateur—he paints by the numbers. Because colors are shifted by the optical effect of water, Verheylewegen keeps his paint tubes straight by coded numbers, not by the hues. □

THE IMPORTANCE OF BEING BRITISH

Perhaps no other nation treats its eccentrics with such gentle tolerance, or creates them in such good-natured multitudes, as Great Britain. Over the centuries, the island kingdom has cheerfully fostered whole communities of oddness: indomitable grannies, nonsensical inventors, rank bibliophiles, and those obsessed—with the good old days, with war or gardens, pets or politics. Some are serious, some playful, and some now and then don the mask of eccentricity to serve a worthy cause.

As the British themselves are keenly aware, the peculiarities of the few often echo the best qualities of the many. Like music-hall comics, eccentrics hold a slightly distorting mirror up to their compatriots. But, in Britain, the different drummer strikes a beat that everyone can hear. Thus, for every house pet that inherits a master's wealth, there are a great many that receive smaller kindnesses. Even the most erratic sportsman is governed by the general insistence that everything must be cricket. And those who rant against others speak, however shrilly, with the brave, centuries-old voice of democracy—one that, like the eccentricity endemic in the land, lives deep in the British heart.

Riding to Pigs

The world has always teemed with eccentrics among the rich and powerful, but England admits the common folk as well—and there was none more colorful than James Hirst, a self-made Yorkshire gentleman. Born in 1738, Jemmy Hirst was sent by his farmer father to become a clergyman, but education never quite fitted the boy, who had a way with animals, not men. Abandoning school, Hirst returned to the village of Rawcliffe and became a tanner. He was successful enough at his trade to acquire property, and his fortune grew bigger by the year. But while others in his position might have discreetly bought land or horses in order to bolster their social status, Hirst blazed his way to notoriety.

Jemmy seems to have had an exotic bent from his early years. He supposedly rode a teacher's pig at school and was expelled for it. In later life, he extended the joke by saddling a bull named Jupiter and regularly riding it when he went shooting. To heighten the effect, he took along a pack of trained pigs, which, he said, served as pointers. Indeed, if legend can be believed, on at least one occasion he rode his bull to hounds. His close companions were a pet black bear named Nicholas, an otter, and a tame fox.

Hirst became a familiar and popular figure at the Doncaster racecourse in his home county of Yorkshire. He was hard to miss in his regular garb: a waistcoat of duck feathers, patchwork breeches, red and white striped stockings, and an otter-skin coat lined with red flannel. His mode of transportation was equally unmistakable. A unique, high-sided wickerwork contraption, the carriage was fitted with a double bed and a wine cellar; it also sported high wheels rigged with a primitive odometer of Hirst's own devising that sounded a bell each time a mile was completed.

In fact, Hirst was something of an inventor, although his inventions often lacked practicality. The pair of feathered wings he contrived for flying from a boat's mast merely earned him a ducking in the river Humber. On one occasion, he fitted sails to his carriage, only to have the vehicle blown into a draper's shop window. He also devised a standing coffin, equipped with folding doors and a window, as a conversation piece for his guests. If a visitor accepted his invitation to step inside, the doors closed automatically, and the guest had to pay a small fine to be let out. Another coffin in his living room—almost lost in the clutter of agricultural implements that were hung or strewn all over the place—served as a drinks cupboard. But Hirst was not a man to waste his money; the funereal bar was built to his own dimensions so it could one day hold his mortal remains.

Word of his famous nonconformity spread beyond the county, eventually reaching the ears of King George III in London, who sum-

Jemmy Hirst *(above)* preferred this colorful wicker gig, equipped with bed and bar, for everyday transportation. The unsigned illustration is from *The Comical Genius*, published in 1841.

moned the Yorkshireman to a royal audience. The story goes that Hirst, who bragged that he had never paid a farthing in taxes, characteristically refused to bow but shook the regal hand. Still, he so pleased His Majesty with his odd clothes and bizarre manners that he was returned home with his wickerwork carriage filled with wine from the royal cellars.

Before his death at the age of ninety in 1829, Hirst arranged to leave life in his own distinctive style. Having a fancy to be carried to his grave by twelve elderly virgins, he bequeathed a little more than a pound apiece to any who would volunteer. Since only two spinsters appeared, however, his executors had to settle for eight widows instead. No doubt the oddball tanner would have loathed the compromise, but he was at last beyond the capacity to protest. For once, Hirst did not go his own way. □

A Dirty Business

Eighteenth-century London was not renowned for its cleanliness, but one shop was so extravagantly filthy as to be known throughout the city—indeed, throughout the world—as the Dirty Warehouse of Leadenhall Street. The hardware it sold lay scattered in bales amid decades of dust. Spiderwebs festooned the ceiling, and half the windowpanes were missing, hidden by shutters improvised from tea trays and box lids chained into place to discourage thieves.

Appropriately, the Dirty Warehouse was occupied by a man universally known as Dirty Dick, who wore patched and ancient clothes he mended himself. He never combed his hair, and it was reputed that he never washed. When a customer chided him for his lack of cleanliness, he replied sadly, "It is of no use, Sir; if I wash my hands today they will be dirty again tomorrow."

The intriguing thing about Dirty Dick—or Nathaniel Bentley, as he had been christened—was that his manners were by general consent exquisite, and he had in his youth been considered a beau. He had spent some time in Paris, where he became something of a social lion, attending salons and achieving an introduction at court. Even when he became slovenly in the shop, he still for a time ventured forth to the theater and other public places in blue and silver finery. "Although involved in dirt," noted one contemporary writer, "his manners bespeak the man of breeding." The Dirty Warehouse likewise had a distinguished history: It had been a splendid Bentley family residence until Nathaniel decided to transform it into his commercial sty.

A streak of miserliness seems partly to explain the change in his personality. Inside the shop, he stood with his feet in a box of straw to save on heating. He kept no servant—an oddity for a wealthy man in his day. Because meat was expensive, he avoided eating it, and he was renowned for the small quantities of vegetables that he bought from the markets. ◊

Some said that his peculiarities were rooted in a disappointment in love. He kept a locked room in the house, and the story was that he had closed it up after preparing a reception for his bride-to-be, who had died suddenly en route to her wedding. But Bentley's Dirty Dick persona may also have been part of his sharp commercial acumen.

When neighbors offered to pay to have the shopfront repainted, he refused, claiming it was so well known as the Dirty Warehouse that cleaning it would ruin him.

Whatever his motive, his filthy little fiefdom achieved a kind of immortality. It is preserved by a popular pub, Dirty Dick's, that stands as Nathaniel Bentley's monument. □

Running Submerged

Like almost everything else, British eccentricity has its fashions, and behavior that in one age seems bizarre might go almost unnoticed in another. The oddities of Matthew Robinson *(below)*, later Lord Rokeby, certainly seemed to be outrageous in his own day. Yet nowadays he might have fitted quite comfortably into the fringes of the environmental movement.

Born in 1713, Robinson spent the first four decades or so of his life as a wealthy country gentleman and served with some distinction as member of Parliament for the city of Canterbury. Scrupulously honest, he was an uncomfortable politician, contemptuous of petty partisan maneuvering. Finally, frustrated by corruption and the wiliness of colleagues, Robinson told his disappointed constituents that he could no longer represent them. He retired to his estate at Monks Horton, in Kent and gave up public life for a life of gentle—and amphibious—eccentricity.

Swimming against the fashions of the day, Robinson let his beard grow, along with everything else requiring cultivation. As his beard lengthened, finally reaching almost to his waist, his lands became wild and overgrown, with animals grazing where they would. He became, as one biographer put it, an Ornamental Hermit. At a time when landed gentlemen were supposed to ride in carriages, Robinson insisted on traveling everywhere on foot; if he took his carriage along, it was generally for the convenience of his servants.

Robinson's dining habits also aroused comment. A firm believer that people should live on local produce, he banished such foreign commodities as tea, coffee, and sugar from his table, making do instead with beef broth and honey. A teetotaler,

his great love was water, and he had spring water in his neighborhood collected in basins for the benefit of passing travelers.

Water was, in fact, the medium of his greatest oddity. He adopted the unusual habit of walking three miles to the beach nearest to his home each day and immersing himself in the sea. There he would often remain until, chilled to the bone, he passed out and had to be rescued by his waiting servant. This strange behavior attracted onlookers, and eventually Robinson decided to preserve his privacy by taking the plunge at home. He built a bath in a greenhouse where sunlight could warm the water, and he spent much of his days soaking. Sometimes he stayed neck-deep in water while he ate his meals.

In 1794, on the death of his uncle, Robinson succeeded to the title of Lord Rokeby at the ripe age of eighty-one, still strong-willed and scholarly—and wealthy. Contrary to dire predictions, his untended estates flourished. To the end of his life, he despised medicine and doctors and firmly believed that fresh air was the best tonic. At eighty-four, the old man was still acute enough to publish a pamphlet on the war in France that was generally admired for its clarity of thought and expression. He even ordered a nephew not to bring a physician to him, warning that if the doctor failed to kill him he would then use his last strength to cut the young man from his will. When Lord Rokeby died at eighty-seven, he had outlived most of his more stylish contemporaries—without living to see an era when his independent ideas about staying close to nature would be, in some circles, conventional wisdom. □

High Spirits

"It will do for Mytton," nineteenth-century Englishmen would say when they wished to describe a foolhardy enterprise no sane man would attempt. For of all the hard-riding, hard-drinking squires of English country lore, none could match the crazy bravado of Mad Jack Mytton, lord of Halston in Shropshire. Born in 1796, the heir to a great estate, he was to squander his patrimony before an early death. The money went on drink—up to eight bottles of port a day, plus copious amounts of brandy—on gambling debts, and on reckless extravagances. Mytton was said to own some 3,000 shirts and 1,000 hats.

Yet it was not his excesses but his wildly unpredictable exploits that assured his place in legend. Often, his stunts involved a horse. He never balked at hedges or ditches that scared off other riders, but that was the least of it. Mytton once rode his mount upstairs into a hotel dining room and then, still firmly in the saddle, jumped the horse from the balcony down into the street. If the horse was attached to a carriage when Mytton's blood was up, so much the better. Late one night, his way blocked by a high hedge, the squire drove his horse to leap the hurdle, taking with him carriage, passengers, and all.

Dining at Mytton's was a nerve-racking affair. On one occasion, he dressed as a highwayman and pulled a gun on his guests as they tried to leave his estate. Another evening he chose to ride into dinner on the back of his pet bear, Nell. As his guests scattered in terror, he spurred the frightened animal on and was badly bitten in the thigh for his pains. For all that he sometimes

put them to strange uses, he loved most animals, reportedly keeping sixty cats and some 2,000 dogs.

Sometimes feared for his recklessness, Mytton was nevertheless loved for his courage and generosity. He gave away money as freely as he spent it. But even his kindnesses could be disastrous. Trying to warm a chilled horse, Mytton fed it a draft of mulled wine. The animal drank the wine—and immediately fell dead. And Mad Jack was no better at taking care of himself.

Mytton's end was sad, if predictable. By 1831, the family coffers had been emptied by his profligacy, and he fled to the Continent to avoid his creditors. By that time, he was ravaged by alcohol, and his eccentricity appeared to be giving way to insanity. In a hotel in the French port of Calais, Mytton attempted to scare away an attack of

Mad Jack Mytton cured his hiccups—and nearly killed himself—by setting fire to his nightshirt. The contemporary illustration is an aquatint by Edward Duncan from a Henry Aiken sketch.

the hiccups by setting fire to his nightshirt, narrowly avoiding death in the ensuing blaze. "Well," the indomitable young squire roared, "the hiccup is gone, by God."

Restless and bored, he returned to England, to the bailiffs, and to debtors' prison. He survived for two more years before succumbing to alcoholism in 1834, aged thirty-eight. But, after his death, people forgot the sadness of his later life, remembering instead the pleasure the tales of his earlier escapades had given. Back in Shropshire, 3,000 mourners turned out to follow the coffin of the roaring squire to his final resting place. □

Volatile Vicar

In the middle of the nineteenth century, pedestrians heading home late at night in the Hertfordshire towns of Hitchin and Baldock were occasionally startled to see an odd figure leap out in front of them swathed in a leopard skin. They would have been more astonished had they known that behind the disguise was a pillar of Hertfordshire society—one of the county's leading landowners, a justice of the peace, and a member of the civic board responsible for the welfare of the district's poor.

But there was much that was surprising about John Alington. Born to a prominent family in 1795, he attended Oxford University and was ordained to the priesthood in 1822. That same year, he married Eliza Frances, a judge's daughter, who would bear him eight children. In 1830, Alington inherited Letchworth Hall, a large Jacobean mansion in the north of the county. Alington moved there in 1838 after the death of his wife.

By then, Alington's behavior had begun to wax peculiar, especially in regard to his professional performance. The vicar garbled the Anglican service, some said. Worse, he used texts from Solomon's richly erotic "Song of Songs" in the Old Testament to preach sermons advocating free love. Investigations were made, and Alington was suspended from his pastoral duties.

But he was not a man to let such setbacks depress him. Deprived of his church, he began holding services in his own home that were blatantly unconventional. Perched upon a four-wheel vehicle—his so-called hobbyhorse—Alington greeted his congregation, then pedaled up and down the aisles, whooping and cheering, offering pinches of snuff to the parishioners on the way. Dismounting at last, he would don his leopard-skin cloak and launch into impassioned sermons castigating the church that had defrocked him. Purple-faced and dripping sweat, he would frequently cap his performance by tearing off his wig and hurling it into the audience. Once the sermon was over, the benches would be cleared away, beer and brandy would be brought in, and gypsy musicians would strike up the dance.

News of the unique Sunday revels spread, and people came from miles around to attend them. And Alington, however unorthodox a preacher, remained a stern magistrate. At the first sign of trouble, brawlers were thrown out of the house; any who resisted were confronted by the erstwhile vicar wielding a shotgun.

As a landowner, Alington showed an unusual degree of concern for his farm hands' education. To teach them geography, he landscaped a pond on his estate to resemble a map of the world, then rowed them around it in a small boat, pointing out the various continents and islands. During the Crimean War, he and his men spent much of one winter turning a ridge on his lands into a replica of the fortifications of Sebastopol, the better to follow news reports of the town's bitter siege. The squire had a seat built in a nearby tree, from which he sniped at imaginary Russian defenders.

In 1851, he decided to take his laborers to London to see the Great Exhibition. Fearing they might get lost in the big city, he had them shift logs in the park to form a street map, then drilled them on the right route to follow. But he lost patience when they made mistakes and abandoned the project, declaring they were too stupid to be trusted on their own.

For all his oddities, Alington was a highly intelligent man with a true passion for literature, chess, and music. He played the violin and collected birds' eggs, butterflies, and moths. He also drank, sometimes to excess; one of his favorite pursuits was to combine hobbies by reading Shakespeare to his farmworkers while he and they proceeded to get drunker and drunker.

Alington died in 1863 at the age of sixty-eight, robustly challenging convention to the end. Ordered to take a medicine by his doctor, he fed it to his gardener for three days before tasting it himself. When a second po-

Unconventional cleric John Alington wears his familiar leopard skin in this Samuel Lucas cartoon, reproduced in Reginald Hine's 1932 *Hitchin Worthies*.

tion was prescribed, even more noxious than the first one, Alington smashed the bottle in a fit of fury and called for half a tumbler of neat brandy instead. He knocked the spirits back in one gulp, settled down on his pillow, and died—presumably a happy man. □

Bookish

Endemic in the United Kingdom, bibliomania is the name given to an obsessive fascination with books. Prominent British bibliomaniacs of the past have included eighteenth-century collector Thomas Rawlinson, whose London apartment was so full of volumes that he had to sleep in the hallway, and Richard Heber, who, after his death in 1833, was discovered to own eight houses in four different countries, all of them stuffed with books.

But the greatest English bibliomaniac of all time was without doubt Sir Thomas Phillipps *(right)*, a Worcestershire landowner who inherited his father's considerable estates in 1818 at the age of twenty-six. For the fifty-four years that remained to him, he lived the life of a miser in order to devote all his energy and resources to his obsession. He ultimately owned upwards of 100,000 books and 60,000 manuscripts—at the time, more than all the libraries of Cambridge University combined.

The vast sums he expended on his purchases nearly beggared his family, and at one stage, Phillipps himself had to go abroad to escape his debtors. The sheer mass of the books also encroached increasingly on the family's living space. When the dining room became clogged with manuscripts, Phillipps simply locked it up, leaving his wife and three daughters to make do as best they could with a sitting room and three poorly furnished bedrooms where wind whistled through the broken windowpanes.

When his wife died at age thirty-seven, worn out by privations and neglect, Phillipps at once set about finding a replacement whose dowry would help finance future purchases. "Do you know of any Lady with £50,000 who wants a husband?" he wrote an acquaintance. "I am for sale." After fierce haggling with a succession of prospective fathers-in-law, one of whom accused him of behaving like a cattle dealer, he eventually settled for a clergyman's daughter with an estate of £3,000 a year.

Even had he forsaken bibliomania, Sir Thomas would not have been much of a catch. He was an irascible man, and his hatreds were almost as intense as his love of books. He hated the Catholic church, for instance, and wrote many pamphlets against it. In later life, he even refused to allow Catholic scholars to consult his library.

But he reserved his most scathing vitriol for his son-in-law, a scholar and bibliophile who had married his eldest daughter without his permission. (He had hoped to wed her to the son of the British Museum's manuscript librarian.) To make matters worse, the groom had been accused of stealing manuscripts from a Cambridge library—in Phillipps's eye, a capital crime.

At first, Phillipps made sporadic attempts to woo his daughter into leaving her husband. When these efforts failed, the concerned parent wrote to inform his errant offspring that she would fall "under the Curse destined for all disobedient children 'unto the 2nd & 3rd Generation,'" adding, "I understand the Curse had already commenced by your eldest Daughter being half witted, & your second is afflicted with a Spinal Complaint."

Phillipps's wrath was the greater because he knew that his home was entailed by the terms of his own father's will to pass to the offending daughter and her detested spouse. Accordingly, Sir Thomas set about rendering the bequest as near to worthless as he could manage. He cut down the avenues of trees that had graced its park, and he abandoned all attempts at maintenance. All that the couple finally inherited was a dilapidated ruin with cows ◊

Swathed in his customary layers of clothing and a trilby hat, pudding fancier Sir Tatton Sykes *(below)* paces as Sledmere, his Yorkshire mansion, burns on May 23, 1911.

wandering freely through the ground-floor rooms.

By that stage, Phillipps had decamped with his library to Cheltenham, where he took a new home so large that he rode on horseback around it to supervise the unpacking of his books. It took two years to complete the move, and many of the wagons used were said to have collapsed under the weight of their loads. Following the death of Sir Thomas in 1872, the collection that had been the pride of his life was sold at auction. But the job of cataloging and selling the accumulated volumes, manuscripts, and miscellaneous papers was so vast that it was not finished until 1946. □

Flowering Rage

Sir Tatton Sykes was the second of that name to rule the great estates around Sledmere Hall in Yorkshire, and he lived all of his life in the shadow of his father. The old man had been a country squire in the tradition of the eighteenth century, even wearing the clothes of that day well into the Victorian era when his son was born. His ideas of parenting were equally old-fashioned: Children had to be beaten into shape. On one occasion, the elder Sir Tatton was seen driving his young heir barefoot and screaming down the driveway with a whip.

The boy doted on his mother, but she, too, gave him little love. Instead she spent her time on gardening,

raising flowers in the magnificent orangery and the hothouses that dotted the estate.

When he finally inherited his father's title at the age of thirty-seven, it was not surprising that the new Sir Tatton set about eradicating the memories of an unhappy childhood. His first acts included selling most of his father's prize livestock and destroying the orangery, hothouses, and flower beds that had been his mother's pride.

But the phobia he subsequently manifested for flowers went beyond all reasonable bounds. He forbade any of his tenants to grow them and would wander through the village, walking stick in hand, ready to slash down any stray blooms that had survived his interdiction. Anyone who dared complain was told to grow cauliflowers instead.

Sir Tatton or-

dered all the front doors in the village to be boarded up, perhaps, some said, because the sight of children playing repelled him. The mandate relegated all social life to the back gardens.

Sir Tatton's floral antipathies were matched by a well-developed hypochondria. Convinced that sudden changes in temperature were bad for his health, he tried to combat them by discarding clothing as the day wore on. He would start out wearing up to six coats—specially tailored to fit well on top of one another—and would steadily remove them as he grew warmer. He also took to wearing two pairs of trousers, and on one occasion, he deeply embarrassed his son by removing the outer pair in public at York station.

His concern for his health also narrowed his diet. He believed his stomach could handle nothing more robust than milk pudding, a British staple made with equal quantities of milk and cream. He took a cook with him on his travels to the grand hotels of Europe solely to produce the familiar pudding.

His oddities hardly equipped him to be an ideal husband, yet he was unwise enough, at the age of forty-eight, to take a wife thirty years his junior. His bride, a spirited woman, soon chafed at his peculiarities. Retreating in search of more congenial company to a town house in London, she sought solace first in good works and the Catholic church, then later in alcohol, adultery, and gambling. The result was a much-publicized lawsuit, in which Sir Tatton sued his wife for forging his signature to a series of promissory notes. She cited his eccentricity in her defense, but even though the presiding judge described him as "an obstinate and extremely whimsical old gentleman," the court found in his favor.

Further unhappiness overtook Sir Tatton and his family when Sledmere was severely damaged by fire. When he was first informed of the conflagration, Sir Tatton refused to allow the disaster to disturb his digestion, insisting that "first I must finish my pudding."

In his last year, following the death of his estranged wife, he became obsessed with the idea that he himself was going to die at precisely 11:30 a.m., a time when he normally went out riding. Frequently he would wave the horse away, muttering, "No, no, can't ride, can't ride, going to die!" In this belief at least, Sir Tatton was simply wrong; when death came for him at last, on May 4, 1914, it was at 3 o'clock in the morning. □

Pursuit of Folly

Faringdon House, the former home of Sir Gerald Hugh Tyrwhitt-Wilson, the fourteenth Baron Berners, still stands on the edge of the Oxfordshire market town whose name it bears. Visitors admire its austere Palladian facade, its beautiful flower gardens, and the lake that graces its grounds. But nothing in the architecture or landscaping is as memorable as the doves that flutter around the house and settle on its window sills and pediments. Pink and yellow and mauve, they come in a variety of pastel shades. Dyeing them those colors was a typical conceit of the artistic lord, and the tradition he established has been kept up to the present day.

Another memorial to Lord Berners's ownership of the house stands across the valley. It is a 140-foot tower built on top of a wooded hillock, commanding fine views of the rolling countryside. It is the last great folly, as such whimsical structures are called, raised in this century. Lord Berners gained permission to build the tower only after a lengthy struggle with the local planning authorities. When asked to explain the purpose of the building, ◊

The doves of Faringdon House are still dyed today, following the fourteenth Baron Berners's custom.

Lord Berners's response spoke for all of Britain's builders of follies over the ages. "The great point of the tower," he declared, "is that it will be entirely useless." Convinced by this cogent argument, planners let Lord Berners pursue his tower. When it finally opened, a neatly printed warning at its entrance cautioned visitors: "MEMBERS OF THE PUBLIC COMMITTING SUICIDE FROM THIS TOWER DO SO AT THEIR OWN RISK."

The tower's builder was a man of considerable artistic talent. Born in 1883, the son of a wealthy family, he entered the diplomatic service before inheriting in 1918 titles, property, and a great fortune. Thereafter, he devoted his time primarily to the arts—and to his considerable bent for off-center behavior. He was to publish five novels and a couple of volumes of autobiography, and his paintings—mostly landscapes—were well received when they were exhibited in London. But he was best known for his music, especially music for the ballet; he was the only English composer to have work commissioned by the great Russian impresario Sergey Diaghilev. Even in composing, however, the baron's sense of humor intervened; one of his compositions—a cheerful piece— was entitled *Funeral March for a Wealthy Aunt.*

A shy man who disliked the company of strangers, Sir Gerald developed an efficient way to secure compartments for his exclusive use when traveling by rail. Donning a skullcap and dark glasses, he would assume a maniacal grin and wave invitingly at anyone who approached him. Most people were repelled. Those who were not usually departed when their odd companion began repeatedly taking his own temperature with a hospital thermometer.

Yet at home Lord Berners was renowned for his elegant hospitality, and his guest lists glittered with the names of famous artists, writers, and musicians. Most were tolerant of the oddity that often crept into his entertainments. Each year he gave a bonfire party; guests were invited to bring effigies of their enemies for burning, a maximum of six being permitted. On one occasion, he gave a tea party in the drawing room of Faringdon House for three friends—and a horse.

When Lord Berners died in 1950, aged sixty-seven, almost everyone in Britain took note of his passing, admiring him not so much as the serious and versatile artist, but as the flippant prankster who dyed his doves and the architect of the Faringdon Folly. □

Lord Berners *(below, right)* hosts a memorable tea at Faringdon House for *(from left)* Bubbles Radclyffe, Penelope Chetwode, Robert Heber-Percy— and Chetwode's favorite horse.

A sportsman to his toes, pugilistic squire Sir Claude Champion de Crespigny posed for Cecil Cutler with gun and hunting tweeds.

The Champ

If ever there was a walking definition of the right stuff, it was Victorian daredevil Sir Claude Champion de Crespigny. From the early days when his steeplechasing exploits won him the nickname the Mad Rider, he was game for anything. "Where there is a daring deed to be done in any part of the world," he declared, "an Englishman should leap to the front to accomplish it."

Other people, however, were not always as willing to accept the derring-do that he volunteered. When Sir Claude offered to accompany Henry Morton Stanley in the search for missing explorer David Livingstone, Stanley turned him down. Similarly, when de Crespigny went to Egypt to help quell the Dervish uprising, the British army declined his services. Even the acrobat Charles Blondin rejected the adventurer's request to join him on the high wire. Frustrated, Sir Claude had to make do with fox hunting and steeplechasing in rural Essex, where he won a reputation for daring. For a little variety, there were trips to shoot big game in Africa and wild turkey in America. And in 1883, Sir Claude and a companion obtained the international medal of the Royal Aero Club by making the first balloon flight over the North Sea, setting down in Holland.

But nothing tested one's mettle like physical combat. Sir Claude was an enthusiastic boxer who regarded a man's fighting ability as the best index to the rightness of his stuff. Putting his ideas into practice, he never hired a manservant without first boxing with him. Passing sturdy beggars while out walking, he would offer them a meal in exchange for a fight. Friends once tricked him by dressing up a professional pugilist in tramp's clothing. Although on that occasion Sir Claude took a drubbing, he held no grudge—and learned no lesson. He continued to challenge all comers.

As a youth, he broke fourteen bones, yet his daredevil ways did not undermine his excellent constitution. At the age of forty-two, he swam the Nile rapids, and in his fifties he volunteered for service in the South African War. (He did not serve in combat, but he did visit the front as an observer.) At sixty-one, he won a bet by walking the forty-five miles from his home in Essex to a London hotel. He rode in his last steeplechase six years later. At seventy-three, he challenged his cousin to a duel, an offer that was turned down, and right up to his death in 1935, at eighty-eight, he continued to indulge his abiding passion for cross-country rambles. "Indifference to danger," he once wrote, "is absolutely essential." □

"The culinary arts," wrote Dr. William Kitchiner, "set humans—the only Cooking Animal"—apart. He also believed a fixation on good food demanded moderation—bed at eleven; early rising. He may have been right. One evening in 1827, a very enjoyable dinner kept him up past 1:00 a.m. He died of a heart attack later that morning, aged only fifty-two.

Ham on Wye

In 1977, a thirty-nine-year-old bookseller named Richard Booth decided that there was room in Great Britain for a second monarch. Thus he duly declared himself king of Hay-on-Wye, a town of 1,200 on the Welsh border. His accession was celebrated with the appropriate proclamations, marches, a coronation ceremony, plus the printing of currency on edible rice paper (so people could put money where their mouth was, he said) and the sale of numerous dukedoms, earldoms, and knighthoods for modest sums. Although publicity was the prime motive for these events, Booth was also convinced that the best political direction for his community was backward, and as king he could lead it that way. He considered the twentieth century a degenerate age.

When the odd but amiable king-to-be took up residence there in 1962, Hay-on-Wye was a humdrum place. He invigorated the economy by purchasing several large buildings and filling them with more than a million secondhand books, bought by the libraryful from throughout the world. The town became a major bookselling center.

For all his entrepreneurial energies, however, Booth frowned on progress, and therefore devised his idea that he would be best equipped to throw obstacles into its path if he were a monarch. After his enthronement, he spared no effort to turn back the clock. He campaigned for the elimination of cars and the return to a horse-based economy.

He urged his subjects to eat only locally grown food: The supermarket, he predicted cryptically, would someday cause "enormous violence." He railed at government meddling and once created a thirty-foot-high effigy of a bureaucrat for the sole purpose of burning it on Guy Fawkes Day. He also devised a decision-making device resembling a roulette wheel, reasoning that random decisions were superior to those made by the government.

The populace of Hay-on-Wye has viewed his reign with a jaundiced eye—particularly such antics as his appointment of a horse as his prime minister. But the tourist traffic and bookselling trade have been boons, and—despite rumbles from below—Booth has so far retained his self-awarded crown. □

Bookseller Richard Booth, the self-proclaimed king of little Hay-on-Wye, holds court with crown and scepter in the library of his Victorian country home in a nearby valley, Cusup Dingle.

Advanced Training

As a boy, Victor Martin wanted to go to work on the British railroads, but he followed his father's wishes instead and became an electrical engineer. Even so, railroads became his life work—but in miniature and suspended in time. In a large shed behind his farmhouse in Kent, he ran a replica of Britain's old London, Midland, and Scottish Railway—as it was in 1938.

Martin started building his railroad with his first wife, Susan, in 1923, when they laid the initial 500 feet of track. He bought his first engine in 1937. After his retirement, and working with his second wife, Louise, the daughter of a railroad stationmaster, Martin saw his model transformed into a true replica of the real thing. For some thirty years, the Martins would rise, have breakfast, and—properly attired in the railroader's brass-buttoned uniform and peaked cap—begin working on their railroad. He provided the rolling stock and track layout—more than 500 engines and cars, and almost a mile of track—and she added the rich background detail: painted scenery, grazing cattle and sheep, and miniature passengers and porters to crowd the station platforms.

Victor and Louise Martin took their duties seriously. They ran extra coaches at Christmas to carry the holiday mail, and they took note of current events. When the queen went on visits, they ran the royal coach. They added more freight trains at the time of a national dock strike. Their busiest time was the Suez crisis of 1956, when they were up all night running troop trains. "Had to do it at night, you see," Martin explained to a reporter, "for the secrecy."

Although they had accidents on the line, Martin, who by 1991 was a ninety-one-year-old widower, claimed that their greatest problem was with mice, attracted by the poultry feed the couple kept in the goods shed. Opposed to taking any life, the vegetarian railroaders set no traps, and let the rodents stuff themselves. "But the little devils," said Martin, "were taking the passengers and staff off our stations

For decades, Victor Martin *(above)*, helped by wife Louise, ran a miniaturized piece of British Rail, duplicated even to train schedules, from this control center on his Kentish farm.

and the goods out of our vehicles till we glued everything down." Once a cat got in to chase the mice, derailing four or five trains.

Louise died on May 28, 1986, and with age encroaching, Victor took to operating the railroad on a weekly rather than a daily schedule, aided by his son-in-law and occasional railroading enthusiasts. But he still received guests, giving them tickets specially produced for the Martins by the firm that prints the real thing for British Rail. Martin never sought attention for his obsession, but he shared it generously with visitors from throughout the world who arrived at his door. Perhaps he hoped to bequeath at least a portion of the joy that his trains gave him. "I've had all my life," he once said, "this great happiness." □

Aloft in the 1988 Winter Olympics in Calgary, Briton Michael David Edwards demonstrates the ski-jumping form that earned him the nickname Eddie the Eagle—and caused his colleagues to fear for his safety.

Lone Eagle

The sudden fame of Michael David Edwards was hardly caused by his sporting prowess. Rather the opposite: He came in last in both the events he entered. But, because his chosen sport—ski jumping—is so daunting to most people, he won respect simply for having the courage to stretch out some thirty stories above his landing point and jump. For two weeks in February 1988, his combination of bravery and bad technique made him a major media attraction at Canada's Calgary Winter Olympics—and earned him the sobriquet Eddie the Eagle. Moreover, the seventy-one-meter-long leap he managed from the ninety-meter run turned out to be a record for Great Britain, where, as one reporter put it, most of the snow comes unfrozen.

For the rest, there was his engag-ing persona. Myopic, with a prominent jaw and unkempt reddish hair, he became the perfect sporting anti-hero. "Sometimes, when my glasses steam up," the Cheltenham plasterer revealed, "I have to guess where to take off from." After completing an eighty-meter jump, he told reporters, "I was terrified. You know, I envy all these people who have been doing this since they were four years old. It comes naturally to them, but I have to think about it every time I'm up there." His refreshingly human fallibility was a pleasant antidote to the steely perfectionism of the other competitors, and the public took him to its heart.

The hapless awkwardness of his jumps echoed through his everyday life at Calgary as well. He arrived an hour late for his first big news conference, having lost his way in the Olympic Village. When he finally found the right building, he was refused admission because he did not have the correct accreditation. Once inside, however, he recovered his aplomb and gleefully told the world's press of the day he had tied his ski helmet on with string because the strap had broken. It was a false economy. "It disappeared in mid-air," he reported, "and finally caught up with me down on the snow, bouncing past my head."

He described a rocky path toward the Olympics. He had boarded in a mental hospital while training in Finland, he said, living with the fear that "someone would come up to my room with an axe." Things were not much better in Switzerland, where the only accommodation he could afford was in a scout camp. "Lived for a week on bread and jam," he recounted laconically, "and if those boys left anything on their plates, it was mine."

As a result of his candor, the story spread that his selection as Britain's only ski jumper had been intended as a joke. Not so, the British Ski Federation insisted. He had performed quite well in pre-Olympic competitions, and there was a desire to expand the number of events in which Britain competed. Even at Calgary, although he won no events, he completed his runs without personal injury—this to the relief of some Games officials who feared for his safety and had urged him to withdraw. Undaunted, Eddie the Eagle had pushed on to his moment of fame.

But a moment was about all that Edwards got. Although he received a rash of sponsorship and personal-appearance offers following the Games, he did not benefit greatly from his commercial endeavors. Before long he was back in Cheltenham and back in debt. His Olympian attempts brought at least one long-term benefit, however. After his performance, there was a rush of interest in ski jumping in Britain, prompting several promising contenders to follow in the Eagle's flight path. Even so, despite his own confident promises that he would compete again, Michael Edwards appeared unlikely to soar among the new contingent. The British Olympic Association raised its ski-jumping standards, and Eddie, twenty-eight years old in 1991, may have passed his peak. □

Fallen Forum

Speakers' Corner of London's Hyde Park is the only place in Britain where the right to free speech, implicit in a democracy, is enshrined in law. The seeds of this unfettered public podium were sown in the 1860s, when Hyde Park became the favored site for radicals to congregate. After attempts to evict demonstrators resulted in serious rioting, the Park Regulations Act of 1872 was passed to concede to orators of any persuasion the right to use that part of the park. The law specified that "anyone with a mind to do so, may now declaim on any subject he chooses, providing he is not obscene, blasphemous or does not constitute an incitement to a breach of the peace."

For years soapbox orators—so called for their improvised platforms—took advantage of the law to preach every kind of minority cause from astrology to vegetarianism. A tradition of good-natured heckling was established, and successful speakers had to be skilled in the art of repartee. Not all of the speakers were obscure. Russian revolutionary Vladimir Ilich Lenin, for example, availed himself of a Speakers' Corner platform, as did the first president of Kenya, Jomo Kenyatta, the American anarchist Emma Goldman, and the union leader Ben Tillett.

Sadly, Speakers' Corner today is not what it was. Traffic noise from nearby roads nearly drowns out speeches, and the more benign eccentrics have largely given way to speakers who, if no less passionate, are surely more vitriolic: People preaching some form of racial or religious hatred abound. The old wooden soapboxes have been replaced by plastic milk crates and aluminum ladders. And even the heckling has turned nasty, often carried out by organized gangs who deliberately set out to bully and disrupt. Thus, while the speakers themselves may still find a safety valve in speaking out, for most listeners Speakers' Corner now offers a jarring reflection of the animosities that underlie modern inner-city life. Still, the tradition is protected by the ideal that first established it, and the eminently British monument to free speech manages to endure. □

Eschewing the traditional, but now rare, soapbox platform, a wartime orator waits for an audience at Speakers' Corner in London's Hyde Park in 1943.

Georgian on My Mind

Stephen Calloway wears a frock coat to work every morning. And not just any frock coat, but one that is correct in every eighteenth-century detail, down to the length of the collar and the size of the buttons. A specialist in period dress at London's Victoria and Albert Museum, Calloway is part of a coterie of revivalists who first began to win attention in the late 1970s. What links the set is a devotion to the lifestyle and architecture of Britain in the years from 1714 to 1830—the Georgian period, so called because four successive kings by the name of George ruled the nation during those years. Dubbed by the media the New Georgians, the group includes in its ranks purists who eschew such twentieth-century conveniences as modern plumbing and electric lighting, preferring to make do with chamber pots and candle flames. ◊

New Georgian Stephen Calloway *(below)*, employed by the Victoria and Albert Museum as a specialist in eighteenth-century dress, relaxes in his west London flat, restored to what it would have been two centuries ago.

Concern for Britain's eighteenth-century heritage is not new. The Georgian Group, an august body that included among its charter members such luminaries as writers Evelyn Waugh and John Betjeman and the art historian Kenneth Clark, was founded more than fifty years ago. Even then the movement had its zealots; to protest the proposed demolition of a London square of Georgian vintage, writer Nancy Mitford offered to chain herself naked to the railings.

The New Georgians trace their origins as a group to a similar, but more decorous, protest. Alarmed by the planned demolition in 1977 of historic buildings in Spitalfields, a run-down area of eastern London, a group of conservationists staged a rally. It was certainly no run-of-the-mill demonstration: Many of the protesters were art historians, and one titled lady sat amid the rubble calmly translating the Bible from Greek into English.

From that point the movement went from strength to strength. Besides saving buildings, a number of devotees turned their attention to restoring them as convincingly as possible to their eighteenth-century state. Historical accuracy became something of a mania; rather than drill into antique paneling, purists preferred to do without central heating, making do instead with log fires—or no heat at all. Others sought authenticity in the details of everyday life. Bath time for the five small children of architect Quinlan Terry meant a dip in a papier-mâché tub. Following eighteenth-century models, one denizen of Spitalfields swept his carpets with damp tea leaves to refresh them. He also darkened the floorboards by rubbing them with soot and beer.

But such revivals stimulate more than cultural memories; they also generate commercial demand. Ironically, in helping to save some old buildings, the New Georgian movement has put others at risk. By setting a fashion for historical accuracy, the neo-Georgians have created a thriving market for period architectural features—often stolen by revival-minded thieves. □

Socket to 'Em

Before eating his regular breakfast of eggs, a cheese made with twenty-seven different herbs, and a bulb of raw garlic, Captain Maurice Seddon (Royal Signals, retired) dons an ancient and ragged dressing gown and plugs himself into an electrical socket. The outlet is one of many such in his house, all connected to a windmill-powered generator in the garden. The current provided by wind power serves to heat elements sewn into the lining of the gown, which warms up in much the same way that an electric blanket does when the power is switched on. If Captain Seddon wishes to move to another room, he has to first unplug himself, then go in search of another socket.

When the British climate requires it, Seddon also wears heated insoles and gloves, and he is particularly renowned for his electrically powered long underwear. The advantage, he is quick to point out, lies in energy saving. In his estimation, it requires only one-thirteenth as

In a sitting room cluttered with his antique gramophones, Captain Maurice Seddon wears an electrically heated jumpsuit while describing another of his inventions: heated insoles.

much power to warm the human body as to heat an entire room. Snug underneath the wires, he can keep the temperature of his Berkshire cottage down to a frigid fifty degrees Fahrenheit even in the coldest English winter. "It may seem very futuristic and funny," he told one reporter. "A lot of people think it frightfully peculiar—but with the cost of heating escalating it could soon become the norm."

Such petty economizing would have seemed irrelevant in Seddon's boyhood. He grew up the son of wealthy parents in a seventy-three-room mansion that had previously belonged to the composer Sir Edward Elgar. But the Second World War and its aftermath of economic austerity dispersed the family funds. Seddon spent twelve years in the armed forces. On his retirement in 1957, he was thrown back on his own ingenuity to earn a living.

Drawing on his army signals experience, he set up a one-man electronics company at his cottage in Datchet, near London's Heathrow Airport, specializing at first in repairing antique audio equipment. But, in the meantime, he began thinking about a new way of keeping warm. The idea came from his passion for motorcycling, a pursuit that can chill a rider even on mild days. Electrical clothing accessories seemed to be the answer. Into the 1990s, Seddon's main customers were still bikers who bought heated gloves, long johns, and insoles to wear with their leathers. His own bike's special feature was an oven—powered, like the clothing, from the machine's alternator; he used it to cook stews. From his heated cycling gear, Seddon moved on to clothing warmed by electricity from a windmill.

The captain, in his sixties, claimed that many people besides bikers had benefited from his thermal wear. His advertising copy specified "Paraplegics, Sclerotics, Arthritics, Wheelchair patients, Disabled, Poor, Maimed, Alone-living, Creative Artists, outside Broadcasters and countless others." His customers also included divers from the North Sea oil fields, mountain climbers, and hunters. There were limits to the market, however. He specified that his clothing should be kept away from children, lunatics, and the senile. Not that they could electrocute themselves on the tiny twelve-volt charge that the clothes run on, he pointed out, but they might trip on the wires. □

The Tortoise and the Heir

Dorothy Duffin was a familiar sight on the sidewalks of Hull, often seen with a perambulator and its carapaced occupant, a tortoise named Fred. In a way, the methodical creature was just the pet for the aging pensioner. Although Duffin loved cats, in her way, she sometimes got impatient with them and thus ran through them quickly. Once, according to a newspaper account, she had fifteen cats put down in one day—and acquired two more a day later. Before the cats, she had kept a pet duck until, deciding it was too much of a nuisance, she ate it for lunch.

Fred the tortoise was more fortunate. Not only did he survive, but, when Dolly Duffin died in 1990, at sixty-one, he became the world's richest reptile.

Duffin left only $1,000 and a number of photograph albums in bequests to her sister and her two brothers. The rest of her assets— ◊

Fred, a tortoise and heir, settles down between negotiable portraits of the queen of England.

estimated to be worth at least $50,000—went to the Royal Society for the Prevention of Cruelty to Animals, on one condition: The estate would be used for "the care, upkeep and maintenance" of Fred for the rest of his life.

Freed from fiscal anxiety, the thirty-four-year-old tortoise found a new home with Susan Kirkwood,

Dorothy Duffin's niece, and her husband, Stuart. With one nine-year-old child, and with Stuart unable to work because of a stroke, the couple had hoped to receive the money themselves. "We were a bit surprised, at first," the niece told a reporter, "because she had promised the money to us. But she was an eccentric lady whom we all loved. We

were not upset and we had a good laugh about it." Susan Kirkwood added, "What we have never had we can never miss. At least Fred has a good home, with all the best lettuce leaves, cucumbers, and the odd boiled peas."

But Fred was not the big winner in the Duffin will. The RSPCA, arguing that turtles can live for up to 100 years, awarded the Kirkwoods only about fifty dollars a year to support him. At that rate, Fred should use up less than one-tenth of his estate if he lives out his full allotment. □

Look! Up in the Sky!

Hew Kennedy of Shropshire has an unusual hobby. He sends dead pigs and horses, irreparable pianos, and various other projectiles flying for considerable distances through the air. The instrument he uses to throw them is a sixty-foot-high, full-scale reconstruction of a medieval siege engine known as a trebuchet.

Kennedy conceived his interest in early weapons more than thirty years ago as a student at Sandhurst, Britain's military academy. He was disturbed to learn that the art of trebuchet making had been lost. In 1988, when cousins in the north of England devised a small machine used to throw gasoline-soaked toilets as an attraction at rural fairs—the local newspaper headline hailed "Those Magnificent Men and Their Flaming Latrines"— he decided to go one better.

One year and $17,000 later, he and neighbor Richard Barr unveiled

their impressive weapon. Giant A-frames supported an axle for a huge central beam that tapered from a lightweight tip at one end to a broad, weighted box at the other. The box held five and a half tons of steel bar. To load the trebuchet, the thin end of the beam was winched down with the help of a tractor, raising the heavy end skyward. With the beam thus poised, a missile— pig, piano, or whatever—was attached to the lowered end by means of a steel-cable sling. When the beam was released, gravity yanked down the heavy end, causing the beam and its projectile to whip upward with terrific force. At the top of this arc, the sling launched the object—the dead pig, for example—on its ballistic trajectory. Hog carcasses, in Kennedy's experience, would often fly for a quite satisfactory 175 yards. The record for a piano was 151 yards. Dead horses

were unwieldy and rarely managed more than 100 yards.

Kennedy had no particular use for his device, other than to entertain neighbors and scare the local sheep. Attempts to interest the makers of the Kevin Costner film *Robin Hood, Prince of Thieves* failed. He had hopes, however, of selling the idea to the operator of an American theme park, though not for slinging farm-animal remains. "It's an amusement in America to smash up motor cars, isn't it?" he hopefully inquired of a reporter. He was recalling, perhaps, having slung an occasional Hillman automobile from his dreadnought.

Aided by a Royal Air Force specialist, Kennedy and his partner were also studying the possibility of slinging live humans—recreationally, of course. "Catapulting off humans is nothing new," Kennedy said. "In the Middle Ages they were

always sending ambassadors back over castle walls; bringing someone down alive in a parachute is another matter." Since the trebuchet's acceleration imposed some twenty times the force of gravity—about the same force that pilots experience when they eject from jet aircraft—the flight was not to be undertaken lightly. One pig carcass literally exploded in its parachute rigging on an early test flight.

Afterward, however, a few hogs were successfully launched and recovered intact. The human flight via Kennedy's trebuchet may, or may not, take place.

The inventor had attracted at least one volunteer by 1991, but no firm launch date was set. And, in fact, Kennedy had begun to tire of his sixty-foot machine by that time. "I'm bloody bored with it now," he told an interviewer, lamenting that he had slung "nearly all the suitable missiles." On his horizon: a transportable eighty-foot trebuchet, and perhaps a replica of the giant crossbow called a ballista, using telegraph poles for arrows. □

After being loaded by designer Hew Kennedy (*inset, wearing cap*) and colleagues, this giant Shropshire trebuchet whips a burning piano some 200 yards through the air at speeds up to ninety miles an hour.

Gardens of Earthly Delights

"Our England is a garden that is full
of stately views,
Of borders, beds and shrubberies
and lawns and avenues . . ."

So wrote Rudyard Kipling, the poetic voice of nineteenth-century empire, and the nation's horticultural pride has in no way dimmed since his day. Gardens are the canvas on which the creative energies of the English people most easily find release. Gardens reveal the poetry hidden behind the apparent conformism of a reserved race. But now and then this floral poetry takes unusual flights.

The concrete zoological garden of John Fairnington was a case in point. In 1935, the fifty-three-year-old master joiner and his wife, Mary, had their first and only child, a handicapped boy named Edwin. When the elder Fairnington retired at age eighty, he embarked on a vision designed solely to amuse his beloved son. He started building a menagerie of concrete animals in the quarter-acre plot behind his semidetached home in the village of Branxton, just south of the Scottish border. First he made a life-size panda, to draw Edwin out to play in the garden. When this worked, Fairnington, helped by two neighbors, began to transform the place into a concrete menagerie. He added camels and cart horses and a unicorn, and myriad other creatures in what he called the Fountain Garden. Overseeing the diverse herd, a concrete Buddha rose from a tree stump.

Eventually there were 75 large statues, each fashioned of concrete on a base of rubbish-filled wire netting, and nearly 150 "minors"—smaller sculptures of rabbits, mice, and the like. By then Fairnington had expanded his original concept to include images of notable personalities, adding a concrete Winston Churchill and Lawrence of Arabia to rub shoulders with the rhinos, hippos, giraffes, and elephants. Edwin played in his strange and beautiful paradise until his death, at thirty-six, when he became, in a way, a part of the garden he loved: His father etched the young man's features into a marble monument. Fairnington died in 1981, nearly ninety-nine, his labor of love completed.

The artifacts of Edward Prynn's passion are perhaps more durable. Forced into early retirement when a quarrying accident left him virtually blind, he found solace in a long-held ambition to create a modern Stonehenge. Inspired by the prehistoric stone circles of his native county of Cornwall, he turned his bungalow garden in the village of St. Merryn into an open-air museum of megaliths. At last count, in 1991, he boasted nineteen stones weighing between two and ten tons each.

Seven of the megaliths made up a circle, and each one was named after one of the women in his life. (One was known only as the Secret Lady, because, Prynn explained, she did not want her husband to find out.) But Prynn's proudest monument was a pair of one-ton blocks of quartzite quarried on the Falkland Islands and shipped 8,000 miles. He had suggested to the islands' governor that the stones might make a suitable monument to British soldiers who fought in the Falklands War.

Prynn chose not to live in the bungalow, staying instead at his parents' home a mile away. But he was mindful that the stones represented his claim on posterity. "Thousands of years from now someone will come down this road and see my stones," he told an interviewer. "They'll say, 'What in heaven's name is that,' and someone will tell them, 'Don't you know, that's Ed Prynn's Temple.' "

Another gardener who came to prefer art to nature was Clifford Davis of St. Anne's on the Lancashire coast. Fed up with the vagaries of the English climate, which prevented his daffodils from coming up on time, this one-time owner of a fish-and-chips shop planted a hand-painted yellow plastic flower among the natural buttercups and was delighted with the result. He subsequently abandoned conventional plants altogether, along with grass and soil, and until his death in 1991 kept an entirely synthetic garden in which manufactured blooms sprouted from beds of corrugated green plastic, separated by concrete or wooden borders. A concrete spaniel, painted bright yellow, guarded the place, and wooden duck decoys sailed the edges of the largest bed, which had an improvised pond with rubber ducks floating on its surface.

Davis built his own flowers with love and care. The pistils were formed from wire, thread spools, and sauce-bottle tops. The petals were of colored plastic, recycled from household rubbish and dipped in hot water to make it malleable. In one respect, however, Davis did stick with tradition: Like most Britons, he made his flowers in a greenhouse. □

Designed to please his handicapped son, Edwin, John Fairnington's garden of mesh-and-concrete animals and famous people *(above)* comprises more than 200 handmade figures.

Immune to destructive shifts of British weather, plastic flowers bloom perpetually in the brilliant garden created by Lancashireman Clifford Davis *(above)*.

Following his dream of building a mini-Stonehenge, a former quarry worker by the name of Edward Prynn *(right)* raised a small forest of megaliths at St. Merryn on the Cornwall coast.

Inventor John Ward *(below)* built the Wogan, named for a television host, entirely from castoff parts.

Rubbish Reborn

John Ward is a peculiar kind of inventor: He specializes in the odd. The machines he has created include a self-propelling wheelbarrow, a personal head shampooer based on the principle of the car wash, and a children's electric trolley that is built from lawn-mower and washing-machine parts and powered by a car battery.

Ward, who in 1991 was living in a modest house in Northamptonshire with his wife and four children, got the raw materials for his contraptions from discarded household machinery. He had no tools more elaborate than a welder and a hand drill, so everything he created was handmade. The purposeful tinkerer devised his machines more for the pleasure of making them than for their practicality. One vehicle twelve feet long by eleven feet high had wings and helicopter-like propellers but could not fly. Another machine, fashioned from piles of household

junk and a minicar gearbox and engine came complete with flashing lights and sirens. Ward called it the Moon Buggy. He had also created a car from washing machines, ironing boards, and soft-drink bottles. He hoped to drive it from Britain's northernmost point, John O'Groats, to Land's End at its southern extremity—for charity.

As word of the oddity inventor got around, he made television appearances in the United States, Australia, Japan, France, Germany, and Holland. Besides a kind of notoriety, the publicity brought him fresh material to work with. Strangers turned up on his doorstep with their junk, and businessmen proffered unwanted goods ranging from a truck to 600 spare flashguns. Ward liked the idea of turning discarded goods into useless inventions. "There's so much waste in the world," he once explained, "so I like to put my rubbish to good use." □

Peer Group

As of 1991, the longest-serving leader of any British political party was still going on the campaign trail in a top hat and a leopard-skin suit. He ran under the name of Screaming Lord Sutch, and the group he represented was called the Monster Raving Loony party. After thirty-one consecutive defeats at by-elections around the country, he and his colleagues had yet to win the five percent of the vote required to recover the £500 deposit demanded of all parliamentary candidates in Britain.

The son of a London policeman, David Sutch first attracted attention in the 1960s as a pop singer whose trademark was making his entrance on stage from a coffin. Sutch had limited success, although a couple of his albums did find their way to the lower rungs of the American charts, and a single, "Jack the Ripper," reached number two in Germany.

Sutch first stood for Parliament in 1963 as the sole candidate of his own National Teenage party. In later years, he liked to point out that many of the issues he once drew ridicule for championing—the reduction of the voting age to eighteen, an end

Perennial Raving Loony candidate David Sutch—Lord Sutch to voters—holds the British record for the most failed attempts to win national office.

to compulsory examinations at age eleven, the abolition of the licensing laws controlling pub hours, the legalization of commercial radio—all became law in Britain.

After changing the party name to the Raving Loonies—slogan, "Vote Insanity: You Know It Makes Sense"—Sutch added other planks to his platform, including one that would force joggers to run on conveyor belts to generate cheap electricity. Throughout his many candidacies, Sutch continued to perform as a rock singer, using the publicity generated by his party to sustain his musical career. In 1990, he fought and lost his thirtieth consecutive by-election, taking the record for the greatest number of failures from Commander Bill Boaks, who had championed road safety until he was killed in a traffic accident.

But all was not bleak for the Raving Loonies. In 1988, they had their first-ever electoral success when a candidate was elected unopposed to a seat on a local council in Devon. Building on that base, they went on to take four seats in the 1990 local-government elections, raising fears among the Loonies themselves that the nation's most ineffective political party might be compromised by an unexpected danger: a taste for victory. □

A Nose for Charity

The British have traditionally shown a willingness to make fools of themselves in a good cause, a trait recently put to use by the charity Comic Relief. Since 1988, several million Britons have been persuaded once a year to don red plastic clown noses that sell for less than a dollar each. Dubbed Red Nose Day, the event centers on a nationwide telethon featuring guest celebrities, all suitably red-nosed, and open telephone lines for viewers to pledge donations.

Across the nation, individuals vie with one another to think up the craziest stunts. One group in Wales put on formal attire to eat a champagne dinner on top of eight tons of cow manure, winning $1,200 in pledges. Another, in London, chose to dine underwater. Across the country individuals filled their boots full of cold porridge, put jelly in their underpants, and lay in baths of custard. A woman from Kent showed a more decorously ingenious imagination: She got a crane to lower a teabag into her cup. Although the general eccentricity lasts for only a day, it is nothing to

sneeze at. Britons have paid handsomely for their compatriots' red-nosed antics: In its short life, Comic Relief had by 1991 raised about $116 million for British charities and for famine relief in Africa. □

Merry Man

In 1959, an event of great sociological significance took place in England that went entirely unnoticed by the news media. Robin and his Merry Men abandoned Nottinghamshire's Sherwood Forest, driven out by army maneuvers and rampant real-estate development. They relocated to the Lake District, a scenic mountainous region 125 miles to the northwest of their original habitat, and at last report, there they remained.

The Robin in question was no Hood, however, but Robin St. Clair, the legendary Sherwood Forest outlaw's most fervent disciple. St. Clair's everyday wear as he roamed the hills and dales was a cloak of Lincoln green, a leather doublet, a sleeveless woolen short coat, woolen hose, thigh-length boots, and a bowman's hat sporting two pheasant feathers. This garb, he hoped, would one day become the national costume of England.

Robin's obsession with his namesake dated from age five, when he saw film star Errol Flynn in *The Adventures of Robin Hood.* Then an unhappy foster child, St. Clair later explained, the experience changed his life. His sense of fellowship with the great outlaw increased when he was taken the following year to visit his grandfather, a lodgekeeper in—of all places—Sherwood Forest. ◊

As Britain's Prince Andrew demonstrates in this 1988 photo, even the royals play on Red Nose Day, an annual spoof that has raised more than $100 million for charity.

When his hometown of Sheffield was bombed during the World War II blitz, seven-year-old Robin ran away from his foster home to join his relative and stayed with him for the rest of the war, cared for by a woman named Rowena, who kept house for the old man.

When Rowena married and moved to Scotland following the war, Robin returned to Sheffield for a time, but he went back to Sherwood Forest in 1957 to rent the lodge, derelict since the death of his grandfather. It was while he was living there and working for British Rail that he founded the Order of the Green Woodpeckers, devoted to the cause of chivalry and to keeping the spirit of Robin Hood alive. In his late fifties as the 1990s rolled around, St. Clair still headed up the Woodpeckers, which claimed to have some 500 members.

His own contributions to the cause included mastering swordplay and the techniques of fighting with the quarterstaff. By way of recapturing medieval skills, he built a working hand-fly-shuttle loom twelve feet wide, based on fourteenth-century models. He also spent some time living in caves with his followers, practicing the woodcraft with which all Green Woodpeckers were expected to become familiar.

But it was his exploits with the longbow that received the most attention. In 1970, in a Lakeland pub, Robin split a cocktail stick perched on the head of a lady tourist. The event got nationwide publicity. Among those alerted by the newspaper articles was Rowena, who had lost contact with young Robin after World War II. Learning of the modern Merry Men, she moved to the Lake District, where her lost charge formally installed her as secretary of the Woodpecker order. The aging housekeeper had a deeper secret, however, which she managed to keep until her death in 1979. Among the papers that she left him, St. Clair discovered an astonishing document: proof that Rowena had been his real mother. □

Armed and attired as the twelfth-century Prince of Thieves, Robin St. Clair is comfortably at home in the branches of his Lake District "lookout tree."

FEATS OF ODDNESS

For an elite of odd achievers, the impulse toward eccentricity is not a summons to peculiar lifestyles or chronic strange behavior, but a call to action. It is the clarion signal that drives its listener—the only one tuned to that narrow channel—to set out on the journey to offbeat, but often remarkable, achievements.

These take many forms, from wooden gardens to modern-day arks, from retrograde marathons to the eating of steel. All are the crystallized result of some private vision that, over a day or a lifetime, cries out for realization: The great vessel must be raised; one must begin to burrow, build, collect, commemorate—one must soar. Inexplicably personal, such feats are the signatures of the eccentric human spirit, grand artifacts and ruins dotting the strange terrain of idiosyncrasy: terrain so rich in private beauty that only a few can look upon it; terrain that, in fact, only a few can even see.

Vermont Autograph and Remarker.

Huntington Vt. October 10, 1834.

I also will show you mine opinion. -Elihu.

Introductory.

We have more than once since our paper was published under its present title been asked what was the meaning of the word 'Autograph'. Although we should think that any person might by consulting a dictionary easily satisfy his mind on that point, still as we are willing to give information as to the meaning of words which we may use, we will condescend to explain it for the edification of those of our readers who may wish to know its meaning. Know then that Autograph means a person's own hand writing, or any copy, or work executed with one's own hand, in distinction from that which struck off upon types at a printing office. We have adopted this word as part of the title of our little paper as being most characteristic of the manner in which it is executed: for there is no one who is at all experienced in reading but can readily percieve that this was done with a pen; and the reader may be assured that every paragraph is composed and written by the Editor himself, and that too without having first to draft it on another piece of paper, which is more than can be said of the

hundreds and thousands of super royal and imperial folios issued from the press. Writing with a pen was the only method of communicating ideas on paper till within four hundred years ago when the art of printing with types was invented; and even all the mighty works of learning that are issued from the press, are originally written with pen and ink under the author's own hand so that the world is still indebted to that simple instrument the pen for all the printed knowledge that ever filled a library from the first invention of letters down to the present day. A word respecting the course we have taken and intend to pursue with regard to the discussion of those subjects which are introduced into the columns of our paper. As it is composed wholly of original matter, it is of course the channel through which we occasionally express our sentiments on political and moral points which we intend to express boldly without fear or favor of any man or set of men. Against Executive usurpation, and against secret societies we feel it our duty to raise our voice and we hope the time will come when both will be put down by the influence of public opinion.

For more than sixty years, James Johns published meticulously pen-printed newspaper pages such as this one from his *Vermont Autograph and Remarker* for October 10, 1834.

Printer's Ink

At the age of twelve, Vermonter James Johns discovered a unique means to get his opinions into print: With pen and ink, Johns hand-lettered his premier opus, the two-page *Huntington Gazette*, in characters patterned faithfully on printing-press type. Published in March of 1810, the *Gazette* was the first of a lifelong flood of pen-printed publications let loose by the energetic chronicler of life in the Green Mountains. Johns also issued works in longhand, but his claim to fame was always his freehand typography—work so fine that the casual reader would have been hard-pressed to distinguish it from the output of a mechanical press.

An inveterate reader and a bachelor farmer with a nose for news, Johns was not shy about expressing himself, and he tried his hand at all manner of literary forms besides his offbeat newspaper—fiction, local history, religious essays, political commentary, speeches, and numerous poems, including the forty-line *Verses composed in 1824 on cutting my foot* and *New Year's address for 1st January 1841.* The latter work recounted the old year's events in thirty-eight rhymed couplets. A lyricist and composer as well, the versatile Johns accompanied his singing on a pianolike instrument of his own invention with tinkling innards of glass.

But it was Johns's pen-printed newspapers that made him a star among the rural literati of his day. For many years he published the pen-printed *Huntington Gazette* erratically and under several titles, finally settling on the *Vermont Autograph and Remarker.* A typical 1,500-word issue contained four double-columned pages measuring a diminutive four and a quarter by six and a half inches. It took Johns a half-day to accomplish the meticulous lettering, so he produced no more than a handful of copies of each issue. Fortunately, he wasted no time fussing with multiple drafts. The contents were, Johns explained, "all written down on the columns directly from the dictates of my mind."

The *Autograph* was posted for Johns's fellow villagers to catch up on births, deaths, accidents, political events, and other items of local interest. On occasion he printed out a second edition for another publisher and mailed it off in the hope of receiving a magazine or book in return. Johns was not primarily interested in selling newspapers, and on the rare occasions when he did sell a copy, it cost twenty-five cents—a remarkable price for a beautifully executed, virtually one-of-a-kind item.

Johns was justifiably proud of his ability to pen so perfectly characters measuring less than one-eighth of an inch tall. Even after he purchased a little printing press in 1857, he chose to continue pen-printing the *Autograph.*

But age and time eventually took their toll, and in an 1867 editorial entitled "Sensible of Failure," the sixty-nine-year-old penman confessed that his hand was no longer so sure as it had been in former times. However, Johns was no quitter, and he vowed to keep the *Autograph* going as long as his fingers and his eyesight allowed. "To make a short story of it," the publisher wrote bravely, "I intend to wear out in harness."

Johns was as good as his word. The last known issue of the *Autograph* appeared on August 28, 1873, just eight months before his death. He had practiced his craft for sixty-three years. □

Dentist to Pope Leo XIII and other famous Italians, Brother Giovanni Battista Orsenigo of the Fatebenefratelli order filled three large crates with an estimated two million souvenirs of his busy practice—the teeth extracted from his patients between 1868 and 1904. Notably peculiar specimens were displayed in a glass case in the dentist's room.

Winchester Cathedral

Sarah Winchester owed her fortune and her fate to the Winchester rifle, nicknamed "the gun that won the West" for its popularity among nineteenth-century settlers. Turned out in huge numbers by her father-in-law's company, the weapon made the family enormously wealthy. In 1881, when her husband, William, died, Sarah Winchester inherited his share—$20 million plus a 48.8 percent share in the Winchester Repeating Arms Company.

But Sarah took little solace in her inheritance. It bore, she feared, a deadly taint. A spirit medium had told the superstitious widow that the recent death of her husband and the death years earlier of their infant daughter had been caused by the vengeful ghosts of thousands of Winchester-rifle victims. Sarah, the medium said, would be their next target unless she took a radical countermeasure: She must go west, begin building a house, and never stop for the rest of her life.

What evolved from the medium's alarming message is a gigantic maze of a house—160 turreted and gabled rooms sprawling across six acres in San Jose, California. Winchester did not start completely from scratch. Instead she purchased an eight-room farmhouse, which soon disappeared from view among the additions built by her crew of carpenters. Taking the medium at her literal word, the obsessive Winchester kept her workers on the job twenty-four hours a day, seven days a week, all year round for almost four decades. A pause, she reasoned, would spell disaster.

From the outset, Winchester kept a tight rein on the project. Undeterred by her complete lack of experience, she acted as her own architect, holding daily conferences with her foreman to go over her endless plans. She made shopping forays to choose building materials, but she remained in her carriage outside the stores. Clerks carried their wares out for the mysterious veiled woman to inspect. Winchester kept her face hidden at home as well as in public. She was said to have dismissed two workers who accidentally saw her face, although she generously sent them on their way with a year's pay each.

The house Winchester built to

The sprawling Winchester mansion *(above)* is a maze of surprises, including the 7-11 staircase *(inset)*, which uses eighteen steps to produce only a three-foot change of elevation.

keep death at bay is decidedly freakish. At the same time, it possesses a careful beauty. With money to burn, she chose gold and silver and exotic woods to appoint her project. Time was never of the essence; one craftsman spent a year laying an intricate parquet floor. The twenty-by-forty-foot grand ballroom is paneled in hand-carved bird's-eye maple joined with glue and wooden pegs. Winchester allowed only a small number of nails in the room's molding and floor—more, she believed, ◊

would interfere with the acoustics.

But peculiarity on a grand scale is the dominant note. There are about forty bedrooms and forty staircases. Some of the stairways go nowhere at all, simply dead-ending at a ceiling or a wall. The V-shaped "7-11" staircase is composed of an eleven-step down flight, a seven-step up flight, with an intervening landing, for a total change in elevation of only three feet. Of the house's thousands of doors, many are unpredictable, even dangerous. One opens smack onto a brick wall, and another offers a two-story plunge to anyone who crosses the threshold without looking. A chimney rises through four stories, only to stop several inches short of the roof. Several fireplaces open onto the truncated chimney, all of them useless.

The structure has some 10,000 windows, many of them in quirky locations. A beautiful stained-glass window made by Louis Tiffany, for instance, is set in the gloom of an interior wall, beyond the sun's illuminating reach. Given Winchester's mind-set, it is not surprising that the mystical number thirteen is a recurrent motif. There are thirteen bathrooms, a thirteen-step staircase, and a chandelier composed of thirteen gas jets.

Such architectural perversities are coupled with admirable innovations, some borrowed and some of Winchester's own devising. Among the first on the West Coast to boast a completely automatic elevator, her house also had state-of-the-art features such as fireplaces that were equipped with trapdoors for disposing of ashes and inside cranks to open and close exterior shutters. Long before recycling was a common concern, Winchester de-signed a clever system for collecting excess water from plants in her conservatory and delivering it to the garden for use there, and she won a patent for a laundry sink that was equipped with a built-in soap holder and scrubboard.

Because construction had to continue without pause, Winchester frequently demolished completed work to make way for a new project. Rooms were also torn down or walled off because of construction errors or the architect's whim. According to one account, when she discovered a hand print in her wine cellar, she interpreted it as an ominous sign and had the room, with its contents still in place, sealed up. Nature also had a hand in the endless metamorphosis of the house: The great earthquake of 1906 destroyed its top three floors, providing the carpenters with a substantial repair job.

Altogether, an estimated 750 rooms were built. After lavishing thirty-eight years and more than five million dollars on her house, ghost-busting Sarah died in her sleep on September 5, 1922, and the house froze in its final form. □

Hide Bound

Trudging along the nineteenth-century rural roads of Connecticut and New York, the Leather Man was an arresting mystery. Always clad in the same homemade leather outfit and always alone, for three decades he doggedly followed a circuit of some 365 miles that took him from the Connecticut River to the Hudson and back again. Like the phases of the moon, the Leather Man was predictable. Farmers and villagers along his route counted on his reappearing every thirty-four days or so, and people liked to say that they set their clocks by his schedule. From 1883 to 1885, for example, he transited Forestville, Connecticut, without deviating from his thirty-four-day rhythm by more than two hours.

No ordinary tramp in search of a night's shelter or a bit of work, the taciturn wanderer called his own shots. He made regular stops at houses of his choosing, and when he knocked on the kitchen door, he made it clear with a gesture or a grunt that he wanted nothing but a meal and perhaps a bit of tobacco. He divulged nothing about himself, not even his name; it was said that he would permanently abandon a habitual way station if someone

there pressed him for information. Even after years of stopping at one New Canaan house, legend holds, the Leather Man's conversation was limited to the telegraphic statement, "Piece to eat." Moreover, what few words he uttered were in broken English, and the consensus was that his native language was French. A passerby was fortunate if his greeting warranted even a grunt or a glance from the wary, self-absorbed pilgrim.

From the first sighting in the late 1850s onward, summer and winter, the Leather Man wore a voluminous patchwork coat and trousers made of leather scraps held together by thongs; a visored cap; and wooden-soled boots. A bag two feet square—of leather, naturally—was slung from his shoulder. Creaking and squeaking like an ill-made shoe, his clothing stood out stiffly and made him appear fat and clumsy, although he was in fact an agile fellow with a spring in his step.

Not surprisingly, people were at first afraid of the Leather Man, and parents occasionally used him as a boogeyman to keep rowdy children in line. Yet, repeated encounters showed him to be peaceable, and it was generally agreed that his peculiar facade concealed a bright and sensitive spirit.

This was merely surmise, however, given the Leather Man's persistent reluctance to talk. Eager for some shred of information about him, villagers sometimes invited him to join them at a tavern, reasoning that alcohol might loosen his reserve. He did occasionally accept such invitations, but after a beer or two drunk in silence, he would take wordless leave of his disappointed audience.

If he intended his reclusiveness to guarantee his anonymity, the Leather Man failed. His oddness unaccounted for, the wanderer engendered endless fascination among the people along his route. Since they had no real information, they gossiped and speculated. (One popular theory held that he was doing penance, however bizarrely, for some misdeed.) So, ironically, the laconic mystery man became something of a celebrity. People clipped newspaper articles about him for their scrapbooks and cherished such photographs as were taken of him. The dishes he ate from became precious objects to some householders, who took pride in being part of his itinerary.

The Leather Man was in the news in December of 1888, after he ran away from a Hartford, Connecticut, hospital where he had been taken for examination of a cancerous lip. The sober reports were followed by a sensational story: The Leather Man's name was Jules Bourglay, the press asserted, and he had fled to the United States from France with a broken heart. Bourglay had, the story went, fallen in love with the daughter of a leather merchant by the name of Monsieur Laron. Laron agreed to the marriage only if Bourglay proved to be a worthy employee in his business. Not only did he fail to pan out, he committed some egregious error that destroyed Laron's enterprise and cost Bourglay his true love.

The story—and the myriad permutations of it that began to circulate—seems to have been a romantic fiction. Still, many people believed that at last they knew the Leather Man's tragic secret. When he died of cancer in March 1889, his meager collection of belongings was examined, but no ties to the fictional Jules Bourglay were found. Dead, the Leather Man frustrated the curious just as thoroughly as he had when alive. □

Peripatetic and punctual, the hide-clad wanderer known only as the Leather Man *(right)* followed roughly the same route for thirty years, taking about thirty-four days to complete each one of his circuits. The route is shown in black on the 1855 map at left.

Rocks of Ages

Abbé Adofe Julien Fouéré had been a priest in Brittany for thirty years when he fell victim to a crushing illness that forced his retirement. The abbé, once both confessor and spokesman for his parishioners, became deaf and mute—the lingering result, some say, of an emotional devastation sustained when he could not save the steel mill that was the economic mainstay of the parish of Paimpont from closing.

No longer able to serve his flock, Fouéré retreated to the tiny coastal village of Rothéneuf near St.-Malo in 1893. Once there, he soon embarked on the project that was to immortalize him as the Hermit of Rothéneuf. "As I did not want to spend an inactive life," he wrote later, "I started to sculpt rocks."

The abbé began to carve into the rocks on a rough cliff overlooking the Gulf of St.-Malo. Working by himself with a hammer and chisel for some sixteen years, Fouéré eventually covered 500 square yards of the cliff with 300 stone figures, most of them in bas-relief. He also filled his simple hut and garden with scores of stone and wood carvings. And, as is the case with many hermits, his life and work became the stuff of legend. As one 1964 account put it, "He dedicated his work to a legendary family, the Rothéneufs," the freebooters and smugglers who "established their empire on these wild coasts and indomitable seas." The isolated abbé's work was said to lay those hardy and restless souls to rest on cliffs "ceaselessly pounded by one of the world's most brutal oceans."

That is the legend. The truth, however, is that Abbé Fouéré realized a complex, personal vision in the granite of those rocky headlands—one that had nothing to do with the Rothéneufs. The sculptures, which seem to rise like spirits liberated from the interior of the rock itself, glorified a number of Breton heroes, including two of Brittany's patron saints. The abbé sculpted an intricate tomb overlooking the sea for Saint Budoc, patron of the shipwrecked. Saint Goberien was carved standing peacefully in front of a gnarled tree that was shaped like a cross. As the solitary sculptor continued, he carved several likenesses of French explorer Jacques Cartier, who was born in nearby St.-Malo, along with Cartier's wife—and, generously, a stone baby for the otherwise childless couple.

Fouéré's granite effigies also encompassed the tragedies of his day. One massive sculpture, replete with scores of recumbent figures, represents the Boer wars in southern Africa. It includes carved portraits of the Transvaalian president Paul Kruger, Great Britain's Queen Victoria, and Colonel Georges-Henri-Victor de Villebois-Mareuil—the Lafayette of austral Africa—who died in combat in the Transvaal. In another bas-relief, the abbé recreated a scene from the Chinese wars of the early 1880s.

Fouéré worked on the sculptures until his death in 1910. Denied a voice, the aging priest had used the rocks of Brittany not to celebrate a pirate legend, but to pray. Although smoothed by time and the elements, these igneous exaltations still proclaim Adofe Fouéré's silenced faith in man. □

His visage as stern as those of his rocky creations, Abbé Adofe Julien Fouéré was photographed among a few of the sculpted multitude of martyrs and heroes that he painstakingly carved on a rough cliff in Brittany.

The walls of his shack adorned with the covers of old magazines, William "Burro" Schmidt posed for cameras in 1938 after finishing a daunting one-man project: a 2,000-foot-long tunnel through a California mountain.

Tunnel Vision

Transporting ore from prospector William Schmidt's mining claim to the nearest smelter was not easy. From Copper Mountain, a peak in Southern California's desolate El Paso range, Schmidt had to follow a long and winding route through the ominously named Last Chance Canyon. One day in 1906, the prospector had a brainstorm: He would ease the journey by tunneling a shortcut to the smelter straight through Copper Mountain.

On the face of it, Schmidt seemed ill-equipped for so mammoth a task. A slight, frail man, he had left his Rhode Island home for the West because of bad health; tuberculosis had killed six of his siblings. In addition to his physical liabilities were his technological ones. He had no training in engineering or mining, and his tools were primitive—a pick, a four-pound hammer, and a hand drill.

Once the idea took hold, however, Schmidt never looked back.

Attacking the granite mountain, he began hacking away to make a cavity seven feet high and five feet wide. At first, the solitary prospector carried the tailings out of the tunnel on his back or in a wheelbarrow. As his excavation lengthened, he installed rails for an ore car and worked by the light of a kerosene lamp. When he could not afford kerosene, he turned to candlelight, allowing himself one two-cent candle per day.

Some fifty feet into the mountain, Schmidt struck potentially valuable veins of gold, silver, copper, and iron. By then, however, the miner in him had been upstaged by the tunneler. Instead of stopping to exploit the deposits, he bored obsessively onward into the heart of the mountain.

Since his obsession was hardly a paying proposition, he hired out as a ranch hand in the summers to grubstake the project. Every fall, he rounded up his two burros, Jack and Jenny, loaded them with a win-

ter's worth of supplies, and headed for Copper Mountain. His only companions for most of the year, Jack and Jenny became the source of Schmidt's nickname, Burro.

The tunneler spent some of his meager funds on blasting supplies, but to economize, he cut his fuses dangerously short. After lighting one, he would run for his life and throw himself flat just before the dynamite blew. On more than one occasion, he was caught in a barrage of flying rock; one particularly dangerous explosion propelled him, shaken and bloody, to a neighboring prospector's shack. "Bad cave-in," Schmidt reported. "Nearly got me that time."

As Schmidt burrowed deeper, the candles he used to illuminate the shaft began to gutter out for lack of oxygen, already somewhat rarefied at the tunnel's 4,400-foot elevation. But no matter what hardships he faced, Burro, stooped and gnarled from decades of labor, persevered.

In 1938, the sixty-seven-year-old prospector finally broke through to daylight on the far side of Copper Mountain. His tunnel, which ran for approximately 2,000 feet, had cost him more than half of his adult life. Ironically, after all that work, Burro Schmidt never carried a single ounce of ore through the tunnel, so completely had it ceased to be a practical undertaking. Simply that it existed was enough, and when someone asked Schmidt why he did not use the tunnel, he just smiled and shrugged.

His labors over, Schmidt sold the claim to another miner and moved to a site farther down Last Chance Canyon. He died there at age eighty-two, sixteen years after the final swing of the pick that fulfilled his mountainous obsession. □

Underground Digs

When Fresno sizzled beneath a blazing California sun in the summer of 1906, newly arrived immigrant Baldasare Forestiere retreated to the shadowy coolness of the cellar he had dug for his little house and longed for his native Sicily's sea breezes. If things had gone according to plan, he would have surrounded the house with tidy rows of young citrus trees, aiming for an orchard like the one his father had tended back home. But the young Forestiere had bought his seventy-acre parcel without testing the soil, which turned out to be an agricultural disaster. Wherever he turned over the earth, his shovel hit a concretelike layer of hardpan about two feet below the surface. Hacking enough planting holes through the hardpan would have been a herculean task, and Forestiere temporarily abandoned his dream of an orchard and went to work as a contract laborer for other farmers.

Forestiere's work schedule left the middle of the day free for him to pursue his subterranean labor at home. It was a logical undertaking for him, since he had become handy with a pick and shovel in Boston and New York, where he had spent two years digging subway and road tunnels before heading west. One day, noting that sunlight streamed down through the cellar door, Forestiere wondered if it would be possible to grow a tree underground. He carved out a small skylighted space some ten feet below the surface and planted an orange tree, and when it grew nicely, he planted two others under their own skylights. Inspired by his successful horticultural experiment, the enterprising tunneler began to transform what had begun as a cellar into an underground estate.

Forestiere added a kitchen, a pantry, a living room, a reading room, two bedrooms, and a large tree-filled courtyard. On one side of the courtyard he made a niche for his bathtub, which was supplied with sun-warmed water from a tank at ground level. Well insulated by the soil, the underground house and garden escaped Fresno's temperature extremes, which range from the 30s in winter to more than 100 in summer.

With hand tools, a wheelbarrow, and occasional help from a horse, Forestiere burrowed on. As the years went by, his cozy abode blossomed into a ten-acre multiple-level maze of more than a hundred rooms, courtyards, and passageways, with an 800-foot-long automobile tunnel. The one-of-a-kind domain included numerous special-purpose spaces such as a reading room, a chapel, a hothouse, a winery, even a fish-viewing room whose skylight opened onto a glass-bottomed pond. In winter some of the skylights were fitted with glass, and the two fireplaces and the wood-burning kitchen stove kept the living quarters comfortable.

What had begun as a retreat from the heat became an obsession. A nephew said of his late uncle, "After a while the rooms ceased to be just places to live. He became completely enamored with his labor. It became a work of art to him." When Forestiere conceived a design for a new space, the only plan he drew was roughly sketched out on his earthen floor, and he

Fleeing hot California summers, Baldasare Forestiere (inset) created a subterranean estate, using skylights (left) to illuminate his rooms and his garden.

```
                          G A D S B Y
on marrying, a man and woman start actually liv-
ing.  It's miraculous, Paul, that's just what it is."
     And so it was; pairs and groups shaking
hands and laughing, until finally a big buxom
woman sang out:—
     "Whoops!!    It was a wow of a grub-
lay-out! It was thot! But this dom thing I calls hoos-
band. Say!  You grub-stuffin' varmint!  Phwat's
that in your hat? A droom-stick, is it? Do you want
His Honor to think I don't cook nuthin' for you?
Goodnight, all! I'm thot full I'm almost a-bustin'!"
     As Lady Standish shook hands, that worthy
woman said:—
     "John, what you did for Branton Hills
should go into our National Library at Washington,
in plain sight."
     "Sally, Youth's part was paramount in
all that work.  All I did was to boss," and Old Doc
Wilkins, coming out, nibbling a bunch of raisins,
said:—
     "Uh-huh; but a boss must know his job!"
     "That's all right," said Gadsby; "but it was
young hands and young minds that did my work!
Don't disqualify Youth for it will fool you, if you
do!"
                         *  *  *  *
                         [ 266 ]
```

Gadsby, Ernest Vincent Wright's 267-page novel published in 1939, was written without a single *e*—the most frequently used letter in English.

would enthusiastically proclaim it *singolare come il mare*—"as unique as the sea."

Although untutored in architecture, Forestiere was an intuitive master of design and construction. When he hacked through the hardpan layer, he used the rocky chunks to build arches, domes, and vaulted ceilings that evoked, some said, the Catacombs of Rome. Forestiere also chiseled the hardpan into a handsome textured surface. No two rooms had the same dimensions or the same shape. To the builder, the great challenge was to make something that was at once irregular and beautiful.

Forestiere had created a unique dwelling—and more. Planting grapevines and fruit trees as he honeycombed the underside of his land, the thwarted orchardist created a thriving underground garden. Grown in huge containers, the plants reached up through the skylights above, making harvesting an easy operation carried out at ground level. Forestiere was a skillful grafter, and one of his favorite trees was a composite that bore seven different types of citrus fruit.

Built for love, his underground garden was also built for a song—by his estimate, about $300. "I have been doing this for fun," Forestiere once explained. "What do I want with money? If I had a million dollars I couldn't spend it. I am broke, but this cavern and all the work it represents is worth more than a million dollars to me." When he died, in 1946, he was in the process of adding a 3,500-square-foot ballroom. Forestiere's million-dollar baby lived on as a tourist attraction until the 1980s, when it became the pawn of litigation and was closed to the general public. □

Eee Gadsby

Writing a 267-page novel proved Ernest Vincent Wright's point: The letter used most frequently in the English language is not indispensable. In *Gadsby,* the sexagenarian author simultaneously shunned the fifth letter of the alphabet and maintained grammatical correctness. "It took a bit of work, but nothing is won without work," said the former U.S. Navy musician, who even preferred to avoid the letter in his interviews.

"At first," recalled Wright in the introduction to his book, "a whole army of little E's gathered around my desk, all eagerly expecting to be called upon. But gradually as they saw me writing on and on, without even noticing them, they grew uneasy; and, with excited whisperings amongst themselves, began hopping up and riding on my pen, looking down constantly for a chance to drop off into some word." Plagued by numerous "erasures and retrenchments," Wright notes with uncharacteristic *e*'s, he eventually put away his pen and used string to tie down his typewriter's *e* key. It never budged during the five and a half months that he spent composing his opus.

Gadsby omits the word *the,* past-tense verbs ending in *ed,* and common pronouns: There are no *he*'s, *she*'s, *we*'s, *they*'s, *thee*'s, *those*'s, *her*'s, *them*'s, or *their*'s. The author also had to dodge most spelled-out numbers: All of those between six and thirty, for example, contain at least one forbidden *e.*

Despite the magnitude of his unusual feat, Wright's prose sometimes reads as if it had been written by a wooden-eared alien. Consider this passage describing the wedding day of two characters: "Now, an approach to a young girl's 'Big Day' is not always just as that girl might wish. Small things bob up which at first look actually disastrous for a joyous occasion; and for Nancy and Frank just such a thing did bob up—for on May third a pouring rain and whistling winds put Branton Hill's spirits way, way low."

However odd his achievement, Wright was not the first to tackle such a compositional challenge. For more than 2,000 years, writers have been intrigued by lipograms, literary works in which one or more letters of the alphabet are excluded. Greek poet Lasus of Hermione may have been the world's first lipogrammatist. His sixth-century-BC *Hymn to Demeter* had to get along without the letter *s* because, according to one scholar, Lasus detested its "unpleasant hissing."

Wright composed his lipogram while living in a California home for war veterans. By the time *Gadsby* was typeset, the author was bedridden; he died on its October 1939 publication date. Although Ernest Wright's book failed to attain best-seller status in its day, its rare copies now carry a high price tag and are prized by collectors. □

Plennie the Walker

A conversation he overheard at his daughter's high-school graduation party set Plennie Wingo on the retrograde road to fame. It was 1930, and Wingo's town, Abilene, Texas, was choked like the rest of the nation in the grip of the Depression. Several teenage boys were gloomily discussing their future prospects, when one of them declared that the only way to get along was to do something that had never been done before. The other boys agreed, but they despaired of coming up with a truly novel feat. Wingo, a thirty-six-year-old former restaurant owner turned twelve-dollar-a-week cook, looked up from his newspaper to put in his two cents' worth: No one, he observed, had ever walked around the world backward. The boys laughed and stumbled about the room for a few minutes, clumsily trying to walk backward.

The teenagers forgot about the comment, but Wingo did not. His grand scheme took shape: He would indeed circumnavigate the globe, walking backward over every step of dry land. He was sure that some company, perhaps a shoe manufacturer, would sponsor such a trek to gain publicity, and money and fame—hard to come by at the time—would then be his.

Wingo began practicing his backward gait diligently and found himself steering an erratic course.

Luckily, he spotted a magazine advertisement for sunglasses fitted with tiny rearview mirrors. Intended for motorcycle drivers, these mirrors suited Wingo's purposes as well, and he soon became adept at retrograde locomotion.

Wingo canvassed first Abilene and then Fort Worth for a sponsor, but none signed on. Even so, on April 15, 1931, he put himself in reverse and set off from Fort Worth. Wingo traveled light, carrying virtually nothing but his coffee-wood walking stick, the sign around his neck reading "Around the World Backwards," a letter of introduction from the Fort Worth Chamber of Commerce, and a Bible. Wingo's pockets were empty, since he had wired all his cash to his wife. He made some money selling postcards bearing his picture to people he met, many of whom invited him in for a meal or a night's rest.

Stepping along smartly, with his whereabouts often making the front page of the local newspaper, Wingo traveled through Dallas to Chicago, then eastward to Washington, D.C. Working his way north, he reached Boston, then backtracked to New York City, where he got a job on a freighter bound for Hamburg. Of necessity face forward during the passage, Wingo resumed his backward journey in Germany and traversed eastern Europe to Turkey. There government officials refused him the visa that he needed to continue his trip.

Returning to the United States, Wingo accepted an acquaintance's offer of a ride to Santa Monica, California. He walked the 1,400 miles from Santa Monica to Fort Worth, backing into town on October 24, 1932. During his eighteen-month trek, he had walked 8,000 backward miles, worn out thirteen pairs of unsponsored shoes, and become a single man again—his wife divorced him in absentia. His back-pedaling had not exactly taken him around the world, but it had certainly been eventful.

Back home in Abilene after his big adventure, Plennie Wingo cheerfully exchanged the limelight for a perfectly

ordinary existence. But when he was eighty-one, wanderlust seized him again, and he took an eighty-five-day, 452-mile walk in fine stern-first form from Santa Monica to San Francisco. Then he hung up his walking shoes for good. □

During the early 1930s, Texan Plennie Wingo *(below and at left)* **walked thousands of miles across America and Europe backwards, guided by two tiny rearview mirrors mounted on his glasses.**

Take a Number

MR. 1069

When high-school teacher and sometime short-order cook Michael Herbert Dengler set about trying to change his name, he had no trouble getting a new Social Security card. His Minneapolis bank and the power company were equally agreeable, but he ran into opposition from the telephone company. It balked when the former Mr. Dengler requested that he be listed in the telephone book as 1069. Nor could he persuade the Minnesota Motor Vehicles Department to issue a driver's license bearing a numerical moniker.

These obstacles were particularly frustrating because they had impeded the would-be 1069 before. In 1975, while living in North Dakota, he had tried to get the state courts to legalize the numerical designation. But the following year, the North Dakota Supreme Court adjudged that 1069 did not, under state law, constitute a legal name. Dengler had the right to call himself anything he pleased, the justices said, but North Dakota would not direct anybody else to accept the new name as legal.

Hoping to do better in Minnesota, Dengler renewed his court battle—as quietly as possible. Obviously averse to being perceived as a publicity seeker engaged in a stunt, he was loath to give interviews or have his picture taken. Nor was he out to irritate government agencies. He wanted the new name because, in his opinion, its four digits expressed in complex and mystical ways his personal and philosophical identity. But the Minnesota Supreme Court did not see things exactly his way. The justices were willing to go along with the alphabetical version One Zero Six Nine, but they would not accept 1069. Determined to be known by digits only, 1069 tried a new tack.

Instead of quibbling over state laws, his attorneys asserted that constitutional issues were at stake: Their client, they argued, had been denied his rights to free speech, privacy, and equal protection under the law. The U.S. Supreme Court, however, summarily dismissed the appeal. Thus the petitioner, in his soul and essence 1069, remained legally Michael Herbert Dengler. □

MR. 1069

...d Haberman, of Tama, Iowa, gathered oil rags to staunch a leaking ice machine back in the 1950s—and became a notable collector. Like a philatelist's first stamps, those rags became the nucleus of Haberman's fabled collection, gathered from highways, service stations, and donors across the land. By 1979, Haberman had collected some 1,300 oil rags.

Kea's Ark

"No seas, weather fair, the keel was laid on the ways at 11:30 hours by myself, it is 6 by 8 inches and assembled will be 60 feet long." So read Captain Kea Tawana's logbook for August 8, 1982, the day she began building her ark. The shipyard's location seemed improbable: a land-locked vacant lot amid the weedy rubble of Newark, New Jersey's dreary and disintegrating Central Ward, twenty-seven blocks from the Passaic River, the nearest navigable body of water.

Nevertheless, the site had its own logic. A longtime Central Ward resident, Tawana had been salvaging materials from the urban wreckage ever since she conceived the project in 1966. The Central Ward was the ark's wellspring and thus the proper place for it to take shape.

From the neighborhood's gutted buildings and rubbish heaps Tawana lugged home lumber, columns from a church, metal vents, stone, tall metal poles that had once supported tiers of clotheslines strung from the rear walls of tenements, even a pipe organ. She also stockpiled more portable treasures such as stained-glass windows, a collection of old books, eighteenth-century hardware, and a forty-eight-star flag destined to fly from the ark's mast. Tawana sold some of the items she salvaged to help support herself. The proceeds augmented her meager earnings as part-time custodian for the Humanity Baptist Church, which was next door to her make-shift shipyard.

Tawana worked by herself and looked after herself, as she had done since childhood. Born to a Japanese mother and an American father, she lost her mother during a World War II bombing raid on Japan. Her father was killed shortly after returning from Japan to the United States with his daughter. When Tawana was scarcely out of elementary school, she ran away from her foster home to ride the rails and work at odd jobs. Along the way she picked up the basics of construction, and when she eventually settled down on her Central Ward homestead, she turned an old bus and a shed perched on a flatbed trailer into a shipshape little dwelling. It even had a hot-water system assembled Rube Goldberg-fashion from a tank for rainwater, a 1907 wood stove, pipes, and radiators from demolished buildings.

Tawana carefully prepared for her building of the ark, studying nineteenth-century shipbuilding techniques and acquainting herself with Coast Guard regulations. Her reading turned up the fact that in wartime the United States government has the right to seize ships more than 100 feet long, so she selected a safe length of 86 feet. Her plan called for three masts that together would support 12,000 square feet of sail. Besides quarters for the captain, two cats, and a crew of eight, the ark was to include a chapel, a library, a greenhouse, an auditorium housing the pipe organ, and an art studio.

With chisel and hammer, Tawana made mortise and tenon joints in the ark's timbers. She also fastened some of the craft's elements with nails that, along with tarpaper, were the only construction materials she needed to buy. Like some skeletal but majestic vessel riding high at anchor in a derelict harbor, the ark slowly materialized. The distance

between the ground and the roof of the auditorium, the ark's topmost space, was twenty-eight feet, and the beam of the vessel was twenty feet. Run up its towering clothes-pole mast, its flapping flag was visible for blocks.

In 1986, trouble began to brew for the shipwright and her unfinished ark. When the lot on which she lived was sold to a developer, the city served her with an eviction notice. With the blessing of the Humanity Baptist Church, Tawana moved both ark and house across the property line to the church parking lot. She soon had unwelcome visitors—city building inspectors who toured the transplanted shipyard, examined the work in progress, and ordered Tawana to tear it down. Although she argued that the ark was a vessel and not a building, the city turned a deaf ear and insisted that she had violated construction and safety codes. The ark was, officials added, an eyesore that could deter redevelopment.

As word spread of her problems with the city, artists, engineers, and architects came to view her work and praise its merit. They also supported Tawana in her battle with official Newark in and out of court. "I've worked a lifetime for this—put my heart and soul, blood and sweat into this—and they want to rob me of what has taken years to put together with my two hands and a lot of guts," she lamented.

In the spring of 1987, the city was poised to tear the ark down, but a sympathetic judge granted Tawana a reprieve that, with two extensions, stretched to a year's time. Estimating that she would need $20,000 to finish the ark and launch it on the Passaic—thus escaping the reach of building inspec-

tors—Tawana began dismantling the auditorium so the ark could pass beneath power lines.

In April 1988, the ark was still in the church's parking lot, and the judge lifted the restraining order that had kept the city at bay. Preferring to dismantle the ark herself, Tawana took up her saw. What had taken six years to build took about two weeks to level. □

Coral Camelot

Jilted by Agnes Scuffs, his sixteen-year-old fiancée, Edward Leedskalnin fled his native Latvia in 1912, prepared to grieve forever. Evidently, the wound inflicted by love still festered when he arrived in the United States several years later. Although Leedskalnin understood that Agnes was lost to him, he did not abandon his affection. On the contrary, he erected a unique monument to her memory: a kind of Camelot in coral.

A masterpiece of engineering if not of art, Coral Castle was begun in Florida City, Florida, after Leedskalnin's arrival there about 1920. It was then trucked piece by piece to Homestead, some ten miles away, where it was completed in 1940, when Leedskalnin was in his fifties. Every part of the three-acre castle—walls and furnishings alike—is made from the coral rock that Leedskalnin quarried on-site in huge blocks. They weigh as much as 6,000 pounds, and how he managed to move them is something of a mystery that Leedskalnin, apparently intentionally, never dispelled.

Because he did all the quarrying, transporting, and sculpting single-handedly, there was no assistant to report on his methods. He was so determined to foil snoopy neighbors that he frequently worked at night by lamplight.

Leedskalnin implied that he had discovered the secrets that allowed the Egyptians to erect the pyramids, and several obscure ruminations he penned on magnetism, electricity, and gravitation hinted at abilities not strictly run-of-the-mill. But the castle rose mainly on his hard labor. As handy as he was secretive, Leedskalnin made all of his own tools and equipment, including a block and tackle, from scrap that had been salvaged from junkyards and the local dump. He owed his considerable skills as mason, mechanic, and engineer to experience, having completed only four years of formal schooling.

Coral Castle's engineering masterpiece is the gate in the wall surrounding the grounds. Eight feet tall and weighing 18,000 pounds, it pivots on rods placed so perfectly that a push of a finger opens the gate. All of Coral Castle's rooms, with the exception of the two in a two-story tower, are unroofed spaces open to the sky. Most of the time, Leedskalnin lived in a shack behind his castle, now and then occupying the roofed tower. But, perhaps envisioning a coral court, he created a throne room with his and hers thrones, another for a child, and a fourth, uncomfortable enough to be dubbed the Mother-in-Law's Chair. The master bedroom features two beds, each eight feet long, and steps that lead up to a children's sleeping area. A circular "sun couch" eight feet across with several billowy coral pillows revolves ◊

Captain Kea Tawana stands on the bow of her eighty-six-foot ark, which she built single-handedly from scraps. Authorities forced her to dismantle the craft about a year after this 1987 photograph was taken.

on a Ford brake drum, allowing a sunbather to rotate the couch as the sun's position changes. Nearby, a heart-shaped table stands ready for happy family meals. On a somewhat darker note, Leedskalnin set aside a "repentance corner" for the castle's imagined youngsters. Its centerpiece is a pillory-like coral slab with a hole chiseled through it. When punishment was called for, the naughty child's head could be thrust through the hole and wedged in place with a wooden block. The captive would thus be unable to escape the parents' lectures. Leedskalnin estimated that an hour in the repentance corner would convince a child to toe the line for several months afterward.

Although Coral Castle was built primarily as a monument to lost domestic bliss, it also has political and scientific aspects. Leedskalnin envisioned the state's governor and his key advisers seated in coral rocking chairs around the conference table he carved in the shape of Florida. A concavity in the table's surface represents Okeechobee, the largest lake in the state. The entabled Okeechobee, Leedskalnin suggested, could function as a finger bowl or a birdbath. Fascinated with astronomy, Leedskalnin sculpted representations of Mars and Saturn and incorporated the Moon's various phases in an elaborate fountain. A twenty-five-foot-long, thirty-ton coral telescope equipped with cross hairs to aid the stargazer is fixed permanently on a point near the Pole Star.

Details of the Coral Castle are known only because, while secretive, Leedskalnin was never much for seclusion. He opened his creation to public tours in the 1920s, charging nominal ten- and twenty-five-cent fees and delighting in explaining his motives, visions, and hopes to visitors. Agnes, his vanished beloved, never saw her ex-beau's monument to her. And, in fact, it appears that Leedskalnin was not brooding over her at the end. Barely self-supporting, and always preoccupied with his eccentric brand of scientific research, the aging Latvian had subsisted for years on a diet of sardines and crackers. In 1951, an experiment with magnetism so occupied Edward Leedskalnin that, one biographer wrote, "he forgot to eat at all." The solitary sixty-four-year-old master of Coral Castle died that same year—not of unrequited love, but of malnutrition. □

An Orange Crush

Reconstructing how it all began, Jeff McKissack said the two words just came to him one day in the late 1960s: Orange Show. Suddenly what had been only a flickering shadow of an idea shifted into focus. He was going to build a monument to the orange.

The idea of building something had been set in motion years earlier, when McKissack, a Georgia-born postal worker in Houston, Texas, began tinkering with a lot he had bought across the street from his own modest, handmade house. He first thought to turn the place into a worm farm but soon gave that up in favor of what seemed a better idea: a beauty salon. In 1956, he got a construction permit, but the salon never materialized. He eventually built a plant nursery on the site and operated it for several years. Then, suddenly and enigmatically, McKissack closed the nursery's doors and gave away all the plants.

From the skeleton structure already in place, the sexagenarian McKissack began to build his

Shaped like the state of Florida, the Coral Castle's coral conference table is shown here with the state's northern panhandle in the foreground; the round declivity is southern Florida's huge Lake Okeechobee.

A beaming Jeff McKissack *(right)* created Houston's Orange Show, an elaborate, idiosyncratic theme park intended
as a tribute to the noble citrus fruit.

Orange Show. He was never at a loss for materials. Given to yearly pilgrimages to the therapeutic waters of Hot Springs, Arkansas, he scavenged through antique shops, junkyards, and roadside stands en route, picking up items as disparate as wagon wheels, butter churns, and tractor seats. He discovered a wealth of material along his postal route as well, and neighbors watched as he unloaded his car in the evenings with the day's haul of bricks, tiles, metal, and the like. For the last few years of his life, McKissack carried the cache home on his bicycle.

Although he knew that his eclectic collection would somehow evolve into the Orange Show, an exact plan of action was slow to crystallize. He later admitted that he was completely lost for the first two years. Still, he plodded on. Finally, "it began to make a pattern," he explained in 1977, "and it grew and grew, until now, without fear or hesitation, I say it is the most beautiful show on earth, the most colorful show on earth, and the most unique show on earth."

Indeed, Jeff McKissack's Orange Show, which opened to the public in 1979, defies easy description. It is a whimsical open-air fantasyland—part amusement park, part sideshow, part exhibit gallery. McKissack built the entire 5,000-square-foot structure by hand, playfully arranging his quarry of found objects into a dazzling, flag-festooned complex that, one observer declared, is "the most deliriously happy place in Houston." There are gaily painted wagon wheels and wrought-iron railings at every turn, thousands of salvaged bricks and tiles, multicolored pieces of farm equipment, and countless bits of scrap metal, some

of them fashioned into a flock of decorative birds.

The show is dedicated, of course, to the orange: McKissack was convinced it was the perfect food, providing pure, undiluted energy. Virtually every inch of available wall space is covered with handcrafted mosaic signs proclaiming the tenets of his orange-based philosophy of health and well-being: LOVE ORANGES AND LIVE, one sign announces. BE SMART—DRINK ORANGE JUICE, says another.

In the exhibit room, a store mannequin has been cast as an ax-wielding woodsman in a crèchelike scene. The accompanying mosaic trumpets the pleas of the woodsman's female counterpart, who urges him to spare an artificial orange tree. A red-nosed clown face offers what some say is the key to McKissack's vision: "I TAKE CARE OF MYSELF EVERY HOUR EVERY MINUTE OF THE DAY," the tiles read. "YOU CAN TOO IF YOU WILL. CLOWNS NEVER LIE."

McKissack had grand visions for the Orange Show, certain that it

would someday attract several hundred thousand visitors a year; about 90 percent of the American public would be interested, he reckoned. He dug out a 175-seat arena and added a stage for musical performances. A second arena, with seating for 250, was dedicated to McKissack's second great preoccupation—steam—and displayed his handmade steel steamboat.

Jeff McKissack saw the Orange Show open in May 1979 to mild and fleeting interest. After he died in 1980, aged seventy-seven, friends banded together to save his work and keep his vision alive. The Orange Show became a draw, although perhaps not what its creator had anticipated. Musical programs are performed on its stage, and it is visited by some 35,000 people a year. Appropriately enough, the Orange Show has become a folk-art foundation, a place to celebrate homespun innovation. At its core, however, it remains the singular vision of one man. "Everyone is interested in the orange from the cradle to the grave," its creator once explained. "But if it had not been for me, Jeff McKissack, the orange industry and the American people would probably have gone another two hundred years without an Orange Show." Or even longer. □

Better Homes and Gardens

For some people, the place where they live must be as unmistakably individual as their fingerprints. Among the arrestingly one-of-a-kind residences on the following pages is a house whose walls portray its owner's life story. Others reveal personality less directly but no less surely in a variety of media: machine parts and beer cans festooning fences and eaves or a newspaper buff's favorite reading matter turned into furniture. In a garden, ordinary greenery gives way to wooden flowers that express one man's personal vision of paradise.

Town-dump treasures take precedence over wares from the local home-improvement emporium for this breed of do-it-yourselfer. The result may never make the pages of a glossy magazine on home decor, but to its creator it is profoundly satisfying. It is home. □

When Sanford Darling peered into his refrigerator *(above)*, he disrupted a mountainous landscape. His front door had more peaks. Darling, an oil-company retiree in Santa Barbara, was seized in 1963 by a painting mania. Nearly every surface of his home, inside and out, was covered in scenes inspired by his life and travels. Its contents bore murals too. After Darling died in 1973, the house was dismantled, and collectors bought some of his work.

Retired mortician David H. Brown built his house in Boswell, British Columbia *(above)*, out of empty embalming-fluid bottles. To indulge what he called his "whim of a peculiar nature," Brown gathered some 500,000 bottles for the 1,200-square-foot house and several smaller structures, including a bridge and a thirty-five-foot lookout tower. Mortared in ranks with their bottoms facing outward *(right)*, the eight-inch bottles are capped for maximum insulation.

Every part of a beer can has its place on or around the late John Milkovisch's house in Houston. Streamers of can bottoms hanging from the eaves tinkle in the breeze *(right)*, and a veneer of flattened labels hides the original clapboards *(below)*. When the six-pack-a-day upholsterer undertook the project around 1970, he already had an attic and a garage full of empties. According to one estimate, Milkovisch used as many as 39,000 cans in his creation. The yellow "ladder of success" he installed in the front yard has one black rung—the rung of failure.

123

Houstonian Robert Harper stands in the gate of his gaily en- crusted chain-link fence, with his dog, Brutus, in the back- ground *(inset)*. Harper, whose fa- vorite material has earned him the nickname Fan Man, has been adorning his yard since 1986 with sculptures and friezes made of offbeat objects. Besides the abun- dance of fans, which he often sepa- rates into their components, Harper makes lavish use of blue plastic bread trays, hubcaps, red crates, beer bottles, television tubes, and cabinets. The symmetrical array of fan blades and grills at left is crowned by a helmeted creature standing on the back of a toy truck under a bottle-fringed canopy.

Tressa Prisbrey poses beside her sculpture entitled the *Leaning Tower of Pisa* in Bottle Village *(below)*, the complex of thirteen pavilions she crowded onto her one-third acre trailer-park lot in Simi Valley, California. She began her project when her pencil collection grew too large for her trailer to accommodate. The dump was Prisbrey's main source of materials, yielding thousands of bottles that she com- bined with concrete to build the pavilions and the wall sur- rounding the village. She packed each pavilion with a dis- tinctive selection of salvaged objects. In the Little Chapel, for instance, Prisbrey displayed dolls adorned with pull tabs from aluminum cans *(far right)*.

From ground to rooftop, Cleveland Turner's decorative tour de force in the East End of Houston explodes with color *(above)*. When he decided his home needed a new look, he first went to work on the garden, and his neighbors soon nicknamed him the Flower Man because of the dozens of varieties of flowers he planted.

Turner, shown here at left wearing a well-chosen outfit, pedals around town on his bicycle, scouting for castoff treasures to ornament the house. "It's not everyone's cup of tea," the Flower Man concedes of his creation. "But it's just the way I want my life to be: beautiful. Without it, it wouldn't be a house to me."

Seven million cigar bands went into the mosaics covering the walls and ceilings of three rooms in Nico Molenaar's house in Volendam, Holland. To create images such as the church at left, the one-time monk often used only the colorful logo in each band's center. More than a dozen logos are pieced together for the right arm of the Venetian gondolier above. Smokers and cigar manufacturers kept Molenaar supplied with his medium for the sixteen years he devoted to the mosaics.

Now yellowed with age, newspaper chairs and a stool surround a piano faced with tightly rolled newspaper cylinders in the newspaper house of newspaper addict Elis Stenman of Pigeon Cove, Massachusetts. The frugal Stenman hated to just throw away the half-dozen or so dailies to which he subscribed, and in 1922, when he was making plans for a summer cottage, he suddenly hit upon his novel recycling scheme.

Stenman enjoyed giving newsworthy themes to individual pieces of handiwork. All of the headlines visible on the piano's cylinders, for example, trumpet a major story of the 1920s, the exploits of polar explorer Richard Byrd.

The fabulous garden that filled the front yard of Romano Gabriel's house *(top)* in Eureka, California, needed painting, not watering. A carpenter by trade, Gabriel *(above)* transformed fruit crates into trees and flowers and peopled his wooden landscape with sloe-eyed beauties in scanty outfits *(left)*, along with priests and nuns, Italian police squads, astronauts, dancers, accordian players, soccer players, and lumberjacks. He liked to hide in a shed near the sidewalk and listen to passersby talk about his garden. Some thirty years in the making, Romano Gabriel's 300 carvings are now sheltered in a glass-fronted pavilion in Eureka.

The Count of Counting

David Wimp first tried his hand at big-time counting when his Riverton, Wyoming, mathematics teacher promised an A-plus to any student who could count by ones from zero to a million in nine weeks. Adding one over and over was slow going with pencil and paper, and Wimp got no further than 25,000. It was nevertheless a propitious beginning, and the self-proclaimed Count of Riverton, who now wields a calculator instead of a pencil, became a celebrated number juggler in his spare time—a wizard of oneness.

When not adding or subtracting, Wimp, a retired army cook, augments his pension by running a lawn service and driving a garbage truck. Beginning to count by ones in 1982, he reached one million after five years of somewhat casual addition. No slave to sequence, he began his second series at two million. He slashed his time dramatically, hitting three million after just 436 days. His uncle had shown him how to use his calculator more efficiently, and Wimp consequently increased his speed to some 1,000 ones per hour. Turning from addition to subtraction, he next counted backward by ones from one million to zero. He finished this feat in 431 days and reduced his rate of error by nearly 40 percent, from 5,800 to a mere 3,600 per million. Then he began adding ones again, this time starting from three million.

Wimp's hobby consumes calculator tape by the mile—more than forty miles to pass three million—and he has burned out about a dozen calculators. To save money, Wimp makes his own tape, cutting paper into strips and neatly taping them together. He finds fluorescent green or orange a nice change from the usual white tape.

Wearing a rubber thimble on his left index finger, southpaw Wimp adds for four or five hours at a stretch, sometimes watching television at the same time. If he keeps to an average of 1,000 numbers per hour, finishing a series of one million requires 1,000 hours.

Wimp cannot explain his devotion to counting. Perhaps, like beauty or art, it is self-justifying. Or, as he puts it, "Everything doesn't have to have a reason, does it?" Until or unless something more interesting comes along, David Wimp's goal is to count to one billion, one by one, and he hopes to be there by 2007. □

David Wimp *(left)* adds to his miles of adding-machine tape in 1989, counting by ones on his way to a billion.

Nuthouse

As she later described her moment of enlightenment, Elizabeth Tashjian was musing on a prized coco-de-mer one day in 1977 when a profound question occurred to her. "Which was created first," she wondered, eying the thirty-five-pound specimen, "this nut or mortals?" For Tashjian, the answer was obvious. In that reflective instant, "I became thoroughly convinced," she explains, "that the nut was first."

Tashjian has since transformed her revelation into a more fully articulated theory. Perplexed by the coco-de-mer's resemblance to female anatomy, she has decided that it demonstrates a flaw in the Darwinian theory of evolution: Humans, she claims, actually descended from the coco-de-mer, which is found only in the Seychelles Islands of the Indian Ocean—the site, some believe, of the Garden of Eden. Not stuffily scientific, she has fashioned a catchy slogan to spread the word: "Out with apes, in with nuts."

Tashjian opened a museum for nuts—presumably the only such shrine—in 1972, in her Old Lyme, Connecticut, home. The Nut Museum, where her prophetic coco-de-mer is enthroned on an appropriately regal antique chair, serves as the focal point of her efforts to reform prevailing evolutionary theory and otherwise give the nut its just desserts. As curator, Tashjian sees the museum's mission as "establishing the entity of nuts through art, music, and lore."

As one would expect, the museum is much more than a simple collection of brazil nuts, almonds, peanuts, and pistachios. Tashjian has collected more than forty different types of nuts from around the world—from the tiny African baobab to the Asian betel nut—and tries to present each as artistically as possible. She also exhibits the fruits of her singular creative labors: nut paintings, jewelry, and souvenirs; aluminum lawn sculptures with a nutty theme; and nut masks made of foam rubber. Tashjian lined the inside of one such mask, called "Almond eye-bags," with sheet music, to stress that "nuts bring a note of happiness and fun."

The silver-haired curator is a veritable

fount of nut folk wisdom and philosophy. In her professed view, nuts are sophisticated entities, worthy of deepest veneration and respect. "They're not just snack treats," declares Tashjian, "they're treats for the soul." She believes they may offer insights into human nature. Like some people, she muses, nuts are "hard and prickly on the outside but soft and sweet on the inside."

Not content with mere hypothesis, however, Tashjian has set some of her views to music. One song, entitled "Sweet Nut in a Burr," further ramifies the parable of a sweet center surrounded by a hard shell.

Her most popular composition, though, is the nut anthem, "Nuts are Beautiful," which she has sung on several occasions on national television. It begins, "Oh, nobody ever thinks about nuts, nuts can be so beautiful if looked aright," and goes on to explain that nuts are "yearly tokens of primeval life," and have been "nourishing man since creation began."

But inevitably she is faced with a dilemma: To wring the central meaning from a nut, one must eat it. "It's very difficult for me because they're so beautiful," she says. "I have to close my eyes." □

Mineral-Rich Diet

Sixteen-year-old Michel Lotito was drinking mint tea with his friends at a French café one day in 1966 when a little accident occurred: The rim of Lotito's glass shattered between his teeth. Instead of spitting the fragments out, Lotito crunched, chewed, and swallowed them, with no ill effects.

It was an enviable display of teenage bravado, the kind that confirms what nearly every male adolescent wants to prove—that he is a man to be reckoned with, capable of doing almost anything. For the majority of young men, a single such incident is enough. But Michel Lotito's feat of derring-do was only a beginning. It spawned a peculiar taste that soon blossomed into an all-consuming passion.

Lotito tested his newfound gastric mettle on other indigesti- ◊

Nut Museum curator Elizabeth Tashjian poses with an eight-foot aluminum nutcracker (said to be the world's largest) and the thirty-five-pound coco-de-mer that proves, she says, that human beings sprang from nuts.

Arch card-carrier Walter Cavanagh *(right)* flashes a cape of plastic wealth: hundreds of credit cards.

ble comestibles: beer cans, razor blades, crockery, bullets, knitting needles, and coins. He downed them all and survived—indeed, he thrived. He put on eating exhibitions at local clubs, to the consternation of his parents and the delight of his Grenoble neighbors, who dubbed him Monsieur Mangetout—Mister Eats-All.

By the late 1980s, Lotito had achieved an international reputation and a measure of wealth, earning as much as $2,000 for every appearance. Traveling the world from Hong Kong to the Americas—sometimes carrying his viands with him—Lotito consumed keys, plates, bowls, spoons, bicycles, chandeliers, shopping carts, television sets (always leaving the poisonous tube on his plate), a camera, a coffin, and a waterbed.

The ultimate omnivore began climbing toward the apex of his career in Caracas, Venezuela, in 1978, when he took the first bite of an airplane, a Cessna two-seater. Like all of Lotito's offbeat meals, the airplane went down his throat piece by tiny piece. (Lotito's traveling kit includes tin snips, pliers, and other tools with which he breaks up his rations into fingernail-size bits.) Carrying the minced craft around with him as he toured, Monsieur Mangetout nibbled on resolutely, finally polishing off the last morsel in 1980. He pronounced the propeller "delicious."

The year after completing his aeronautical triumph, Lotito received a brief setback when a friend stabbed him in the abdomen for paying too much attention to the friend's wife. About a month later, after doctors repaired the damage, Lotito was back on his metallic diet.

Monsieur Mangetout, who had an offstage preference for choice steaks, was still going strong with his less-mundane munchables in the early 1990s. The secret of his success, he said, was concentration, though the rapt attention to his mineral-rich meals left him drained. "I am always exhausted," Lotito stated, "at the end of a performance."

In recognition of his remarkable talent, the *Guinness Book of World Records* dubbed Lotito the world's greatest omnivore and presented him with a handsome brass plaque. He ate it. □

Give the Guy Credit

"Some people read," Walter Cavanagh explains; "I fill out credit applications."

His usual pace is one or two a week, but one winter month he applied for no fewer than 300 credit cards. The California financial planner's love affair with plastic began about 1973, when he and a friend vied to see who could collect more cards in one year. The diligent Cavanagh was a runaway victor, with a score of 143.

By 1991, his collection had grown to more than 1,200. Worth some $1.7 million in credit, Cavanagh's piles of plastic have come from all fifty of the states and

French omnivore Michel Lotito *(left)*, dubbed Mr. Eats-All by bemused compatriots, munches his way through an alloy hors d'oeuvre of bicycle spokes.

Lucy Pearson *(below)* shows off some shining examples of her 80,000 hubcaps—a collection that made little Pearsonville, California *(inset below)*, the Hubcap Capital of the World.

seven foreign countries. Besides obvious sources such as banks, gasoline companies, and department stores, the credit cards also represent specialty stores, as varied as a San Francisco tall-woman dress shop and a Reno casino.

Cavanagh occasionally totes an 850-card, 250-foot-long wallet—the world's largest known—in a capacious briefcase, but more often the cards are tucked away in a safe-deposit box. Most of them are unsigned, and Cavanagh estimates that he has used no more than five percent of the cards he owns. Like a person with a more ordinary relationship to credit cards, Cavanagh normally carries only two or three, and he pays his balance off entirely each month—a prudent practice for a man whose goal is to collect every card in the world. □

The Hubcap Queen

When a woman has 80,000 hubcaps, she may find it convenient to have a town of her own to store them in. Such is the arrangement enjoyed by Lucy Pearson, who got into the hubcap game on Pearson Road in Pearsonville, California—scarcely more than a wide spot on U.S. 395 between Los Angeles and Reno. Kentuckians who pulled up stakes to go west, Mrs. Pearson and her auto mechanic husband, Andy, founded their town in 1959, when they settled down on eighty barren desert acres and opened a wrecking yard.

When Mr. Pearson salvaged tires and wheels from the frequent accidents along the busy highway, it was his habit to throw away the hubcaps. This distressed his wife. "I hate to see anything go to waste," Lucy Pearson explains, "so I started collecting hubcaps, and I've been doing it ever since."

Now hubcaps hang from fences and cover the walls of Mom and Pop's Cafe, another Pearson establishment, and are stacked all over Pearsonville. Cheerfully obsessed, Mrs. Pearson is no longer content merely to collect. She swaps, buys, and sells, and with her granddaughter's help, makes hubcap clocks. As long as she wishes to wear the crown, the self-declared Hubcap Queen's reign in the Hubcap Capital of the World seems secure. □

Up, Up, and Away

The Wright brothers would have applauded truckdriver Larry Walters's inventiveness: From readily available and inexpensive materials, he built an aircraft, of sorts, flew it to an altitude of 16,000 feet near Long Beach, California, then landed safely. The ninety-minute maiden voyage took place on the sunny morning of July 2, 1982, fulfilling Walters's twenty-year dream of free-floating airborne adventure.

The amateur's flying machine could scarcely have been simpler: It consisted of an aluminum lawn chair buoyed by forty-odd helium-filled weather balloons arranged in four tiers. When Walters took off from his girlfriend's backyard in San Pedro, his equipment included a portable CB radio and a BB pistol, with which he planned to pop balloons for his descent. Sensibly cautious, Walters wore a parachute and, of course, buckled his seat belt before the chair's tether cables were finally cast off.

Although Walters had no experience flying any kind of aircraft, he felt reasonably confident that the wind would waft him to the Mojave Desert, located some fifty miles northeast of San Pedro. He was mistaken. His chair zipped upward at a startling rate and headed southeast toward Long Beach.

It was chilly up there and dangerous besides, for Walters soon found himself bobbing amid commercial jets approaching the Long Beach airport. He radioed air-traffic controllers, shot ten weather balloons with his BB pistol, and began his descent, praying earnestly. Floating low over a Long Beach neighborhood, Walters ran into a power line, but the police had seen him coming and had shut off the electricity. He disembarked unscathed fifteen miles from his liftoff point.

The free-spirited Walters earned the stern disapproval of the Federal Aviation Administration. The agency cited him for various offenses, including flying an aircraft for which there was no airworthiness certificate. After some wrangling, the FAA let Walters off with a $1,500 fine. Evidently, the flight was worth every penny to Walters, who explained, "It was something I had to do to achieve inner peace." □

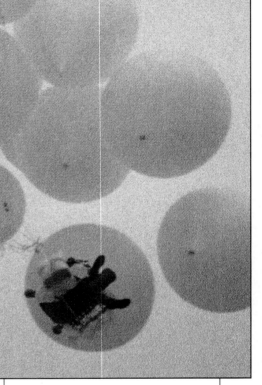

Drawn by more than forty helium-filled weather balloons, truckdriver Larry Walters lifts off into the Los Angeles sky in 1982 for a ninety-minute flight—his first and only—in a lawn chair.

Making Rupee

The pomp and splendor of the procession that wound for five miles through the streets of Ahmadabad, India, on June 1, 1991, would have done a Mogul emperor of centuries past proud. Wearing a gold-encrusted red costume, a turbaned young man rode in a silver-plated chariot drawn by seven elephants draped with gorgeous caparisons. Gold rings gleamed on his fingers, and diamonds hung from his ears and glittered in chains around his neck. In the chariot's wake came fifty beautifully ornamented horses, forty camel carts, and dozens of dance troupes. Waves of spectators surged around the bespangled charioteer, eagerly extending their hands for the favors that he scattered—millions of rupees' worth of gold and silver coins, pearls, and diamonds.

A prince by commerce if not by blood, the twenty-nine-year-old multimillionaire diamond merchant Atul Shah was paying a spectacular farewell to his life of luxury: The parade came on the eve of his becoming a Jain priest. The ceremonial splash was totally at odds with the simplicity and austerity that Jains traditionally practice, but the young man was determined to do it his way.

Besides the small fortune that was tossed to parade viewers, the gold and gems adorning Atul Shah's person were valued at some six million rupees—about $290,000. The 5,000 calendar-size invitations to the ini-

In June 1991, diamond merchant and aspiring priest Atul Shah (right) of Ahmadabad, India, said goodbye to wealth with days of opulent feasts and lavish parades (opposite page, top).

tiation ceremony that was held on the day after the parade must have seemed a bargain at a mere two million rupees.

Before a stadiumful of witnesses, Shah cast aside his fabulous ornaments for a priest's plain white robe. Then, in a final convulsion of his extravagant withdrawal from wealth, he threw a lunch for 150,000—a caterer's nightmare, according to one cynical witness, but surely a grand and satisfying gesture for the metamorphosing merchant. □

Spudnik

"I suppose you could say I have a potato-centric view of the world," Alan Fairweather ruminates. In his opinion, potatoes are "the most interesting plants in the world," and for a number of years Fairweather's life has been guided by his vegetable lodestone. A botanist and agronomist by training, he has steeped himself in the techniques of growing and propagating the potato and is an expert on its impact on social and political history.

Given his interests, Fairweather has a dream assignment analyzing Scotland's potato crop annually, and he is frequently called upon to sift for traces of the tuber in archaeological excavations.

A favorite holiday spot for the botanist-agronomist is the International Potato Center in Peru, the vegetable's native country. According to the fixated Fairweather's taste, the world's best potato is a yellow variety grown in the Andes.

Not surprisingly, Fairweather relishes potatoes, which are his staff of life. He eats them at every meal, consuming some two or three pounds per day. Spurning such variations as potato chips, Fairweather likes his potatoes plain and simple. The unpeeled potato is plunged into boiling salted water for twenty minutes, and at the end of the allotted time, it is dried in a hot pan until its flesh is fluffy. He eats the finished potato with salt and sometimes a little butter.

After his tuberous evening meal, Fairweather beds down for sweet potato dreams on the floor of his study, which is stuffed with books on his obsession. He rents out the four bedrooms of his house, declaring, "I don't see the point in having a special room set aside to fall unconscious in." □

Up to his neck in topsoil, spudmeister Alan Fairweather imitates his favorite vegetable, the potato.

ACKNOWLEDGMENTS

The editors wish to thank these individuals and institutions for their valuable assistance:

Frédéric Altmann, Nice; Betty Bailey, Conwood Company, L.P., Memphis, Tennessee; Sarah Bolce, Haverford College, Haverford, Pennsylvania; Henri Bordillon, Vitré, France; Michael Brescia, St. Mary's Church, Perth Amboy, New Jersey; Mike Cassidy, *San Jose Mercury News*, San Jose, California; Walter Cavanagh, Santa Clara, California; Phillip Danzig, Upper Montclair, New Jersey; Timothy Dickinson, *Paris Review*, Washington, D.C.; Hal Bernard Dixon, Jr., Pentecostal Research Center, Cleveland, Tennessee; Marc Forestiere, Fresno, California; Sherry Fowble, Winterthur, Delaware; Patricia Gandy, Perth Amboy Free Public Library, Perth Amboy, New Jersey; Pietro Gargano, Naples; Paul Gayot, Collège de Parapsychologie, Reims, France; R. A. Gilbert, Bristol, England; Denny G. Hair, Houston Police Academy, Houston; Hearst San Simeon State Historical Monument, San Simeon, California; Istituto Storia della Medicina, Universita La Sapienzà, Rome; Marie Jett, Tulsa; Curt Johnson, *Long Beach Press-Telegram*, Long Beach, California; Thomas Lockney, University of North Dakota School of Law, Grand Forks; Diana McCain, Connecticut Historical Society, Hartford; National Capital Commission, Ottawa; Newport Historical Society, Newport, Rhode Island; New York State Historical Association, Cooperstown; Christopher Peterson, Department of Psychology, University of Michigan, Ann Arbor; Dominique Remaude, Bibliothèque Municipale, de Laval, France; Luisa Ricciarini, Milan; H. Ames Richards, Jr., Stamford, Connecticut; Bob Rickard, London; Donald A. Ritchie, Senate Hart Building, Washington, D.C.; George Robeson, *Long Beach Press-Telegram*, Long Beach, California; Seymour Rosen, SPACES, Los Angeles; Jean A. Schoenthaler, Drew University, Madison, New Jersey; Tonie Seger, Randsburg, California; Paul Sieveking, London; Ken Soltesz, South Salem, New York; Ben Z. Swanson, Jr., National Museum of Dentistry, Baltimore; Elizabeth Tashjian, Old Lyme, Connecticut; Kea Tawana, Upper Montclair, New Jersey; Susanne D. Theis, The Orange Show, Houston; John Walden, Kern County Library, Bakersfield, California; Westerly Public Library, Westerly, Rhode Island; David Wimp, Riverton, Wyoming; Jack Zink, Tulsa, Oklahoma.

PICTURE CREDITS

The sources for the illustrations that appear in this book are listed below. Credits from left to right are separated by semicolons, from top to bottom by dashes.

Cover: Jean-Alain Marie/Gamma Liaison, New York, background, Craig Aurness/Westlight, Los Angeles. **3:** Jean-Alain Marie/Gamma Liaison, New York. **7:** Courtesy of the New-York Historical Society, New York, background, W. Woodworth/Superstock, New York. **8:** Sonia Halliday Photographs/Weston Turville, Buckinghamshire, England. **9:** Tokyo National Museum, Toyko. **10:** Courtesy of the New-York Historical Society, New York. **11:** By permission of the British Library, London. **12, 13:** Library of Congress LC-16402, hand colored by Karen Doyle. **14:** From *Food & Drink: A Pictorial Archive from Nineteenth-Century Sources*, selected by Jim Harter, Dover Publications Inc., New York, 1983 (2); UPI/Bettmann, New York; from *Animals: 1419 Copyright Free Illustrations of Mammals, Birds, Fish, Insects, etc.*, selected by Jim Harter, Dover Publications Inc., New York, 1979. **15:** The Hulton Picture Company, London. **16:** California State Library, Sacramento. **17:** Brown Brothers, Sterling, Pennsylvania. **18:** Isabella Stewart Gardner Museum, Boston. **19:** UPI/Bettmann, New York. **21:** Library of Congress LC-115596—Culver Pictures, New York; from *Animals: 1419 Copyright Free Illustrations of Mammals, Birds, Fish, Insects, etc.*, selected by Jim Harter, Dover Publications Inc., New York, 1979. **22:** UPI/Bettmann, New York. **23:** Brown Brothers, Sterling, Pennsylvania, hand colored by Karen Doyle. **24:** UPI/Bettmann, New York. **25:** Ken Raveill Photo, Kansas City, Missouri (2); Library of Congress LC-64751. **26:** National Capital Commission, Ottawa. **27:** Photographed by Jerry Cornelius, courtesy of Marie Jett. **28, 29:** Evan Sheppard, courtesy of Old Town Coin & Jewelry Exchange Inc., Alexandria, Virgnia—The Bettmann Archive, New York; AP/Wide World Photos, New York. **31:** UPI/Bettmann, New York. **32:** Courtesy Prince Leonard, Australia. **33:** FPG International, New York, background, Comstock, Inc., New York. **34:** Alinari, Florence. **35:** From *Portraits, Memoirs and Characters of Remarkable Persons: From the Reign of Edward the Third to the Revolution*, Vol. 1, by James Caulfield, R. S. Kirby, London, 1813. **36:** The National Portrait Gallery, Smithsonian Institution, Washington, D.C. **37:** Mansell Collection, London. **38:** The Bodleian Library, Oxford, hand colored by Karen Doyle. **39:** Mansell Collection, London. **40:** From *Food & Drink: A Pictorial Archive from Nineteenth-Century Sources*, selected by Jim Harter, Dover Publications Inc., New York, 1983—Mansell Collection, London. **41:** Mary Evans Picture Library, London. **42:** Art by Time-Life Books; Culver Pictures, New York. **43:** Brown Brothers, Sterling, Pennsylvania, hand colored by Karen Doyle. **44:** From *The Recluse of Herald Square: The Mystery of Ida E. Wood*, by Joseph A. Cox, The Macmilian Co., New York, 1964. **45:** Courtesy of Conwood Company, L.P., Memphis, Tennessee. **46:** AP/Wide World Photos, New York. **47:** FPG International, New York. **48:** Brown Brothers, Sterling, Pennsylvania. **49:** The Granger Collection, New York. **50:** Drew University Library, Madison, New Jersey, hand colored by Karen Doyle. **51, 52:** Vasili Peskov. **53:** Courtesy of R. H. Ellis & Sons, Worthing, Sussex, England. **54, 55:** ACME/Bettmann, New York; UPI/Bettmann, New York. **56, 57:** Curt Johnson, *Long Beach Press-Telegram*, Long Beach, California. **58:** Courtesy of Time Inc. Magazines Picture Collection—UPI/Bettmann, New York. **59:** Arthur Pollack/*Boston Herald*, Boston. **61:** *The Yorkshire Post*, Leeds, England, background, M. Angelo/Westlight, Los Angeles. **62:** Courtesy of the Trustees of the British Museum, London. **63:** Mary Evans Picture Library, London. **64, 65:** University College London. **66:** By permission of the British Library, London. **67:** Mary Evans Picture Library, London. **68:** Courtesy of the National Portrait Gallery, London. **69:** Courtesy of the Royal Dublin Society, Dublin. **70:** Mary Evans Picture Library, London, except bottom left, art by Time-Life Books. **71:** Mary Evans Picture Library, London, except center, art by Time-Life Books. **72:** The Hulton Picture Company, London. **73:** Reproduced by kind permission of the President and Council of the Royal College of Surgeons of England, London. **74:** Library of Congress LC-116549. **76:** BMG Music, photo by James McInnis. **77:** Library of Congress LC-116548—Kobal Collection/Super Stock Intl., New York; Sony Classical—UPI/Bettmann, New York. **78, 79:** C. S. Perkins/Magnum, New York; Sony Classical—UPI/Bettmann, New York. **80:** *The Yorkshire Post*, Leeds, England. **81:** UPI/Bettmann, New York. **82:** Mike Daines/Sky Picture Group. **83:** Michael Ward, Higham Ferrers, Northants, England, background, Uniphoto, Inc., Washington, D.C. **84:** By permission of the British Library, London. **85:** Mary Evans Picture Library, London; The Hulton Picture Company, London. **86, 87:** Mary Evans Picture Library, London. **88:** From *Hitchin Worthies*, by

Reginald L. Hine, published London 1932 by George Allen and Unwin Ltd. of HarperCollins Publishers Ltd., London. **89:** Roy Davids Collection, London—from *Goods and Merchandise: A Cornucopia of Nineteenth-Century Cuts*, compiled and arranged by William Rowe, Dover Publications Inc., New York, 1982. **90:** Courtesy of Sir Tatton Sykes, Bt., Sledmere, East Yorkshire, England—from *Goods and Merchandise: A Cornucopia of Nineteenth-Century Cuts*, compiled and arranged by William Rowe, Dover Publications Inc., New York, 1982. **91:** Eric Crichton, London. **92:** By permission of Candida Lycett-Green, Marlborough, Wiltshire, England. **93:** The Illustrated London News Picture Library, London; from *Men: A Pictorial Archive from Nineteenth-Century Sources*, selected by Jim Harter, Dover Publications Inc., New York, 1980. **94:** Topham Picture Source, Edenbridge, Kent. **95:** Tony Ray-Jones/The John Hillelson Agency Ltd., London—from *Transportation: A Pictorial Archive from Nineteenth-Century Sources*, selected by Jim Harter, Dover Publications Inc., New York, 1984. **96:** ©Greg Mortimore/Allsport, London. **97:** By permission of the British Library, London—art by Time-Life Books. **98:** Peter Jordan, London. **99:** Michael Freeman, London—

art by Time-Life Books. **100:** *Hull Daily Mail*, Hull, England. **101:** Solo/Sipa, New York. **103:** Eric Crichton, London. **104:** Michael Ward, Higham Ferrers, Northants, England—photo Phil Carpenter © Express Newspapers, London. **105:** Rex USA Ltd., New York. **106:** Derek Hudson/Sygma, New York. **107:** Jim Selby/Rex USA Ltd., New York, background, M. Angelo/Westlight, Los Angeles. **108:** Courtesy of American Antiquarian Society, Worcester, Massachusetts. **109:** Winchester Mystery House, San Jose, California. **110:** Private collection. **111:** The Connecticut Historical Society, Hartford. **112:** Roger-Viollet, Paris. **113:** Robert Franklin. **114:** Jan Wampler picture, from *All Their Own: People and the Places They Build*, by J. Wampler, Schenkman Publishing Company, John Wiley & Sons, New York, 1977, Oxford University Press, Oxford, 1978; Fresno Bee, photo courtesy of the Forestiere family. **115:** Vicki Warren, courtesy of Library of Congress, Rare Book Room. **116, 117:** UPI/Bettmann, New York (6); art by Time-Life Books. **118:** Camilo J. Vergara, New York. **120:** Gregg Blasdel, Burlington, Vermont. **121:** Susan Boger Stern, The Orange Show Foundation, Houston; Paul Hester/The Orange Show Foundation, Houston—from *Food & Drink: A Picto-*

rial Archive from Nineteenth-Century Sources, Dover Publications Inc., New York, 1983. **122:** Ralph Crane for *LIFE*—© 1975 Seymour Rosen, Los Angeles. **123:** Jan Wampler picture, from *All Their Own: People and the Places They Build*, by J. Wampler, Schenkman Publishing Company, John Wiley & Sons, New York, 1977, Oxford University Press, Oxford, 1978 (2)—John Milkovisch/The Orange Show Foundation, Houston—Fran Brennan, Houston. **124:** Paul Hester, Houston (2)—Gregg Blasdel, Burlington, Vermont; Seymour Rosen, Los Angeles. **125:** Paul Hester, Houston. **126:** Dijkstra, Uithoorn (2)—Mark Alcarez, Boston. **127:** Jan Wampler picture, from *All Their Own: People and the Places They Build*, by J. Wampler, Schenkman Publishing Company, John Wiley & Sons, New York, 1977, Oxford University Press, Oxford, 1978, except bottom left, Gregg Blasdel, Burlington, Vermont. **128:** Mark Alcarez, Boston—photo by Chuck Woodbury, *Out West Newspaper*, Grass Valley, California. **129:** Mark Alcarez, Boston. **130:** Reuters/Bettmann, New York—Jim Selby/Rex USA Ltd., New York. **131:** Courtesy of Lucy Pearson. **132:** Ruth Ann Wunderman Gottlieb for *LIFE*—Sudhir C. Shah, Bombay. **133:** Sudhir C. Shah, Bombay—D. Hudson/Sygma, New York.

BIBLIOGRAPHY

Books

Aidala, Thomas R. *Hearst Castle, San Simeon.* New York: Harrison House, 1981.

Altmann, Frédéric. *La Vérité sur L'Abbé Fouéré: "L'Ermite de Rothéneuf."* Nice: Editions A.M., 1985.

Amory, Cleveland:
The Last Resorts. New York: Harper & Brothers, 1952.
Who Killed Society? New York: Harper & Brothers, 1960.

Arntzen, Sonja. *Ikkyū Sōjun: A Zen Monk and His Poetry.* Bellingham, Wash.: Program in East Asian Studies, Western Washington State College, 1973.

Arntzen, Sonja (Trans.). *Ikkyū and the Crazy Cloud Anthology.* Tokyo: University of Tokyo Press, 1986.

Avery, Gillian. *Gillian Avery's Book of the Strange and Odd.* Harmondsworth, Middlesex: Penguin Books, 1975.

Baeyer, Edwinna von. *Garden of Dreams: Kingsmere and Mackenzie King.* Toronto: Dundurn Press, 1990.

Baker, Paul R. *Richard Morris Hunt.* Cambridge, Mass.: MIT Press, 1980.

Barnes, Alison. *Essex Eccentrics.* Ipswich, England: Boydell Press, 1975.

Barrett, Richmond. *Good Old Summer Days.* New York: D. Appleton-Century, 1941.

Beebe, Lucius. *The Big Spenders.* Garden City, N.Y.: Doubleday, 1966.

Bentley, James. *A Calendar of Saints.* New York: Facts On File, 1986.

Berg, Stephen. *Crow with No Mouth: Ikkyū.* Port Townsend, Wash.: Copper Canyon Press, 1989.

Bergheim, Laura A. *Weird Wonderful America.* New York: Tilden Press, 1988.

Berry, A. J. *Henry Cavendish: His Life and Scientific Work.* London: Hutchinson, 1960.

Bickley, Francis (Ed.). *The Diaries of Sylvester Douglas (Lord Glenbervie)* (Vol. 1). London: Constable, 1928.

Birmingham, Stephen:
California Rich. New York: Simon & Schuster, 1980.
The Grandes Dames. New York: Simon & Schuster, 1982.

Boller, Paul F., Jr. *Presidential Anecdotes.* New York: Oxford University Press, 1981.

Bramhall, William. *The Great American Misfit.*

New York: Clarkson N. Potter, 1982.

Bridgeman, Harriet, and Elizabeth Drury. *The British Eccentric.* New York: Clarkson N. Potter, 1975.

Burgess, G. H. O. *The Eccentric Ark: The Curious World of Frank Buckland.* New York: Horizon Press, 1968.

Burgess, Stanley M., and Gary B. McGee (Eds.). *Dictionary of Pentecostal and Charismatic Movements.* Grand Rapids, Mich.: Regency Reference Library, 1988.

Burke, John. *Duet in Diamonds.* New York: G. P. Putnam's Sons, 1972.

Burst, Ardis. *The Three Families of H. L. Hunt.* New York: Wheatland, Weidenfeld & Nicholson, 1988.

Bushell, Peter. *Great Eccentrics.* London: George Allen & Unwin, 1984.

Carter, Morris. *Isabella Stewart Gardner and Fenway Court* (2nd ed.). Boston: Houghton Mifflin, 1940 (reprint of 1925 edition).

Caufield, Catherine. *The Emperor of the United States of America and Other Magnificent British Eccentrics.* New York: St. Martin's Press, 1981.

Caulfield, James. *Portraits, Memoirs, and*

Characters of Remarkable Persons: From the Reign of Edward the Third to the Revolution (Vol. 1). London: R. S. Kirby, 1813.

Coblentz, Edmond D. (Ed.). *William Randolph Hearst: A Portrait in His Own Words.* New York: Simon & Schuster, 1952.

Colson, Percy. *Their Ruling Passions.* London: Hutchinson, 1970.

Corn, Kahane, and Jacki Moline. *Madcap Men and Wacky Women from History.* New York: Simon & Schuster, 1987.

Costigan, Giovanni. *Makers of Modern England.* New York: Macmillan, 1967.

Cott, Jonathan. *Conversations with Glenn Gould.* Boston: Little, Brown, 1984.

Cox, Joseph A. *The Recluse of Herald Square: The Mystery of Ida E. Wood.* New York: Macmillan, 1964.

Crowther, J. G. *Scientists of the Industrial Revolution.* London: Cresset Press, 1962.

Davenport-Hines, Richard. *Sex, Death and Punishment: Attitudes to Sex and Sexuality in Britain since the Renaissance.* London: Collins, 1990.

de Crespigny, Claude Champion. *Forty Years of a Sportsman's Life.* London: Mills & Boon, 1925.

Denison, Frederic. *Westerly (Rhode Island) and Its Witnesses: For Two Hundred and Fifty Years, 1626-1876.* Providence: J. A. & R. A. Reid, 1878.

The Eccentric and Extraordinary History of Nathaniel Bentley, Esquire. London: Tegg & Castleman, 1803.

Edwards, Paul (Ed.). *The Encyclopedia of Philosophy* (Vol. 1). New York: Macmillan, 1967.

Elliot, Hugh Samuel Roger. *Herbert Spencer.* Freeport, N.Y.: Books for Libraries Press, 1970 (reprint of 1917 edition).

Elliott, Maude Howe. *This Was My Newport.* Cambridge, Mass.: Mythology, 1944.

Erskine, Helen Worden. *Out of This World.* New York: G. P. Putnam's Sons, 1953.

Facts and Fallacies. Pleasantville, N.Y.: Reader's Digest Association, 1988.

Fairholt, F. W. *Eccentric and Remarkable Characters.* London: Chard Bentley, 1853.

Falk, Bernard. *The Bridgewater Millions: A Candid Family History.* London: Hutchinson, 1942.

Felton, Bruce, and Mark Fowler:
Felton and Fowler's Best, Worst, and Most Unusual. New York: Thomas Y. Crowell, 1975.

Felton and Fowler's Famous Americans You Never Knew Existed. New York: Stein & Day, 1979.

Fitzpatrick, William John. *Memoirs of Richard Whately: Archbishop of Dublin* (Vol. 1). London: Richard Bentley, 1864.

Florence, P. Sargant, and J. R. L. Anderson (Eds.). *C. K. Ogden: A Collective Memoir.* London: Elek Pemberton, 1977.

Forrest, D. W. *Francis Galton: The Life and Work of a Victorian Genius.* New York: Taplinger, 1974.

Fowler, Gene. *Skyline.* New York: Viking Press, 1961.

Friedrich, Otto. *Glenn Gould: A Life and Variations.* New York: Random House, 1989.

Frost, David, and Michael Deakin. *David Frost's Book of Millionaires, Multimillionaires, and Really Rich People.* New York: Crown, 1984.

Galton, Francis. *The Art of Travel.* Harrisburg, Pa.: Stackpole Books, 1971 (reprint of 1872 edition).

Gordon, W. Terrence. *C. K. Ogden: A Bio-Bibliographic Study.* Metuchen, N.J.: Scarecrow Press, 1990.

Grant, John (Ed.). *Essex: Historical, Biographical and Pictorial.* London: London & Provincial, 1928.

Griffin, Bulkley S. (Ed.). *Offbeat History: A Compendium of Lively Americana.* Cleveland: World, 1967.

Gualdi, Abbe (Gregorio Leti). *Biography of Donna Olimpia Maldachini.* Philadelphia: Barrett & Jones, 1846.

Gunnis, Rupert. *Dictionary of British Sculptors, 1660-1851* (rev. ed.). London: Abbey Library, 1969.

Hadley, Rollin van N. *Museums Discovered: The Isabella Stewart Gardner Museum.* Ft. Lauderdale, Fla.: Woodbine Books, 1981.

Hickey, D. J., and J. E. Doherty. *A Dictionary of Irish History since 1800.* Totowa, N.J.: Barnes & Noble, 1981.

Hine, Reginald L. *Hitchin Worthies.* London: George Allen & Unwin, 1932.

Hoare, Philip. *Serious Pleasures: The Life of Stephen Tennant.* London: Hamish Hamilton, 1990.

Holbrook, Stewart H. *The Age of the Moguls.* Garden City, N.Y.: Doubleday, 1953.

Hurt, Harry, III. *Texas Rich: The Hunt Dynasty from the Early Oil Days through the Silver Crash.* New York: W. W. Norton, 1981.

Hutchison, Bruce. *The Incredible Canadian.* New York: Longmans, Green, 1953.

James, Edward T. (Ed.). *Notable American Women, 1607-1950: A Biographical Dictionary* (Vol. 1). Cambridge, Mass.: Harvard University Press, 1971.

Johnson, Allen, and Dumas Malone (Eds.). *Dictionary of American Biography* (Vol. 2). New York: Charles Scribner's Sons, 1958.

Keay, John. *Eccentric Travellers.* Los Angeles: Jeremy P. Tarcher, 1982.

Kent, William (Ed.). *An Encyclopedia of London.* London: J. M. Dent & Sons, no date.

Kirby's Wonderful and Eccentric Museum (Vol. 5). London: R. S. Kirby, 1815.

Kramer, Dale. *Charles Robert Maturin.* New York: Twayne, 1973.

Lamont-Brown, Raymond. *A Book of British Eccentrics.* London: David & Charles, 1984.

Larsen-Martin, Susan, and Lauri Robert Martin. *Pioneers in Paradise: Folk and Outsider Artists of the West Coast.* Long Beach, Calif.: Long Beach Museum of Art, Department of Parks and Recreation, 1984.

Lee, Sidney (Ed.). *Dictionary of National Biography* (Vol. 60). London: Smith, Elder, 1899.

Lewis, Arthur H. *The Day They Shook the Plum Tree.* New York: Harcourt, Brace & World, 1963.

Livingston, Bernard. *Their Turf: America's Horsey Set and Their Princely Dynasties.* New York: Arbor House, 1973.

McBride, Barrie St. Clair. *Farouk of Egypt.* South Brunswick: A. S. Barnes, 1968.

McGonagall, William. *Poetic Gems.* London: Duckworth, 1989.

The McGraw-Hill Encyclopedia of World Biography. New York: McGraw-Hill, 1973.

McLeave, Hugh. *The Last Pharaoh.* New York: McCall, 1970.

Masters, Brian. *The Dukes: The Origins, Ennoblement and History of 26 Families.* London: Blond & Briggs, 1980.

Michaud, M. (Ed.). *Biographie Universelle: Ancienne et Moderne.* Paris: Thoisnier Desplaces, 1855.

Michell, John. *Eccentric Lives and Peculiar Notions.* San Diego, Calif.: Harcourt Brace Jovanovich, 1984.

Munby, A. N. L.:
The Formation of the Phillipps Library from 1841 to 1872. Cambridge: Cambridge University Press, 1956.
Portrait of an Obsession. London: Constable, 1967.

Murray, Ken. *The Golden Days of San Simeon.* Garden City, N.Y.: Doubleday, 1971.

Nash, Jay Robert. *Zanies: The World's Greatest Eccentrics.* Piscataway, N.J.: New Century, 1982.

The National Cyclopedia of American Biography (Vol. 14). New York: James T. White, 1926.

Nicholas, Margaret. *The World's Greatest Cranks and Crackpots.* New York: Exeter Books, 1984.

O'Connor, Richard. *The Golden Summers: An Antic History of Newport.* New York: G. P. Putnam's Sons, 1974.

Ogden, C. K. *Jeremy Bentham, 1832-2032.* London: Kegan Paul, Trench, Trubner, 1932.

Osgood, Herbert L. *The American Colonies in the Eighteenth Century* (Vol. 2). New York: Columbia University Press, 1980.

Oursler, Fulton. *The True Story of Bernarr Macfadden.* New York: Lewis Copeland, 1929.

Owen, Jane. *Eccentric Gardens.* New York: Random House, 1990.

Page, Tim (Ed.). *The Glenn Gould Reader.* Toronto: Lester & Orpen Dennys, 1984.

Paine, Ralph D. *The Book of Buried Treasure.* New York: Arno Press, 1981.

Paletta, Lu Ann, and Fred L. Worth. *The World Almanac of Presidential Facts.* New York: World Almanac, 1988.

Panati, Charles. *Panati's Extraordinary Endings of Practically Everything and Everybody.* New York: Harper & Row, 1989.

Pastor, Ludwig, Freiherr Von. *The History of the Popes: From the Close of the Middle Ages* (Vol. 30). London: Kegan Paul, Trench, Trubner, 1940.

Pearson, Karl. *The Life, Letters and Labours of Francis Galton* (2 vols.). Cambridge: Cambridge University Press, 1924.

Perec, Georges. "History of the Lipogram." In *Oulipo: A Primer of Potential Literature,* translated and edited by Warren F. Motte, Jr. Lincoln: University of Nebraska Press, 1986.

Piper, David. *The Companion Guide to London.* London: Collins, no date.

Pitch, Anthony S. *Congressional Chronicles.* Potomac, Md.: Mino Publications, 1990.

Portland, the duke of. *Men Women and Things.* London: Faber & Faber, 1937.

Priestley, Harold E. *Truly Bizarre.* New York: Sterling, 1979.

Raimo, John W. *Biographical Directory of American Colonial and Revolutionary Governors, 1607-1789.* Westport, Conn.: Meckler Books, 1980.

Redding, Cyrus. *Memoirs of Remarkable Misers* (Vol. 1). London: Charles J. Skeet, 1863.

Rosen, Seymour. *In Celebration of Ourselves.* San Francisco: California Living Books, 1979.

Rosenman, Mervin. *Forgery, Perjury, and an Enormous Fortune.* New York: Beach Hampton Press, 1984.

Ross, Ishbel. *Charmers and Cranks: Twelve Famous American Women Who Defied Convention.* New York: Harper & Row, 1965.

Schuyt, Michael, Joost Elffers, and George R. Collins. *Fantastic Architecture: Personal and Eccentric Visions.* New York: Harry N. Abrams, 1980.

Seale, William. *The President's House: A History.* Washington, D.C.: White House Historical Association, 1986.

Shepherd, Chuck, John J. Kohut, and Roland Sweet. *News of the Weird.* New York: New American Library, 1989.

Sifakis, Carl. *American Eccentrics.* New York: Facts On File, 1984.

Silitch, Clarissa M. (Ed.). *Mad and Magnificent Yankees.* Dublin, N.H.: Yankee, 1973.

Sills, David L. (Ed.). *International Encyclopedia of the Social Sciences* (Vol. 15). New York: Macmillan, 1968.

Sirén, Osvald. *Chinese Painting: Leading Masters and Principles* (Vol. 2, part 1). New York: Ronald Press, 1956.

Sitwell, Edith. *The English Eccentrics.* London: Dennis Dobson, 1950.

Skinner, Cornelia Otis. *Madame Sarah.* Boston: Houghton Mifflin, 1967.

Slonimsky, Nicolas (Ed.). *Baker's Biographical Dictionary of Musicians.* New York: Schirmer Books, 1984.

Somerville-Large, Peter. *Irish Eccentrics.* London: Hamish Hamilton, 1975.

Sparkes, Boyden, and Samuel Taylor Moore. *The Witch of Wall Street: Hetty Green.* New York: Doubleday, Doran, 1935.

Stacey, C. P. *A Very Double Life: The Private World of Mackenzie King.* Toronto: Macmillan, 1976.

Stein, Susan R. (Ed.). *The Architecture of Richard Morris Hunt.* Chicago: University of Chicago Press, 1986.

Stern, Michael. *Farouk.* New York: Bantam Books, 1965.

Strange Stories, Amazing Facts. Pleasantville, N.Y.: Reader's Digest Association, 1976.

Swanberg, W. A. *Citizen Hearst.* New York: Charles Scribner's Sons, 1961.

Sykes, Christopher Symon. *The Visitors' Book.* New York: G. P. Putnam's Sons, 1978.

Tebbel, John. *The Life and Good Times of William Randolph Hearst.* New York: E. P. Dutton, 1952.

Thompson, Jacqueline. *The Very Rich Book.* New York: William Morrow, 1981.

Thorndike, Joseph J., Jr. *The Very Rich.* New York: Bonanza Books, 1981.

Thornton, Willis. *The Nine Lives of Citizen Train.* New York: Greenberg, 1948.

Thurston, Herbert, and Donald Attwater (Eds.). *Butler's Lives of the Saints* (Vol. 1). New York: P. J. Kenedy & Sons, 1956.

Timbs, John. *English Eccentrics and Eccentricities.* Detroit: Singing Tree Press, Book Tower, 1969 (reprint of 1875 edition).

True Life Stories of . . . Freaks, Fate & Fortune. New York: Castle Books, 1973.

Turner, James. *The Dolphin's Skin: Six Studies in Eccentricity.* London: Cassell, 1956.

Vail, Robert W. G. "James Johns, Vermont Pen Printer." In *The Papers of the Bibliographical Society of America* (Vol. 27). Chicago: University of Chicago Press, 1933.

Vaizey, Marina. *Christo.* New York: Rizzoli, 1990.

Vaux, Roberts. *Memoirs of the Lives of Benjamin Lay and Ralph Sandiford.* Philadelphia: Solomon W. Conrad, 1815.

Wallace, Irving. *The Square Pegs.* New York: Alfred A. Knopf, 1957.

Wallace, Irving, David Wallenchinsky, and Amy Wallace. *Significa.* New York: E. P. Dutton, 1983.

Wampler, Jan. *All Their Own: People and the Places They Build.* Oxford: Oxford University Press, 1978.

Wecter, Dixon. *The Saga of American Society: A Record of Social Aspiration, 1607-1937.* New York: Charles Scribner's Sons, 1970.

Weeks, David Joseph, and Kate Ward. *Eccentrics: The Scientific Investigation.* Stirling, Scotland: Stirling University Press, 1988.

Weslager, C. A. *The Garrett Snuff Fortune.* Wilmington, Del.: Knebels Press, 1965.

Whately, Elizabeth Jane. *Life and Correspondence of Richard Whately, D.D.* London: Longmans, Green, 1866.

Who Was Who in America (Vol. 3). Chicago: Marquis—Who's Who, 1963.

Wilson, George. *The Life of the Honorable Henry Cavendish.* New York: New York Times, Arno Press, 1975 (reprint of 1851 edition).

Wilson, James Grant, and John Fiske (Eds.). *Appleton's Cyclopedia of American Biography.* New York: D. Appleton, 1898.

Wingo, Plennie L. *Around the World Backwards.* Austin, Tex.: Eakin Press, 1982.

Wood, Clement. *Bernarr Macfadden: A Study in Success.* New York: Lewis Copeland, 1929.

Wright, Ernest Vincent. *Gadsby.* Los Angeles: Wetzel, 1939.

Wright, Richardson. *American Wags and Eccentrics: From Colonial Times to the Civil War* (American Classics series). New York: Frederick Ungar, 1965 (reprint of 1939 edition).

Periodicals

"A. Stuyvesant Jr., Last of Line, Dies." *New York Times,* August 12, 1953.

" 'The Aladdin's Cave' Sale Makes £26,000." *Worthing Herald,* September 27, 1974.

Albee, Allison. "The Leather Man." Parts 1-3. *The Quarterly Bulletin of the Westchester County Historical Society,* April, July, October 1937.

Amory, Cleveland. "Gone Are the 'Royal' Stuyvesants." *New York Journal-American,*

September 3, 1958.

"Author Bans Letter E in New 50,110 Word Novel." *Los Angeles Times,* April 7, 1937.

"Baron Harden-Hickey's Death." *New York Times,* February 13, 1898.

Barry, Richard:
"The Fate of the Wendel Millions." *New York Times,* February 28, 1916.
"The Passing of the 'Recluse of Fifth Avenue.' " *New York Times,* December 6, 1914.

Beers, Cody. " 'The Count' Hasn't Quit." *Riverton Ranger,* January 11, 1991.

Beggy, Carol. "Fire Destroys Home, Belongings of Hermit." *Boston Globe,* May 3, 1987.

Bell, William A. "End of a Scramble for the 26,000." *Philadelphia Bulletin,* September 23, 1951.

Berg, Steve. "The Continuing Saga of 1069, Changing His Name to a Number." *Minneapolis Tribune,* November 25, 1977.

"Biggest Robbery in U.S. History Ends in Murder." *Indianapolis Star,* May 15, 1977.

Birmingham, Stephen. "Our Celebrated Eccentrics." *Harper's Bazaar,* October 1982.

"Black Mountain Tunnel." *Time,* December 12, 1938.

Block, Jean Libman. "Misers." *Cosmopolitan,* March 1957.

Braithwaite, Dennis. "Reclusive Gould Wasn't Always So." *Toronto Star,* April 28, 1978.

Brown, Chip. "Kea's Improbable Ark." *Chicago Tribune,* April 22, 1987.

Brown, Joe David. "Whooping Baron of the Prairie." *Sports Illustrated,* November 4, 1963.

Brown, Patricia Leigh. "Living for Folk Art, and in It, Too." *New York Times,* January 3, 1991.

"Building of Ark Allowed to Continue." *New York Times,* April 14, 1987.

Burgess, Michele. "This Is the House That Sarah Built." *Travel-Holiday,* March 1986.

Calvin, Michael:
"The Eagle Soars and Survives to Fail Another Day." *Daily Telegraph,* February 24, 1988.
" 'Eddie the Eagle' Takes Lone Leap in the Dark for Britain." *Daily Telegraph,* February 12, 1988.

Canby, Vincent. "Son of W. C. Fields Toasts Him in Tea." *New York Times,* February 19, 1966.

Carpenter, Dan. "Rich Heiress' 'Ghost' Haunts Jackson Place." *Indianapolis Star,* May 3, 1981.

Cash, William:
"He Flies through the Air." *Spectator,* May 4, 1991.
"When Pigs Do Fly." *Spectator,* December 22-29, 1990.

Cassidy, Mike. "S. J. Family Lived amid 25 Tons of Rotting Garbage." *San Jose Mercury News,* August 3, 1988.

Chadwick, Susan. "Houston's Fan Man Humbly Rejects the Notion His Decorated Home Is Art." *Houston Post,* May 18, 1990.

"Chestnut Hill Hermit Reunited with Son, Daughter after 20 Years." *Boston Globe,* March 1, 1987.

"Coins Hoarded in the Oven." *Worthing Herald,* February 28, 1975.

Cole, Wilford P. "Henry Dawkins and the Quaker Comet." *Winterthur Portfolio 4,* Richard K. Doud (Ed.). Charlottesville: University Press of Virginia, 1968.

"Collyer Mansion Yields Junk, Cats." *New York Times,* March 26, 1947.

Commager, Steele. "Words upon the Greatness of William McGonagall." *Atlantic,* December 1980.

Connor, Lawrence S. "The Six Million Dollar Murder." *Saturday Evening Post,* November 1977.

Corwin, Miles. "Buried Treasure." *Los Angeles Times,* August 13, 1989.

"A Crazy Man's Awful Act." *New York Times,* December 5, 1891.

Cullen, Kevin. "Britt: A Gregarious Hermit Who Guarded Privacy Publicly." *Boston Globe,* March 8, 1988.

Cunningham, John. "Focus on the Georgian Group." *Guardian,* April 10, 1986.

Czarnecki, Mark. "Glenn Gould, 1932-1982." *Maclean's,* October 18, 1982.

Davis, Forrest. "The Wendels: A Fabulous Family." *New York World-Telegram,* March 24-April 4, 1931.

Deacon, Jeremy. "Relatives Shell-Shocked at £26,000 Bequest for Upkeep of Pet Fred." *Yorkshire Evening Post,* June 13, 1990.

"Decision of Honorable William T. Collins, Surrogate. In the Matter of the Estate of Mary Bullock Powers, Deceased." *New York Law Journal,* November 29, 1949.

Deitz, Paula. "Painshill Park, Surrey." *Antiques,* June 1991.

"Diamond Jim Brady Dies while Asleep." *New York Times,* April 14, 1917.

"Ella Wendel Dies; Last of Her Family." *New York Times,* March 15, 1931.

"Ella Wendel's Dog Dies at Old Home." *New York Times,* October 5, 1933.

"English Eccentrics," *Horizon,* Winter 1972.

"English Homes. No. XXXVIII. Welbeck Abbey." *Illustrated London News,* August 3, 1895.

Faber, Harold:
"Body of Collyer Is Found Near Where Brother Died." *New York Times,* April 9, 1947.
"Homer Collyer, Harlem Recluse, Found Dead at 70." *New York Times,* March 22, 1947.

"Facing Eviction from His Boston Hovel, Hermit Bill Britt Pleads There's No Place like Home." *People,* April 13, 1987.

"$500,000 More Found in Mrs. Wood's Room; Recluse, 93, Carried $10,000 Notes since 1907." *New York Times,* October 10, 1931.

Flanagan, Mike. "Sarah Winchester's Mystery House." *Empire,* October 27, 1985.

"Forty Two Years in the Wilderness." *Fortean Times,* No. 45.

Fraser, Blair. "The Secret Life of Mackenzie King, Spiritualist." *Maclean's,* December 15, 1951.

"Fred (34) Settles to a Life of Luxury." *Daily Mail,* June 13, 1990.

"Fred Can Afford to Take It Easy." *Yorkshire Evening Post,* June 13, 1990.

Frederic, Harold. "An Opera Bouffe Kinglet: Baron Harden Hickey as a Limited Liability Sovereign." *New York Times,* August 18, 1895.

"From Rags to Riches? Not Exactly for Iowan." *Des Moines Register,* May 29, 1979.

"Funeral for Stephen Senior." *Perth Amboy Evening News,* January 30, 1924.

Gelarden, R. Joseph. "Mrs. Jackson Withdrew $7.88 Million, Bank Official Testifies." *Indianapolis Star,* December 1, 1977.

Gibson, Helen. "Where Books Are King." *Time,* March 6, 1989.

Gillard, Colleen. "San Jose House Was a Dump." *San Francisco Chronicle,* August 4, 1988.

Gould, Allan M. "Glenn Gould: The Way He Was." *CBC Radio Guide,* January 1983.

"The Greatest Capital-Goods Salesman of Them All." *Fortune,* October 1954.

Greenfield, Verni. "The Story of the Bottle Village." *Raw Vision,* Spring 1991.

Groux, Nathalie. "Moral D'Acier et Santé de Fer." *Le Dauphiné Libéré,* September 9, 1988.

Hall, Mary Louise. "The Story of the Leather Man." *New Canaan Gazette,* May 1, 1934.

Hamilton, Alan. "Monster Mould Breakers Re-Invent the Liberals." *London Times,* September 30, 1988.

"Harden-Hickey a Suicide." *New York Times,* February 11, 1898.

Harris, Martyn. "Lord of Misrule: Sutch a Level-Headed Loony." *Sunday Telegraph,* November 11, 1990.

Hay, Robert. "McGonagall: Perhaps He Had the Last Laugh." *Scots Magazine,* July 1956.

"The Heiress." *Time,* February 20, 1950.

Henderson, Jim. "A Zink Bash Is Something." *Tulsa World,* June 8, 1969.

Hess, Skip. "Going, Going to Jackson Auction." *Indianapolis News,* June 22, 1977.

"He's Unknown Now, but the World's Top Underwater Artist Is Waiting for His Reputation to Surface." *People,* November 30, 1987.

"High Chair." *Time,* January 3, 1983.

Hill, Hal. "A Legacy Greater than Dollars: Forestiere's Underground Gardens." *Desert,* July 1981.

Hillinger, Charles. "Queen Lucy Leads a Tireless Life in Hub of the Desert." *Los Angeles Times,* November 9, 1990.

Hillman, Judy. "A King Who Makes Hay." *Guardian,* March 29, 1978.

Holliday, Richard. "A Medieval Slingalong: You Hum It, I'll Throw It." *Mail on Sunday,* August 4, 1991.

Hooper, Carl. "Remembering Mister West." *Parade,* August 16, 1981.

"How an Eccentric Inventor Is Warming Up for Winter." *Observer Weekender,* September 8, 1989.

"How to Have Fun with 100 Million Dollars." *Collier's,* May 2, 1953.

"The Inimitable Maurice Seddon." *Motorcycle Sport,* February 1990.

"In Quiet Reflection." *Time,* October 23, 1950.

"Inventor Plugs in to a Very Hot Idea." *Observer,* January 20, 1987.

"J. G. Wendel Dead; A Realty Croesus." *New York Times,* December 14, 1914.

Jobson, Robert. "Falklands Stones for Garden Stonehenge." *Western Morning News,* August 20, 1985.

Jones, Bob. "Kern Tunnel: Monument to Old Man's Dream." *Bakersfield Californian,* March 6, 1977.

Jones, Jack:

"Flying Chair Act May Buzz S. D." *Los Angeles Times,* September 11, 1982.

"Lawn Chair 'Pilot' Runs into Flak." *Los Angeles Times,* December 18, 1982.

"Postscript." *Los Angeles Times,* October 18, 1988.

Jones, Ken. "Edward Flies beyond a Joke." *Independent,* February 12, 1988.

"Just a Country Boy." *Time,* December 9, 1974.

Kaplan, David. "This Man Loves 'Junk' Food." *Houston Post,* March 1, 1988.

Kendall, Ena. "Richard Booth." *Observer,* July 17, 1983.

Kernan, Michael. "The Collyer Saga and How It Grew." *Washington Post,* February 8, 1983.

"The Kiddie-Car That Jack Built." *Chronicle and Echo,* June 29, 1962.

"King's Secret." *Time,* December 24, 1951.

Koehler, Albert, and David G. Wittels. "The Scramble for the Garrett Millions." *Saturday Evening Post,* September 11, 1948.

Kozinn, Allan. "Moondog Returns from Hippie Years." *New York Times,* November 16, 1989.

LaMarche, Robert J. "Grocery Heiress Found Slain." *Indianapolis Star,* May 8, 1977.

"Landlocked Ark Caught in Storm." *New York Times,* May 1, 1988.

"Langley Collyer Dead near a Month." *New York Times,* April 10, 1947.

Laurie, Alison. "The Happy Extremists." *Sunday Times Magazine,* October 18, 1970.

Lenman, Bruce. "McGonagall's Dundee." *Scots Magazine,* May 1969.

"Life Candle Burns Out; Smitty Dies." *Bakersfield Californian,* February 2, 1954.

"The Life of Archbishop Whately." *Fraser's Magazine,* April 1897.

"Life with a Genius." *Time,* April 20, 1953.

Littler, William. "Glenn Gould Remains Enigma despite Book." *Toronto Star,* June 10, 1978.

"Lives of Wendels Pictured as Happy." *New York Times,* March 30, 1931.

Lockney, Thomas M., and Karl Ames. "Is 1069 a Name?" *Names: Journal of the American Name Society,* March 1981.

"Macfadden Dead; Health Cultist, 87." *New York Times,* October 13, 1955.

"Mackenzie King, 75, Is Dead." *New York Times,* July 23, 1950.

McNamara, Sheila. "The Man Who Did for Dr. Death." *Observer,* June 17, 1990.

Mahurkar, Uday. "Diamonds Are Not Forever." *India Today,* June 30, 1991.

Mapes, Glynn. "A Scud It's Not, but the Trebuchet Hurls a Mean Piano." *Wall Street Journal,* July 30, 1991.

Martin, William. "What's Red, White, and Blue . . . and Orange All Over?" *Texas Monthly,* October 1977.

Mayman, Jan. "And Now . . . the Prince of Iceberg." *The Australian,* December 31, 1977.

Meade, Laura. "The Paper House." *Gloucester Daily Times,* April 17, 1982.

Meney, Patrick. "Soviet Geologists Discover Clan 'Living in Stone Age.' " *Omaha World-Herald,* October 21, 1982.

Meredith, Jo. "TV Fame for Oddball." *Chronicle and Echo,* June 23, 1989.

Metz, Holly. "Grass-Roots Art Seeks a Haven." *Progressive,* October 14, 1987.

Minsky, Terri. "It's His Choice: A 15th Winter Living Outdoors." *Boston Globe,* January 10, 1985.

"Mr. Darling Paints His Dream House." *Life,* June 25, 1971.

Mok, Michel. "Ida Wood's Parentage Traced . . . ." *New York Post,* November 8, 1934.

"Monsieur Mange-Tout à la Diète." *Le Dauphiné Libéré,* August 14, 1981.

Muller, Claude. "Le Grenoblais Michel Lotitio (Monsieur Mangetout) Va Bientôt Déguster . . . un Avion!" *Le Dauphiné Libéré,* June 22, 1978.

Narvaez, Alfonso:

"A Battle over Newark Ark's Future." *New York Times,* March 28, 1987.

"Newark's Ark Is Coming Down." *New York Times,* March 13, 1988.

Nelson, Nigel, and Rose Sheppard. "The Bizarre Lives of People Driven by Overwhelming Passion." *Sunday Mirror,* August 31, 1986.

"The 90 Best Things about Houston." *Houston Metropolitan,* July 1990.

"Nosing after Funny Money." *Time,* March 20, 1989.

"O. H. P. Belmont Dead after Brave Fight." *New York Times,* June 11, 1908.

"The Old Leather Man: The Strange Life of an Old Man Clad Entirely in Leather." *Hartford Globe,* July 12, 1885.

Owen, Russell. "Something for O. Henry: Story of the Collyers." *New York Times,* March 30, 1947.

Parisi, Albert J. "Newark Ark Faces Need to Move Again." *New York Times,* October 18, 1987.

Parker, Joan. "Emperor Norton I." *American Heritage,* December 1976.

"A Passion for Potatoes." *Newsweek,* May 30, 1988.

Perry, Dave. "The Count of Riverton." *Riverton Ranger,* October 10, 1989.

Pickering, Carolyn. "A Recluse Heiress Who Mistrusted Banks." *Indianapolis Star,* May 15, 1977.

Pierce, Arthur D. "A Governor in Skirts." *Proceedings of the New Jersey Historical Society,* January 1965.

Pipe, Simon. "The New 'Wreckers.' " *Courier,* September 8, 1983.

"Prince Len's Got Big Plans, Right Royal Cocky!" *Daily News Express,* August 11, 1989.

Purcell, Steve. "Sutch a Loony after all." *Daily Star,* May 28, 1991.

"Rebecca Swope, 5th Av. Recluse, Dies at Quogue." *New York Times,* August 4, 1930.

"The Recline of Stephen Tennant." *Observer,* September 21, 1986.

"Recluse Carries Mystery to Death." *New York Times,* July 22, 1948.

"Recluse Worth $500,000 Frozen to Death in Shack He Had Occupied Alone 40 Years." *New York Times,* January 28, 1924.

Revelle, Mark. "Hot Wired." *Event,* January 8-14, 1982.

Ribadeneira, Diego:

"Autopsy Shows Hermit Froze to Death at

Campsite in Brighton Cemetery." *Boston Globe,* March 9, 1988.

"Chestnut Hill Hermit Bill Britt Is Found Dead at His Campsite." *Boston Globe,* March 8, 1988.

Richard, Paul. "Dali and the Realm of Dreams." *Washington Post,* January 24, 1989.

Rickey, Gail. " 'Silver Dollar' Jim West: Oilman with a Golden Heart." *Houston Business Journal,* February 4, 1985.

Robertson, Heather. "Kingsmere: Retreat for an Eccentric." *Reader's Digest* (Canada), February 1987.

Robeson, George. "Concrete Clint Creates Chaos." *Long Beach Press,* May 7, 1975.

Robinson, Dana. "Depression Made Man Turn His Back on World." *Abilene Reporter-News,* August 2, 1980.

Ross, Irwin. "The Stingiest Man in History." *Commerce,* March 1976.

Ross, Ishbel. "Wood Souvenir Hoard Gives Up Rare Valentines." *New York Herald Tribune,* December 4, 1931.

"Russell Sage Dies Leaving $80,000,000." *New York Times,* July 23, 1906.

Russotto, P. Gabriele, O. H. "Fatebenefratelli Denitsi." *Vita Ospedaliera,* March 1971.

Rust, Carol. "The Orange Show." *Texas* (*Houston Chronicle* magazine), November 26, 1989.

"The Sad State of Eccentricity." *Time,* March 14, 1969.

Sandford, Jeremy. "King Richard the Haymaker." *Guardian,* March 5, 1983.

Sargeant, Winthrop. "An Excitable Spanish Artist, Now Scorned by His Fellow Surrealists, Has Succeeded in Making Deliberate Lunacy a Paying Proposition." *Life,* September 24, 1945.

"A Scavenger, Harvard '01, Leaves $400,000 Fortune and a Mystery." *Life,* February 4, 1952.

Schmemann, Serge. "Deep in Siberia, 3 Centuries of Faith in God." *New York Times,* November 30, 1982.

Schmitt, Hugh. "The Prince of Hutt Gets Tough." *Sun-Herald* (Sydney), January 22, 1978.

Sedgwick, John. "The Museum That Eccentricity Built." *GQ,* November 1989.

"Seminaries Share Big Wendel Legacy." *New York Times,* March 24, 1931.

"The Shy Men." *Time,* April 7, 1947.

"Siberian Hermit Family 45 Years in Wilderness." *Daily Telegraph,* October 22, 1982.

Skulley, Mark. "Mighty Take a Slight Stumble." *Western Mail,* August 25, 1986.

Spencer, Charles Worthen. "The Cornbury Legend." *New York State Historical Association Proceedings,* 1914, Vol. 13.

Spilman, Ed. "John Steele Zink." *Oklahoma Today,* Spring 1959.

Springer, Katie. "Ed's Granite Temple to the Women in His Life." *Western Morning News,* April 13, 1985.

"Statesman's Other Side." *Life,* March 23, 1953.

"Strange Case of the Collyer Brothers." *Life,* April 7, 1947.

"Stuyvesant Rites End an Era Here." *New York Times,* August 15, 1953.

Sweeney, Joan, and Jack Jones. "Seat-of-the-Pants Pilot Goes Aloft in Lawn Chair." *Los Angeles Times,* July 3, 1982.

"A Tale of Two Autocrats." *Time,* March 26, 1965.

"To Be Prince of Trinidad." *New York Tribune,* November 5, 1893.

"Tortoise Fred's Fame Spreads." *Daily Mail,* June 18, 1990.

Trimel, Suzanne. "Museum Curator Convinced Man Descended from Nuts." *New London Day,* August 9, 1978.

"TV Spotlight on Madcap Inventor." *Chronicle and Echo,* September 30, 1988.

"$22,000 Steel Grave for Russell Sage." *New York Times,* July 25, 1906.

"A Unique Tour of San Simeon." *Life,* August 26, 1957.

"Uplift." *Life,* January 1983.

Vergara, Camilo J. "Kea, the New Ark and Newark." *SPACES,* Winter 1988.

Vergara, Camilo J., and Holly Metz. "Update on Kea's Ark." *SPACES,* Winter/Spring 1989.

Vergé, Bernard. "La Legende de Rothéneuf: Où L'Incroyable Entreprise de L'Abbé Fauré." *Spar,* August 1964.

Violet, Ultra. "Goodbye, Dali—It's Been Surreal." *New York Times,* January 30, 1989.

Wallis, Neil. "Eddie's Ready to Make a Million." *Sun,* February 18, 1988.

Ward, John. "All in a Day's Work." *Northamptonshire Businessman,* March 1989.

"W. C. Fields Dies on Christmas Day." *Life,* January 6, 1947.

"W. C. Fields Estate Seeks $5,000 in Bank He

Forgot." *New York Herald Tribune,* December 10, 1952.

Weisman, Steven R. "Christo's Intercontinental Umbrella Project." *New York Times,* November 13, 1990.

"Wendel Dog Loses Perquisites of Old." *New York Times,* December 23, 1931.

"Wendel Will Aids Flower Hospital." *New York Times,* March 20, 1931.

Whitworth, William. "Profiles: Bishop Homer A. Tomlinson." *New Yorker,* September 24, 1966.

Williams, Robert J. "Philadelphia Had a Hughes Case of its Own." *Philadelphia Bulletin,* September 7, 1981.

Williamson, Samuel T. "Life with Bernarr Macfadden." *New York Times Book Review,* April 20, 1953.

"Woman Might Get Reprieve to Build Ark." *New York Times,* April 13, 1987.

Wooldridge, Ian. "The Eddie Enigma." *Daily Mail,* February 25, 1988.

Yagoda, Ben. "The True Story of Bernarr Macfadden: Life and Loves of the Father of the Confession Magazine." *American Heritage,* December 1981.

"You Gotta Give a Card like Walter Some Credit." *People,* January 30, 1989.

"Zero for 1069." *U.S. News and World Report,* June 2, 1980.

Other

Bendiner, Milton. "Florence Foster Jenkins." Brochure. New York: Melotone Recording Studio, 1946.

"Coral Castle: An Engineering Feat Almost Impossible to Believe!" Brochure. Homestead, Fla.: Coral Castle, 1988.

"Coral Castle English Tour Guide." Pamphlet. Homestead, Fla.: Coral Castle, no date.

"Fact Sheet." Pamphlet. San Jose, Calif.: Winchester Mystery House, March 3, 1991.

"History of the Paper House." Pamphlet. Pigeon Cove, Mass.: Paper House, no date.

"The Orange Press." Newsletter. Houston, Tex.: The Orange Show, A Folk Art Foundation, March/April 1991.

"The Story of the Famous Glass House." Pamphlet. Boswell, British Columbia: The Glass House, no date.

"Winchester Mystery House." Brochure. San Jose, Calif.: Winchester Mystery House, no date.

INDEX

Numerals in italics indicate an illustration of the subject mentioned.

A

Abbey Ruins (Kingsmere), *26,* 27
Adams, John Quincy, 10
Adventures of Robin Hood, The, 105
Alexander, William: portrait by, *62*
Alexander VII, 34
Algardi, Alessandro: sculpture by, *34*
Alington, John, *88*
Alpaca (Hunt), 24
American Revolution, 37
Amory, Cleveland, 46
Andrew, duke of York, *105*
Anne, queen of England, 9, 10, 30
Anthon, Marian, *23*
Ark: built by Tawana, *118-119*
Around the World in Eighty Days (Verne), 17
Artists: Sarah Bernhardt, *74-75;* Enrico Caruso, *76-77;* Christo, *78-79;* Robert Coates, *67;* Salvadore Dali, *78;* W. C. Fields, *77;* Glenn Gould, *79-80;* Louis T. Hardin, *81;* Florence Foster Jenkins, *75-76;* Mi Fei, *65;* Jamy Verheylewegen, *82.* See also Sculptors and sculptures
Art of Travel; or Shifts and Contrivances Available in Wild Countries, The (Galton), 72
Astor, John Jacob, 50
Australia: Casley's Province of Hutt River, 31-32

B

Bach, Johann Sebastian, 79
Backwards walking: Wingo's tour, *116-117*
Balzac, Honoré de, 71
Barr, Richard, 100
Basic English, 66
Baudelaire, Charles-Pierre, 71
Beecher, Henry Ward, 17
Beer-can house, *123*
Belmont, August, 21
Belmont, Oliver Hazard Perry, *21*
Bentham, Jeremy, *64-65,* 66
Bentinck-Scott, William J. C., 41
Bentley, Nathaniel, *85-86*
Benton, Thomas Hart, 29
Berners, Baron, *91-92*
Bernhardt, Sarah, *74-75*
Bernstein, Leonard, 79
Betjeman, John, 98
Bibliomania, 89
Black, Joseph, *62*
Blagden, Charles, 63
Blondin, Charles, 93
Bolin, Clinton, 56-57
Books: collection of Collyer brothers, 56; collection of Phillipps, 89-90
Booth, Richard, *94*
Bottle Village, *124*

Bourglay, Jules, 110-*111*
Brady, James Buchanan, *19*-20
Bridgewater, the earl of, *11*
British characters: John Alington, *88;* Jeremy Bentham, *64-65,* 66; William J. C. Bentinck-Scott, 41; Nathaniel Bentley, *85-86;* Richard Booth, *94;* Trevelyan Buckland, *73;* Henry Cavendish, *62-63;* Robert Coates, *67;* Comic Relief stunts for charity, 105; Thomas Cooke, *40;* Roger Crab, *35;* Daniel Dancer, *39;* Claude Champion de Crespigny, *93;* Dorothy Duffin, 99-100; Michael David Edwards, *96;* Francis Henry Egerton, *11;* John Meggot Elwes, 36-*37;* Francis Galton, *72;* gardeners, 102-*103;* Charles Hamilton, 38; James Hirst, *84*-85; Edward Hyde, 7, 9, *10;* Hew Kennedy, 100-*101;* William Kitchiner, *93;* Wilfred Makepeace Lunn, *61, 80;* Victor Martin, *95;* Jack Mytton, *87;* New Georgians, *97*-98; Joseph Nollekens, *63*-64; Charles Kay Ogden, *66;* Thomas Phillipps, 89-90; Matthew Robinson, *86;* Robin St. Clair, *105*-106; Maurice Seddon, *98-99;* soapbox orators, *97;* Herbert Spencer, *70;* David Sutch, *104*-105; Tatton Sykes, 90-*91;* Gerald Hugh Tyrwhitt-Wilson, *91-92;* John Ward, *104;* Richard Whately, *15*
Britt, Bill, *59*-60
Brown, David H., *123*
Buckland, Francis Trevelyan, *73*
Buckland, William, 73
Byron, Lord, *71*

C

Calloway, Stephen, 97, *98*
Cambridge University, 89
Caruso, Enrico, 75, *76-77*
Casley, Ian, 31, *32*
Casley, Leonard, 31-*32*
Casley, Richard, 31
Casley, Shirley, 31, *32*
Casley, Wayne, 31, *32*
Cavanagh, Walter, *130*-131
Cavendish, Charles, 62
Cavendish, George, 63
Cavendish, Henry, *62-63*
Chestnut Hill Hermit, *59*-60
Christo, 78-79; art by, *78-79*
Churchill, Winston, 30, 66
Cigar mosaics, *126*
Citizen Kane, 24
Clark, Kenneth, 98
Coates, Robert, *67*
Coco-de-mer: and Tashjian's theory of evolution, 128-*129*
Collyer, Homer, 54-55
Collyer, Langley, 54-55
Comic Relief charity, 105
Connors, Bob, *59*
Cooke, Thomas, *40*

Copper Mountain: tunnel, 113
Coral Castle, 119-*120*
Cornbury, Lord, 9-*10*
Costner, Kevin, 100
Counting: project of Wimp, *128*
Count of Riverton, *128*
Crab, Roger, *35*
Creativity, 61. *See also* Artists; Sculptors and Sculptures
Credit cards: collection of Cavanagh, *130*-131
Curare: Waterton's experiments with, 68

D

Dali, Salvador, *78*
Dancer, Daniel, *39*
Dancing: and Maturin, *71*-72
Darling, Sanford, *122*
Darwin, Charles, 70, 72
Davis, Clifford, 102, *103*
Davis, Jefferson, 16
Death: Bernhardt's obsession with, 74
de Crespigny, Claude Champion, *93*
Dengler, Michael Herbert, 117
Dexter, Timothy, 11, *12-13*
Diaghilev, Sergey, 92
Diamond Jim, *19*-20
Dirty Dick, *85-86*
Dirty Warehouse, *85-86*
Dogs: dining with Bridgewater, *11;* Fields's phobia of, 77; and King, *26-27;* tree climbing, 15; and Wendel, *50*-51; and Whately, 15
Douglas, William, 28
Doves: dyed by Berners, *91*
Dowie, John Alexander, 13
Duffin, Dorothy, 99-100
Dukenfield, William Claude, *77*
Dumas, Alexandre, 75
Duncan, Edward: illustration by, *87*

E

Eccentricity: creativity and, 61; described, 7
Eddie the Eagle, *96*
Edison, Thomas, 69
Edmonstone, Anne, 68
Edward III, *62*
Edward VII, 75
Edwards, Michael David, *96*
Egerton, Francis Henry, *11*
Elgar, Edward, 99
Elijah the Restorer, 13
Elwes, Harvey, 36-37
Elwes, John Meggot, 36-37
Embalming house, *123*
The English Hermite, or, Wonder of this Age (Crab), 35
Enlightenment: age of, 62, 65; in Zen Buddhism, 9
Euthanasia: The Aesthetics of Suicide (Harden-Hickey), 21
Evil Eye, 77

Time-Life Books is a division of Time Life Inc.,
a wholly owned subsidiary of
THE TIME INC. BOOK COMPANY

TIME-LIFE BOOKS

PRESIDENT: Mary N. Davis

Managing Editor: Thomas H. Flaherty
Director of Editorial Resources: Elise D. Ritter-Clough
Director of Photography and Research: John Conrad Weiser
Editorial Board: Dale M. Brown, Roberta Conlan, Laura Foreman, Lee Hassig, Jim Hicks, Blaine Marshall, Rita Thievon Mullin, Henry Woodhead
Assistant Director of Editorial Resources/Training Manager: Norma E. Shaw

PUBLISHER: Robert H. Smith

Associate Publisher: Ann M. Mirabito
Editorial Director: Russell B. Adams, Jr.
Marketing Director: Anne C. Everhart
Production Manager: Prudence G. Harris
Supervisor of Quality Control: James King

Editorial Operations
Production: Celia Beattie
Library: Louise D. Forstall
Computer Composition: Deborah G. Tait (Manager), Monika D. Thayer, Janet Barnes Syring, Lillian Daniels
Interactive Media Specialist: Patti H. Cass

© 1992 Time-Life Books. All rights reserved.
No part of this book may be reproduced in any form
or by any electronic or mechanical means, including
information storage and retrieval devices or systems,
without prior written permission from the publisher,
except that brief passages may be quoted for reviews.
First printing. Printed in U.S.A.
Published simultaneously in Canada.
School and library distribution by Silver Burdett
Company, Morristown, New Jersey 07960.

TIME-LIFE is a trademark of Time Warner Inc. U.S.A.

Library of Congress
Cataloging-in-Publication Data
Odd and eccentric people / by the editors of Time-Life
Books.
p.   cm.   (Library of curious and unusual facts).
Includes bibliographical references and index.
ISBN 0-8094-7723-8 (trade)
ISBN 0-8094-7728-9 (lib. bdg.)
1. Eccentrics and eccentricities.
I. Time-Life Books. II. Series.
CT9990.O33 1992
920.02—dc20   91-28256 CIP

LIBRARY OF CURIOUS AND UNUSUAL FACTS

SERIES EDITOR: Laura Foreman
Series Administrator: Roxie France-Nuriddin
Art Director: Cynthia Richardson
Picture Editor: Sally Collins

Editorial Staff for
Odd and Eccentric People
Text Editors: Carl A. Posey (principal), Sarah Brash
Assistant Editors/Research: Ruth Goldberg, Jennifer A. Mendelsohn, Terrell Smith
Assistant Art Director: Alan Pitts
Senior Copy Coordinators: Jarelle S. Stein (principal), Anthony K. Pordes
Picture Coordinator: Jennifer Iker
Editorial Assistant: Terry Ann Paredes

Special Contributors: Tony Allan, George Constable, Peter Pocock, George Russell (text); Andra H. Armstrong, Catherine B. Hackett, Kathryn B. Pfeifer (research); Louise Wile Hedberg (index)

Correspondents: Elisabeth Kraemer-Singh (Bonn), Christine Hinze (London), Christina Lieberman (New York), Maria Vincenza Aloisi (Paris), Ann Natanson (Rome).
Valuable assistance was also provided by Caroline Alcock, Judy Aspinall (London); Trini Bandrés (Madrid); Meenakshi Gahguly (New Delhi); Elizabeth Brown, Katheryn White (New York); Leonora Dodsworth (Rome); Dick Berry, Mieko Ikeda (Tokyo).

The Consultants:
William R. Corliss, the general consultant for the series, is a physicist-turned-writer who has spent the last twenty-five years compiling collections of anomalies in the fields of geophysics, geology, archaeology, astronomy, biology, and psychology. He has written about science and technology for NASA, the National Science Foundation, and the Energy Research and Development Administration (among others). Mr. Corliss is also the author of more than thirty books on scientific mysteries, including *Mysterious Universe, The Unfathomed Mind,* and *Handbook of Unusual Natural Phenomena.*

Other Publications:

THE NEW FACE OF WAR
HOW THINGS WORK
WINGS OF WAR
CREATIVE EVERYDAY COOKING
COLLECTOR'S LIBRARY OF THE UNKNOWN
CLASSICS OF WORLD WAR II
AMERICAN COUNTRY
VOYAGE THROUGH THE UNIVERSE
THE THIRD REICH
THE TIME-LIFE GARDENER'S GUIDE
MYSTERIES OF THE UNKNOWN
TIME FRAME
FIX IT YOURSELF
FITNESS, HEALTH & NUTRITION
SUCCESSFUL PARENTING
HEALTHY HOME COOKING
UNDERSTANDING COMPUTERS
LIBRARY OF NATIONS
THE ENCHANTED WORLD
THE KODAK LIBRARY OF CREATIVE PHOTOGRAPHY
GREAT MEALS IN MINUTES
THE CIVIL WAR
PLANET EARTH
COLLECTOR'S LIBRARY OF THE CIVIL WAR
THE EPIC OF FLIGHT
THE GOOD COOK
WORLD WAR II
HOME REPAIR AND IMPROVEMENT
THE OLD WEST

For information on and a full description of any of the Time-Life Books series listed above, please call 1-800-621-7026 or write:
Reader Information
Time-Life Customer Service
P.O. Box C-32068
Richmond, Virginia 23261-2068

This volume is one in a series that explores astounding but surprisingly true events in history, science, nature, and human conduct. Other books in the series include:

Feats and Wisdom of the Ancients
Mysteries of the Human Body
Forces of Nature
Vanishings
Amazing Animals
Inventive Genius
Lost Treasure
The Mystifying Mind
A World of Luck
Hoaxes and Deceptions
Crimes and Punishments